THE ULTI
TREK TRIVIA
CHALLENGE FOR
THE NEXT
GENERATION

C000121103

THE ULTIMATE
TREK TRIVIA
CHALLENGE FOR
THE NEXT
GENERATION

JAMES HATFIELD
AND
GEORGE "DOC" BURT

KENSINGTON BOOKS

This book was not prepared, approved, licensed, or endorsed by any entity involved in creating or producing the Star Trek series or motion pictures.

KENSINGTON BOOKS are published by

Kensington Publishing Corp.
850 Third Avenue
New York, NY 10022

Copyright © 1996 by Omega Publishing Endeavors

All rights reserved. No part of this book may be reproduced in any form or by any means without the prior written consent of the Publisher, excepting brief quotes used in reviews.

If you purchased this book without a cover you should be aware that this book is stolen property. It was reported as "unsold and destroyed" to the Publisher and neither the Author nor the Publisher has received any payment for this "stripped book."

Kensington and the K logo Reg. U.S. Pat. & TM Off.

ISBN 1-57566-063-6

First Printing: August, 1996
10 9 8 7 6 5 4 3 2 1

Printed in the United States of America

CONTENTS

This book is dedicated to:

The late Gene Roddenberry,
the "Founder of the Federation,"
for creating a wondrous world full of optimism and
hope for tomorrow.

Nancy,
who lovingly made me realize that
the best things in life come to those
who wait patiently, and
Dad and "Bet,"
for standing by me through
the good times and bad.

—J.H.

My late father, a giant of a man,
who sacrificed so much in his
short life so that I could have the
success and prosperity that he
always dreamt of having. This
book is dedicated to you, Dad,
for "making it so."

—Doc

And to our mothers,
who both died the same year and are now teaching the angels a few things.

ACKNOWLEDGMENTS

Research for a trivia book this size turned out to be quite a project. We owe a deep gratitude to so many people, all of whom had the kindness and patience to assist us in our neverending quest for fascinating and obscure facts about *Star Trek: The Next Generation*. To its fans, the world of *TNG* is wonderfully full of facts, figures, production notes, and peculiar details. To the non-Trekker, *TNG* is nothing more than a wildly imaginative science-fiction show with a cult following the equivalent of a religious movement. Of necessity, a book of this nature brings both groups together, and we found it a rewarding challenge to be working with both fans and non-fans alike.

First, special thanks go out to author and fellow Arkansawyer Ruby Jean Jensen, whose introducing us to Zebra kept this book from being just another manuscript collecting dust, and our editor, Tracy Bernstein, for her professionalism and faith in this book's worth.

We would also like to especially thank those on the home front: Theresa Burt, who typed large parts of the manuscript with exemplary thoughtfulness and meticulous care while keeping one eye on the calendar to beat the *first* deadline, and Nancy Bledsoe, for her patience and support above and beyond the call of duty while we made the last-minute changes before the *second* deadline.

For their assistance, information, support, and generosity, the following individuals deserve a special note of thanks: Ralph and Raymond Hatfield, Betty Henderson, Susan and Mike Bradshaw, Judy and Ed Echols, Carla and Bryan Grayson, Jeanette and Tom Mentzel, Pam Barnett, Teddy Kuan, Ian Spelling, John Scognamiglio, "Admiral" Harold Skidmore, and Dr. Richard Waldie (for realigning the back after hours upon hours at the computer).

And finally, our deepest thanks to the various *Star Trek* fan clubs who cared so much and provided invaluable help.

All the others who helped us in some way to produce the ultimate *TNG* trivia challenge have our heartfelt thanks, and if we omitted your name please forgive us.

James Hatfield and George "Doc" Burt

INTRODUCTION

Great Trekspectations

In the summer of 1994, after seven seasons and 178 episodes, *Star Trek: The Next Generation* (commonly referred to by fans as *TNG*) warped off the air and boldly went where few television series have gone before—the big screen. *Star Trek: Generations,* the first *Trek* film to feature *The Next Generation* cast, had the most successful debut weekend at the box office of any previous *Trek* movie.

From its premiere in 1987 with the two-hour episode "Encounter at Farpoint," *TNG* was the highest-rated syndicated drama in the history of television, with as many as 20 million viewers a week. Among males ages 18 to 49 *TNG* was the #1 show on TV, period. Syndicated episodes from its seven seasons show nightly in 142 markets across the country, while video stores are busy renting the same episodes.

Trek conventions are held in cities all over the country throughout the year. Thousands of fans (Trekkers) show up dressed outrageously as Starfleet officers, Vulcans, Ferengi, Cardassians, Klingons, Romulans, Borg, or any number of *Trek*'s myriad alien life forms. And they love to talk *Trek* trivia.

Obviously, there was a need for a book of nothing but *TNG* trivia. With remote controls in hand like phasers, we played, rewound, and played again every *TNG* episode from 1987's "Encounter at Farpoint" to the record-breaking grand finale in 1994, "All Good Things. . . ." The book you now hold is the end result of hundreds of hours of painstaking research.

You wanted the ultimate *Star Trek: The Next Generation* trivia challenge and now you've got it. Get your mind set for hours of enjoyment and mental stimulation. Test yourself and test your friends. The Prime Directive to guide you through this challenge is very simple— just have fun!

HOW TO DETERMINE YOUR SCORE ·

In the spirit of any worthwhile trivia game, there are a variety of categories in this book. For example, the questions in the "It's About Time" sections are about episodes having to do with time travel, distortions, rifts, etc.; "The Time to Play" sections deal with holodeck programs. Testing methods are just as varied. Some categories are strictly short answer, others are multiple choice or matching, and still others are a combination of methods. There's also a little true/false and fill in the blank thrown in for good measure.

All trivia questions count as 1 point, except the specially designated **Prime Memory Bonus.** Because these questions may short-circuit your memory bank, it would be logical to count them as 5 points each. Every category has one or more Prime Memory Bonus questions. You will find the answers in the back of the book, plus a line to enter your score for each category. We gave serious consideration to placing an answer key after each category, but we thought you might be too tempted to sneak a peek. On the very last page you will compute your total score for this book's trivia challenge and determine your Starfleet rank:

1. Admiral
2. Captain
3. Commander
4. Lieutenant
5. Ensign
6. Academy cadet

Note that Trekkers have christened the original *Star Trek* series *"TREK-classic"* and *Star Trek: The Next Generation* as *"TNG."* In the interest of continuity and brevity, we shall adhere to these same designations.

Good luck, contestants, and as the Klingons say, *"Qapla'."*

Q AND A

Q was a powerful cosmic superbeing with the temperament of a spoiled child. The *Enterprise*-D made first contact with Q when he detained the starship and put the crew's away team on trial for being "grievously savage." Over the course of *TNG*'s seven seasons Q was a recurring character, appearing in the two-hour pilot, "Encounter at Farpoint" and in the two-hour series finale, "All Good Things. . . ." Almost every episode in which Q appeared had the letter *Q* in the title, so it's only natural to begin our pursuit of *TREK* trivia with a little Q and A.

1. On his second visit to the *Enterprise*-D, to which senior bridge officer did Q offer a gift of Q-like supernatural powers?

2. Q later sent the *Enterprise*-D across the galaxy, where first contact was made with the immensely powerful and dangerous Borg. What was the name of this second season episode?

3. Q appeared in the form of an Aldebaran serpent during his second visit to the *Enterprise*-D. How many heads did this reptile have?

4. How many light years beyond Federation space did Q transport the *Enterprise*-D into the flight path of the Borg vessel?

5. What was the name of the extradimensional domain in which Q and others of his kind exist?

6. When Q was stripped of his powers and sought refuge aboard the *Enterprise*-D, which officer did he claim was the nearest thing he had to a friend?

7. Which race of gaseous creatures attacked the *Enterprise*-D in an attempt to seek revenge on Q?

8. Who was seriously injured while protecting Q from attack?

9. Name the *Enterprise*-D shuttlecraft that Q commandeered in an effort to save the starship from further hostile action.

10. Q cast Captain Picard, Vash, and other members of the *Enterprise*-D crew into an elaborate Robin Hood re-creation in an attempt to teach Picard a lesson about love. Which *Enterprise* officer was cast in the minstrel part of Alan-a-Dale?

11. What role did Q play in the Sherwood Forest fantasy?

12. How many years did Vash explore unknown parts of the galaxy with Q?

13. In the "True-Q" episode, which *Enterprise*-D officer did Q transform into a barking dog?

14. Name the student intern aboard the *Enterprise*-D who left with Q to discover her new identity.

15. A severely injured Picard relived his reckless youth in what Q claimed was the afterlife. How many Nausicaans did young Ensign Picard get into a fight with while on leave at Starbase Earhart?

16. How many centuries had Q and Guinan known and hated each other?

17. What was Q's IQ?

18. In "All Good Things ...," Captain Picard quantum-leaped through three time periods, with Q secretly controlling his trips.

What was the cosmic wisenheimer doing when Picard first encountered him in the past?

Prime Memory Bonus

Name the life form of unknown origin from TREK-classic who many fans speculate was related to Q.

IT'S ABOUT TIME

Part I

From temporal rifts to distortions in the space–time continuum, the *Enterprise*-D and her crew quantum-leaped through numerous episodes in seven seasons. Test your knowledge of the *Enterprise*-D's time-traveling voyages with the following trivia questions.

1. What was the name of the humanoid alien from Tau Alpha C who had the ability to exploit the interchangeability of time, space, and thought?

2. In the episode "Where No One Has Gone Before," a failed warp-drive experiment caused the bizarre distortion of time aboard the *Enterprise*-D. Which officer's long-deceased mother materialized in the corridors of the starship?

3. In the episode "Remember Me," who was the *Enterprise*-D officer trapped in a private universe or reality after a warp physics experiment went awry?

4. The Vorgons were a humanoid race capable of time travel. In "Captain's Holiday," how many 27th-century Vorgons transported backward in time to locate Captain Picard?

5. In the seventh season episode "Parallels," Worf and Deanna Troi had become lovers and "mated" in another quantum reality. What was the name of their son?

6. What type of explosion created the temporal rift in "Yesterday's Enterprise," accidentally sending the *Enterprise*-C some 22 years in the future?

Prime Memory Bonus

Which Enterprise-D officer was killed in "Parallels" when the Cardassians attacked the starship?

---

7. Which *Enterprise*-D crew member in "Yesterday's Enterprise" was the only one aware of the damage to the "normal" flow of time?

8. Although Tasha Yar died without ever having a child, her alternate version from the *Enterprise*-C gave birth to a daughter named Sela. In which episode was Sela first seen as a Romulan operative?

9. In which episode was the *Enterprise*-D and a Romulan ship frozen in time, moments away from an explosion that would destroy both ships?

10. Name the episode in which a duplicate of Captain Picard from six hours in the future was found drifting in space, the aftermath of the destruction of the *Enterprise*-D.

11. In "Cause and Effect," which Federation starship was trapped in a temporal causality loop, causing it to collide time and time again with the *Enterprise*-D?

12. In "Time's Arrow, Parts I and II," members of the *Enterprise*-D crew traveled back in time to 19th-century San Francisco. Who was the bellboy working at the hotel where Data took up lodging?

13. In "Time's Arrow, Parts I and II," which alien race was using the cholera plague of the time to conceal their murder of humans?

14. Which Shakespeare play was "Mr. Pickerd's" troupe of itinerant actors planning to perform in the "Time's Arrow" episodes?

Prime Memory Bonus

What was the name of the landlady in "Time's Arrow, Parts I and II," who had the misfortune of renting an apartment to Picard and other Enterprise-D *crew members?*

---

15. In the "Future Imperfect" episode, which Enterprise-D officer woke up, apparently 16 years in the future, having lost all memory of the past 16 years?

16. What was the name of the episode in which a time-traveling professor, evidently on a research project from the future, turned out to be a petty thief from the past?

17. In which episode was Picard given the opportunity to relive the three-day period in his youth leading up to a fight that cost him his heart?

18. In the first season episode "Where No One Has Gone Before," the Traveler encouraged Captain Picard to support Wesley Crusher's unusual talents because he was a "prodigy." In which seventh season episode did Crusher discover he, too, was a time "traveler"?

19. In "The Neutral Zone," the Enterprise-D revived a group of 20th-century humans who were frozen some four centuries earlier. One of the "thawed" humans, dissatisfied with services aboard the Enterprise-D, suggested that Captain Picard could use a few lessons from which ocean-going passenger ship?

20. In "The Inner Light," how long did it take for an unconscious Picard to experience Kamin's entire adult life?

21. Captain Montgomery Scott survived the crash of a Federation transport ship in "Relics" by suspending himself for 75 years in a modified transporter beam. What was the name of Scotty's crashed ship?

Prime Memory Bonus

What was the alcoholic beverage Data served Scotty in Ten-Forward after Scotty expressed displeasure with synthehol-based scotch?

A TIME TO PLAY

Part I

Match the listing of holodeck simulation programs from the *Enterprise*-D to the episode in which it appeared.

1. _____ Martial-arts exercise program

2. _____ Ancient West

3. _____ *The Three Musketeers* reinterpreted by Barclay

4. _____ Natural setting with a stream

5. _____ Tanuga Research Station simulations used in extradition trial of Commander Riker

6. _____ Sherlock Holmes

7. _____ Chula Valley on Romulus

8. _____ Grassy hill for Tasha Yar's memorial service

9. _____ Stand-up comic

10. _____ Klingon Age of Ascension

11. _____ Simulation of Albert Einstein

12. _____ Bridge of *Enterprise* NCC-1701

A. "Nth Degree"

B. "The Outrageous Okona"

C. "Code of Honor"

D. "Hollow Pursuits"

E. "Relics"

F. "The Defector"

G. "Skin of Evil"

H. "The Icarus Factor"

I. "A Matter of Perspective"

J. "Encounter at Farpoint"

K. "A Fistful of Datas"

L. "Elementary, Dear Data" "Ship in a Bottle"

Prime Memory Bonus

In which episode did La Forge simulate a moonlit beach on the holodeck?

A TIME TO PLAY

Part II

1. _____ Horse riding in open countryside

2. _____ Dixon Hill gumshoe

3. _____ Dancing lesson

4. _____ Paris' Champs Élysées

5. _____ French sidewalk cafe

6. _____ Boreth monastery

7. _____ White-water kayaking

8. _____ Klingon calisthenics program

9. _____ Shakespeare's *Henry V*

10. _____ Poker with great scientists

11. _____ The Low Note club on Bourbon Street in New Orleans

12. _____ Skiing the Denubian Alps

A. "Rightful Heir"

B. "11001001"

C. "Where Silence Has Lease" "The Emissary" "New Ground"

D. "Descent, Part I"

E. "Angel One"

F. "The Perfect Mate"

G. "Pen Pals"

H. "Data's Day"

I. "The Big Goodbye" "Manhunt" "Clues"

J. "We'll Always Have Paris"

K. "The Defector"

L. "Transfigurations"

Prime Memory Bonus

In which episode was the Kriosian Temple of Akadar re-created on the holodeck?

BEHIND THE SCENES

Part I

1. Which two *TNG* stars shared the same birthday with the late Gene Roddenberry?

2. Andreas Katsulas, Romulan commander Tomalak in several episodes, co-starred in the Oscar-winning movie *The Fugitive*. Who did he portray?

3. Suzie Plakson, Worf's murdered mate K'Ehleyr, had previously played the Vulcan Dr. Selar in which episode?

4. Lwaxana Troi's attendant, Mr. Homn, was portrayed by Carel Struycken. Which recurring role did he play in the Addams Family movies?

5. Michelle Forbes, who played the Bajoran national Ensign Ro on *Enterprise*-D, also portrayed Dara, the daughter of Dr. Timicin, in which episode?

6. Ben Vereen, LeVar Burton's co-star in the landmark T.V. mini-series *Roots*, also guest-starred on an episode of *TNG* during the seventh season. What role did he play?

7. The character of Geordi La Forge was named in memory of which late, handicapped *Star Trek* fan?

8. Which LA Lakers basketball star played a minor role as a Klingon in an episode from the seventh season?

9. Armin Shimerman (Quark on *Deep Space 9*) played Letek, one of the first three Ferengi in "The Last Outpost," and Bractor, another

Ferengi in "Peak Performance." What non-Ferengi role did he perform in "Haven"?

10. Michael Dorn, the actor who played Worf, the Klingon security officer on *Enterprise*-D, also portrayed a policeman for three years on which T.V. cop show?

11. The episode "Attached," in which Dr. Crusher and Captain Picard finally expressed their love for each other, was directed by which regular cast member?

12. "The Icarus Factor," a Klingon episode, and *Star Trek V: The Final Frontier*, were filmed about the same time, causing a run on the costume department's supply of Klingon boots. How was the boot shortage remedied?

13. Captain Picard brought back a Horga'hn, a wooden statuette representing sexuality, when he visited Risa in the "Captain's Holiday" episode. The Horga'hn could sometimes be seen adorning whose quarters in later episodes?

14. What was the name of the episode in which Wil Wheaton made his final regular appearance as Ensign Crusher?

15. Who was the noted rock musician who played the bomb-carrying Antidean ambassador in "Manhunt"?

16. Commander Riker turned down a chance to command the U.S.S. *Aries* in "The Icarus Factor." The starship was named for the moon landing shuttle from which non-*Trek* sci-fi motion picture?

17. Who was the well-known science fiction writer and friend of Gene Roddenberry who was credited in "Datalore" for 20th-century employment of positronic computing devices in robot brains?

18. Stephanie Beacham played Professor James Moriarty's love interest in the "Ship in a Bottle" episode. The following season, Ms. Beacham became a cast member on which T.V. sci-fi series?

19. Patrick Stewart portrayed the ironweaver Kamin in "The Inner Light" episode. Who played Kamin's son, Batai?

20. Ray Walston played Boothby, the old but wise groundskeeper at Starfleet Academy. Name the popular 1960s T.V. series in which Walston played an E.T.

21. Dwight Shultz, who played systems diagnostic engineer Reginald Barclay in a recurring role was once a co-star on a very popular action-adventure series. Can you name the show?

22. Who was the *LA Law* star who appeared as a member of the Q Continuum in the "Déjà Q" episode?

23. How many pairs of gold contact lenses did Brent Spiner go through per season for the role of Data?

24. Which *TREK-classic* cast member's son directed *TNG* episode "Timescape"?

25. What was the name of the motion picture Gates McFadden filmed while on leave from *TNG* during the second season?

26. In which episode was the audience shown what it looks like to be beamed from the transport subject's point of view?

Prime Memory Bonus

Who designed the triangle-circle IDIC pendant, which is also known as the Vulcan symbol?

---

27. Marina Sirtis originally auditioned for the part of which *Enterprise*-D officer?

28. The set for the Ten Forward lounge was re-dressed to serve as the office of the Federation Council President in *Star Trek VI: The Undiscovered Country*. Which city could be viewed outside the windows of the President's office?

29. One of the computer readouts studied by Dr. Timicin in "Half a Life" bore the numeric code 4077. What was the connection between this number and the actor who played Timicin?

30. George Murdock portrayed Starfleet Admiral J. P. Hanson in "The Best of Both Worlds, Parts I and II." Hanson had been in charge of Starfleet Tactical's effort to develop a defense against the Borg, but he was killed along with 11,000 others at Wolf 359. What role had Murdock previously played in *Star Trek V: The Final Frontier?*

31. David Warner played Gul Madred, the Cardassian officer who interrogated and tortured Captain Picard in "Chain of Command, Part II." Warner also played diplomat St. John Talbot in *Star Trek V: The Final Frontier.* What role did he play in *Star Trek VI: The Undiscovered Country?*

32. The late Kevin Peter Hall portrayed Leyor, a Caldonian negotiating for rights to a wormhole in "The Price." What role did he play in the movie *Predator?*

33. Who provided the voice for the *Enterprise*-D's main computer?

34. In which episode was the *Enterprise*-D barber shop first seen?

35. Michelle Phillips played Captain Picard's old flame, Jenice Manheim, in "We'll Always Have Paris." Which famous musical group was Phillips a member of in the 1960s?

36. Walter Gotell portrayed Kurt Mandl, the director of an aborted terraforming station in the episode "Home Soil." What role did Gotell make famous in several James Bond movies?

37. In which episode was the weekly poker game between some of the *Enterprise*-D's senior officers seen for the first time?

Prime Memory Bonus

Which episode won the 1993 Hugo Award for Best Dramatic Presentation from the World Science Fiction Society?

---

38. What type of lionfish lived in the saltwater aquarium in Picard's ready room?

39. Charles Cooper portrayed K'mpec, the leader of the Klingon High Council in "Sins of the Father." What role did he play in *Star Trek V: The Final Frontier?*

40. In the popular episode "Relics," what was the technical blooper that *Star Trek* fans repeatedly pointed out?

41. What was different about the Starfleet communicator pins in the episodes "Future Imperfect" and "Parallels"?

42. Name the *Lethal Weapon* villain who played Kyle Riker, father of *Enterprise*-D executive officer William Riker.

43. Which episode was being filmed at the time of the death of *Star Trek* creator Gene Roddenberry?

44. Who portrayed Dr. Stephen Hawking, one of the most brilliant theoretical physicists of 20th-century Earth, in the episode "Descent, Part I"?

45. The character of Guinan was named after which famous Prohibition-era saloon bartender?

Prime Memory Bonus

Actress Tricia O'Neil played Rachel Garrett, captain of the Enterprise-C *in "Yesterday's Enterprise." What character did she portray in the "Suspicions" episode?*

TO SEEK OUT NEW LIFE . . .

Part I

The *Enterprise*-D's exploration of space has revealed the galaxy to be home to myriad life forms of virtually every imaginable design, shape, and size. Match the life forms listed below with their correct description.

1. ____ Crystalline Entity

2. ____ Armus

3. ____ Pakleds

4. ____ Nanites

5. ____ Lycosa tarantula

6. ____ J'naii

7. ____ Klabnian eel

8. ____ Exocomps

9. ____ Gatherers

10. ____ Zylo eggs

11. ____ Tarkassian razor beast

12. ____ Wompats

A. Spaceborne ship-sized life form

B. Resembled a giant snowflake

C. Nomadic offshoot of the Acamarians

D. La Forge's first pet

E. Life form that was Guinan's imaginary friend

F. Humanoids who tried to gain control of Starfleet with addictive mind game

G. Intelligent humanoid race despite slow speech

H. Androgynous humanoid species

13. _____ Ktarians

14. _____ Junior

15. _____ Circassian cat

I. Pet often kept by
    Cardassian children

J. Small robotic
    servomechanisms that
    attained sentience

K. Life form Data chose as
    subject of his first painting

L. Submicroscopic robotic
    life form

M. Malevolent life form on
    Vagra II

N. Miles O'Brien kept one as
    a pet

O. Life form Q disliked

Prime Memory Bonus

What was the name of the Klingon insect one-half the size of an Earth mosquito mentioned in "The Outrageous Okona"?

TO SEEK OUT NEW LIFE . . .

Part II

1. Starfleet code-named this ancient, spaceborne organism "Tin Man," the last of a species of living spacecraft.
   A. Aldean
   B. Gomtuu
   C. Calnoth

2. In "The Price," this humanoid race attempted to bid for rights to use the Barzan wormhole.
   A. Caldonians
   B. Mintakans
   C. Tellarites

3. They were life forms that existed in a deep subspace domain, forcibly abducting *Enterprise*-D crew members during their sleep for medical testing.
   A. Iconians
   B. Solanagen-based aliens
   C. Troglytes

4. This last remaining protector of the once grand TKon Empire was awakened from stasis by the presence of Ferengi and Federation spacecraft.
   A. Tosk
   B. Kelvan
   C. Portal 63

5. This sentient reptilian race applied for admission to the Federation in "Lonely Among Us."
    A. Selay
    B. Anticans
    C. Bandi

6. Possessing awesome powers of creation and destruction, this race of energy beings was fond of assuming the appearance of other life forms.
    A. Dresci
    B. Droxine
    C. Douwd

7. He was a marooned alien child who lured Riker into a virtual reality fantasy in which he hoped Riker would remain as a playmate.
    A. Vedek
    B. Barash
    C. Pomet

8. In the episode "Pen Pals," this little humanoid girl from the endangered planet Drema IV communicated with Data via subspace radio.
    A. Denorios
    B. Sarjenka
    C. Natira

9. These Rubicun III inhabitants demanded the lawful execution of Wesley Crusher for infraction of a minor regulation.
    A. Angosians
    B. Gemarians
    C. The Edo

10. The beings of this ancient, highly advanced civilization were once known as "Demons of Air and Darkness."
    A. Iconians
    B. Iotians
    C. Kohms

11. This humanoid race was nearly wiped out by a deadly biological weapon.
    A. Tarellians
    B. Talarians
    C. Tamarians

12. This humanoid race had vaguely reptilian features. Dr. Crusher discovered in "Suspicions" that they were able to control the rate of their cellular physiology, allowing them to put themselves into a state resembling death.
    A. Ullians
    B. Takarans
    C. Barzans

13. This race of humanoids could be distinguished by a light blue skin and a midfacial dividing line. Captain Rixx, seen in the "Conspiracy" episode, was a member of this species.
    A. Bolians
    B. Bringloidi
    C. Elasians

14. In "The Nth Degree," the *Enterprise*-D was contacted by this species that resided on a planet near the center of the galaxy.
    A. Cygians
    B. Cyalodins
    C. Cytherians

15. This race of fishlike humanoid creatures found spaceflight extremely traumatic and survived the ordeal by entering a self-induced catatonic state.
    A. Antideans
    B. Denebians
    C. Dopterians

16. What was the name of the terrorist group on the western continent of Rutia IV that abducted Captain Picard and Dr. Crusher?
    A. Lenarian
    B. Kalandan
    C. Ansata

17. This ancient intelligent culture was composed of two different life forms, one of energy and the other of matter.
    A. Gunji
    B. Koinonians
    C. Eymorg

18. Establishment of diplomatic relations with this reclusive insectoid race in "Samaritan Snare" was a Federation priority because of their planet's strategic importance.
    A. Jarada
    B. Mondor
    C. Eminiar

19. This humanoid race entered into trade negotiations with the Romulans in "Unification, Part I."
    A. Baryons
    B. Barolians
    C. Barokies

20. This blue-green skinned race breathed with the assistance of a respirator.
    A. Zeons
    B. Tagrans
    C. Benzites

21. This humanoid race was faintly reptilian in appearance and their spoken language was based entirely on metaphors.
    A. Tamarians
    B. Mikulaks
    C. Ophidians

22. This race was known for their need to hibernate for six months at a time. Captain Picard chose them as mediators in an evacuation dispute in "The Ensigns of Command."
    A. Frunalain
    B. Grisella
    C. Calnoth

23. These Bronze Age proto-Vulcan humanoids were reported to be very peaceful and lived in a matriarchal, agricultural society. In "Who Watches the Watchers?," a Federation anthropological

field team accidentally exposed them to advanced Federation technology.

    A. Mintakans

    B. Yangs

    C. Rakhari

24. In "Coming of Age," this humanoid race was characterized by webbed hands. Their cultural values rejected human courtesy as a form of dishonesty.

    A. Zaynars

    B. Zayras

    C. Zaldans

25. This race from "The Loss" episode utilized cloaking technology, and their ships were armed with disruptor-type weapons.

    A. Thasians

    B. Haliian

    C. Breen

Prime Memory Bonus

In "Time's Arrow, Part I," they were a single-celled microscopic life form indigenous to Devidia II. A cellular fossil of one of these life forms was discovered buried beneath San Francisco, near Data's severed head.

    A. LB10445

    B. 487818

    C. 486719

STARFLEET INTELLIGENCE OFFICER DOSSIER
Captain Jean-Luc Picard

1. What was Picard's serial number?
   A. SF-487-818
   B. SP-937-215
   C. SF-22530-077

2. Which one of Picard's parents opposed his ambitions of voyaging among the stars?

3. What was the name of the French town where his family's vineyard was located?

4. As a boy, what was young Picard's favorite pasttime?
   A. Building ships in bottles
   B. Playing the piano
   C. Gardening

5. (True or false) Picard failed to gain entrance to Starfleet Academy at the age of 17, but was admitted a year later.

6. What distinction did Picard hold as a runner while at the Academy?

7. Cadet Picard committed a serious offense while at the Academy. Years later, whom did he credit for making it possible for him to graduate by helping him to "do the right thing"?
   A. Robert, his brother
   B. Marta, his friend
   C. Boothby, the Academy groundskeeper

8. On leave with several classmates at Starbase Earhart, Picard picked a fight with some Nausicaans. One of them stabbed Picard through the heart, necessitating what type of medical procedure?

9. As a young lieutenant, who was the famous Federation ambassador Picard met at a wedding?

10. What was the name of the young woman whom Picard loved very deeply and regretted breaking off the relationship for many years?

11. In his early career, Picard distinguished himself when he led an away team to save an endangered ambassador on which planet?
    A. Beto II
    B. Milika III
    C. Legaran

12. Lieutenant Picard was a bridge officer on the U.S.S. *Stargazer* when the ship's captain was killed. Which class of Federation starship was the *Stargazer*?

Prime Memory Bonus

What was the first name of Captain Picard's father (as seen on Jean-Luc's bio computer screen in "Conundrum")?

---

13. During an exploratory mission to Section 21503, the *Stargazer* was attacked by forces of which alien race?
    A. Ferengi
    B. Romulan
    C. Cardassian

14. Picard commanded the *Stargazer* for some 20 years until it was nearly destroyed by an unprovoked sneak attack near which star system?
    A. Maxia Zeta
    B. Triona
    C. Volchok Prime

15. What was the name of the defensive tactic (and required reading
     at Starfleet Academy) that was devised by Picard aboard the
     Stargazer during the battle with the Ferengi spacecraft?

16. Following the loss of the *Stargazer*, Picard was court martialed per
     standard Starfleet procedure, but cleared of wrongdoing. Who
     was the prosecutor in the case with whom Picard had been ro-
     mantically involved?

17. Years later, a Ferengi returned the hulk of the *Stargazer* to Picard
     as part of a plot to discredit the captain for what the Ferengi be-
     lieved to be Picard's part in his son's death. What was the venge-
     ful Ferengi's name?

18. (True or false) 2365 was the stardate that the *Enterprise*-D was
     launched under the command of Captain Picard.

19. Picard was offered a promotion to the admiralty when Admiral
     Gregory Quinn claimed there was a threat to the Federation and
     he needed men whom he could trust in positions of Starfleet au-
     thority. What was Picard to have been in charge of had he ac-
     cepted the promotion?

20. What time-space disturbance was responsible in the Endicor
     system for creating a duplicate of Picard from six hours in the fu-
     ture?
     A. Energy vortex
     B. Temporal rift
     C. Temporal distortion

Prime Memory Bonus

*When complications developed, who was the doctor that per-
formed an emergency cardiac replacement procedure on Picard at
Starbase 515?*

---

21. Picard mind-melded with Ambassador Sarek when the Vulcan's
     last mission was jeopardized by an emotionally debilitating dis-
     ease. Which *Enterprise*-D officer remained with Picard while
     Sarek's savage emotional outbursts ripped through Picard?

22. Picard was abducted and incorporated forcibly into a Borg as part of the powerful race's assault on the Federation. What was the name of the "transformed" Picard?

23. Picard was forced to cooperate in the devastating battle of Wolf 359, in which 40 Federation starships tried in vain to prevent a Borg invasion of Earth. How many ships in the armada were destroyed?

24. Following the destruction of the Borg and his rescue by an *Enterprise*-D away team, Picard spent several weeks in rehabilitation from the terrible physical and psychological trauma. While the *Enterprise*-D was undergoing repairs, Picard stayed with his brother and his family. What was the name of Picard's nephew?

25. During this time, Picard considered leaving Starfleet to accept the directorship of the Atlantis Project. What was the name of Picard's boyhood friend who was a supervisor on the project?

26. What was the unprecedented role Picard assumed in Klingon politics following the death of K'mpec, the Klingon High Council leader?

27. Under Picard's outsider mediation, which council member emerged as the sole challenger for leadership of the High Council?
    A. K'nera
    B. Gowron
    C. Duras

28. A molecular reversion field reduced Picard and other crew members to children when their shuttlecraft passed through the mysterious energy field. Who were the other three affected *Enterprise*-D crew members?
    A. Guinan, Ro, and Keiko
    B. Guinan, Ro, and Troi
    C. Guinan, Ro, and Beverly

29. Picard suffered profound emotional scars when he was captured and tortured by Cardassians during a failed commando raid on Celtris III. What was the new type of weapon the Cardassians were allegedly experimenting with on Celtris III?

30. Gul Madred, the Cardassian expert in extracting information, implanted a pain-inducing device in Picard in an attempt to gain tactical plans from the Starfleet captain. Picard resisted, but later confessed to which *Enterprise*-D officer that he would have told Madred anything had he not been rescued?

Prime Memory Bonus

What were the four words Picard screamed at Gul Madred when refusing to bow to the Cardassian's demands for the last time before returning to the Enterprise-D?

---

31. Picard was an avid amateur archaeologist, occasionally publishing papers and lecturing on the subject. Who was the noted archaeologist and teacher who urged Picard early in his career to seriously consider archaeology as a profession?

32. Picard was also an accomplished horseman, and one of his favorite holodeck programs was a woodland setting in which he enjoyed riding an Arabian mare. How long had Picard owned the saddle that he kept with him aboard the *Enterprise*-D?

33. Captain Picard was an aficionado of the 1930s and 1940s gumshoe Dixon Hill stories and enjoyed holodeck simulations based on them. The Dixon Hill adventures were set in which early 20th-century North American city?

34. Which musical instrument did Picard play when he was young?

35. Picard's deep love of music may have stemmed from an encounter with an alien probe when his mind received a lifetime of memories from a man named Kamin, whose planet's sun had gone nova centuries earlier. How many years had Kamin been dead?

36. Who was the accomplished pianist, scientist, and *Enterprise*-D officer with whom Picard became romantically involved?
    A. Neela Daren
    B. Tess Allenby
    C. Norah Satie

37. What was the name of the archaeologist and adventurer with whom Picard first met and developed a relationship while on vacation on Risa?

38. Who was the beautiful empathic metamorph from the Krios system that bonded with Picard?

Prime Memory Bonus

The private detective character that Picard enjoyed playing on the holodeck first appeared in the short story "The Big Goodbye" in which pulp magazine?

---

39. Picard was vaporized and the *Enterprise*-D proceeded to hold a funeral for the captain in the seventh year of their continuing mission. Who refused to believe Picard was dead?
     A. Worf
     B. Riker
     C. Troi

40. Picard was alive and had been posing as a mercenary in an attempt to solve the mystery of a looted archaeological site. What was the name of the Romulan mercenary?

41. After Picard's old nemesis, DaiMon Bok, bought his way out of a Ferengi prison, he sent a holographic message to Picard telling the Federation captain that he would finally get his revenge for Picard killing his son. How did he plan to exact his revenge?

42. On the *Enterprise*-D, Captain Picard's ready room was a small office located directly adjacent to the bridge. Which one of the following items did *NOT* decorate the captain's room?
     A. A crystalline sailing ship model
     B. An ancient nautical sextant
     C. A hardbound edition of the collected works of Henry David Thoreau

43. In 2370, the reactivated dormant gene of a crew member caused the *Enterprise*-D's personnel to mutate to an earlier form of themselves. Where was Captain Picard when he and his com-

rades began to de-evolve, leaving the *Enterprise*-D aimlessly adrift in space?

44. Also in 2370, Picard became the source of a rupture in time that threatened to annihilate all humanity. The hellraiser Q sent Picard hopscotching through three time periods—the present, the past, and 25 years in the future. In what year did the past time frame take place?

Prime Memory Bonus

What was Captain Picard's security access code, or identification code, as of stardate 42494?

STARFLEET INTELLIGENCE OFFICER DOSSIER

Commander William Thomas Riker

1. Riker was born in 2335 in Alaska. Name the city.

2. How old was Riker when his mother died?

3. At what age was Riker when his father, Kyle, abandoned him?

4. What was Riker's rank in his graduating class at Starfleet Academy?

5. Riker's first assignment after graduating from the Academy was aboard which Federation ship?
   A. U.S.S. *Gandhi*
   B. U.S.S. *Hermes*
   C. U.S.S. *Pegasus*

6. Early in his Starfleet career, Riker was stationed on Betazed, where he became romantically involved with psychology student Deanna Troi. What rank in Starfleet was Riker at the time he met Troi?

7. While aboard the U.S.S. *Potemkin*, Riker led a rescue mission to which planet?
   A. Nervala IV
   B. Taurus II
   C. Korris II

8. (True or false) Riker was promoted to lieutenant commander and commended for "exceptional valor" after the rescue mission.

9. An exact duplicate of Riker was created during a transporter accident when the *Potemkin* was evacuating a science team. One copy of Riker returned safely to the *Potemkin*. Where did his duplicate materialize?

10. Once rescued, the other Riker decided to use another first name to distinguish himself from his duplicate. What name did he choose?

11. The Riker copy indicated a desire to continue in Starfleet and was assigned to which Federation ship?
    A. U.S.S. *Melbourne*
    B. U.S.S. *Gandhi*
    C. U.S.S. *Gettysburg*

12. Riker presented his identical copy with a cherished gift when the two men parted company. What was the going away present?
    A. A trombone
    B. A Horga'hn statuette
    C. A kiss from Troi

Prime Memory Bonus

During a crisis aboard the Potemkin, *where did Riker position the starship above a planet in an attempt to confuse his opponent's sensors?*

---

13. Riker was later promoted to executive officer aboard the U.S.S. *Hood*, where he served under the command of which captain?
    A. Paul Rice
    B. Walker Keel
    C. Robert DeSoto

14. After being transferred to duty aboard the *Enterprise*-D, Riker became the first Federation officer to serve on a Klingon warship when he participated in an Officer Exchange Program. What position did Riker assume while posted on the Klingon vessel?

15. Riker suffered a near brush with death while on a survey mission to an unexplored planet, where contact with a poisonous

plant caused him to lose consciousness for several hours. What was the name of the planet?

A.   Tanuga IV
B.   Surata IV
C.   Dytallix B

16.   Riker was charged with the murder of Dr. Nel Apgar after Apgar's science station exploded. Riker was acquitted after a holodeck re-creation demonstrated who was really responsible for Apgar's death. Alright, you Data/Sherlock Holmes fans, who killed Dr. Apgar?

A.   Dr. Apgar, when he tried to kill Riker
B.   Mauna Apgar, the doctor's wife
C.   Tayna, Dr. Apgar's research assistant

17.   Riker was granted a temporary field promotion to captain and given command of the *Enterprise*-D following the abduction of Captain Picard by the Borg. When Picard hailed the *Enterprise*-D and spoke for the Borg, Captain Riker replied with only three words. What were they?

18.   (True or false) Data once observed that Riker relied upon traditional problem-solving techniques in his approach to command less than one-quarter of the time.

19.   Which musical instrument did Riker play fairly well?

20.   One of Riker's passions was for what type of old Earth music?

21.   As *Enterprise*-D executive officer, what was Riker's favorite hobby?

22.   Which three starships did Starfleet offer Riker the opportunity to command?

A.   U.S.S. *Drake*, U.S.S. *Aries*, U.S.S. *Melbourne*
B.   U.S.S. *Drake*, U.S.S. *Hornet*, U.S.S. *Saratoga*
C.   U.S.S. *Drake*, U.S.S. *Zapata*, U.S.S. *Intrepid*

Prime Memory Bonus

What was Riker's identification code while aboard the Enterprise-D?

WHEN THE STARSHIPS SHINE

Starships were interstellar spacecraft capable of faster-than-light travel using warp drive. Of course you know the *Enterprise*-D was the Federation's flagship, but what do you know about other starships in the fleet?

1. In the episode "Too Short a Season," this *Constellation*-class ship was Mark Jameson's last command before becoming an admiral.
   A. U.S.S. *Renegade*
   B. U.S.S. *Gettysburg*
   C. U.S.S. *Lantree*

2. This starship suffered a warp containment breach near Turkana IV, and the crew was captured by members of the Alliance.
   A. U.S.S. *Antares*
   B. U.S.S. *Endeavour*
   C. U.S.S. *Arcos*

3. This *Miranda*-class starship was destroyed by the Borg in the battle of Wolf 359.
   A. U.S.S. *Zhukov*
   B. U.S.S. *Saratoga*
   C. U.S.S. *Yamato*

4. Commanded by Captain Rixx, this *New Orleans*-class ship met the *Enterprise*-D at Dytallix B for a covert meeting between captains Rixx and Picard.
   A. U.S.S. *Thomas Paine*
   B. U.S.S. *Magellan*
   C. U.S.S. *Lalo*

5. This starship underwent a computer system upgrade by the Bynars and was Ensign Ro's assignment before the *Enterprise*-D.
   A. U.S.S. *Republic*
   B. U.S.S. *Wellington*
   C. U.S.S. *Merrimac*

6. In "Redemption, Part II," this starship served in Picard's armada to blockade Romulan supply ships.
   A. U.S.S. *Phoenix*
   B. U.S.S. *Excalibur*
   C. U.S.S. *Rutledge*

7. This *Ambassador*-class starship was commanded by Walker Keel and destroyed by parasitic aliens seeking to control Starfleet Command.
   A. U.S.S. *Farragut*
   B. U.S.S. *Gorkon*
   C. U.S.S. *Horatio*

8. In "Encounter at Farpoint," this *Excelsior*-class starship transferred Riker, Dr. Crusher, and La Forge to the *Enterprise*-D.
   A. U.S.S. *Hood*
   B. U.S.S. *Grissom*
   C. U.S.S. *Hathaway*

9. In "Ménage à Troi" this starship was scheduled to transport Wesley Crusher to Starfleet Academy.
   A. U.S.S. *Cairo*
   B. U.S.S. *Bradbury*
   C. U.S.S. *Eagle*

10. This starship suffered a hull breach near Gravesworld in "The Schizoid Man."
    A. U.S.S. *Constantinople*
    B. U.S.S. *Bozeman*
    C. U.S.S. *Lexington*

11. In "Redemption, Part II," Data temporarily commanded this ship in Picard's armada at the Romulan Neutral Zone.
    A. U.S.S. *Horizon*
    B. U.S.S. *Endeavour*
    C. U.S.S. *Copernicus*

12. Dr. Pulaski served on this *Constitution*-class starship prior to her posting aboard the *Enterprise*-D.
    A. U.S.S. *Goddard*
    B. U.S.S. *Ajax*
    C. U.S.S. *Repulse*

13. Commanded by Riker's good friend Paul Rice, this starship was destroyed at planet Minos by an ancient, but still active, weapons system.
    A. U.S.S. *Denver*
    B. U.S.S. *Texas*
    C. U.S.S. *Drake*

14. In the episode "Unnatural Selection," the entire crew of this Federation ship was killed by exposure to genetic superchildren at Gagarin IV.
    A. U.S.S. *Lantree*
    B. U.S.S. *Roosevelt*
    C. U.S.S. *Horohito*

15. This starship was the first ship to respond to Klingon distress calls after the Khitomer massacre and was Sergey Rozhenko's former ship.
    A. U.S.S. *Reliant*
    B. U.S.S. *Intrepid*
    C. U.S.S. *Yorktown*

16. Data served aboard this starship before his posting on the *Enterprise*-D.
    A. U.S.S. *Trieste*
    B. U.S.S. *Sutherland*
    C. U.S.S. *Arizona*

17. This *Constellation*-class starship was La Forge's assignment as an ensign prior to his transfer to the *Enterprise*-D.
    A. U.S.S. *Tripoli*
    B. U.S.S. *Adelphi*
    C. U.S.S. *Victory*

18. This *Ambassador*-class starship transported Vulcan ambassador T'Pel to the *Enterprise*-D, participated in a scientific mission to

Phoenix Cluster, and was Reginald Barclay's previous assignment.
- A. U.S.S. *Tolstoy*
- B. U.S.S. *Zhukov*
- C. U.S.S. *Tsiolkovsky*

19. Commanded by Picard's old friend, Donald Varley, this *Galaxy*-class starship was destroyed by an ancient Iconian computer virus weapon.
- A. U.S.S. *Yamato*
- B. U.S.S. *Tian An Men*
- C. U.S.S. *Valiant*

20. In "The Naked Now," this Federation science vessel's crew was killed by the Psi 2000 virus.
- A. U.S.S. *Gage*
- B. U.S.S. *Tsiolkovsky*
- C. U.S.S. *Howard*

21. Which three starships were destroyed by the Borg at the battle of Wolf 359?
- A. U.S.S. *LaSalle*, U.S.S. *Gorkon*, U.S.S. *Exeter*
- B. U.S.S. *Monitor*, U.S.S. *Essex*, U.S.S. *Cochrane*
- C. U.S.S. *Tolstoy*, U.S.S. *Melbourne*, U.S.S. *Kyushu*

22. This starship discovered Data on planet Omicron Theta IV.
- A. U.S.S. *Vico*
- B. U.S.S. *Tripoli*
- C. U.S.S. *Archon*

23. This early Starfleet vessel, *Daedalus*-class, was destroyed and her crew of 229 were killed on a moon of planet Mab-Bu VI in the episode "Power Play."
- A. U.S.S. *Essex*
- B. U.S.S. *California*
- C. U.S.S. *Shining Star*

24. In "The Most Toys," this starship was requested to stand by for possible help with the underground tricyanate contamination of planet Beta Agni II.
    A. U.S.S. *Grissom*
    B. U.S.S. *Hood*
    C. U.S.S. *Carolina*

25. In "Peak Performance," this decommissioned starship was temporarily returned to duty for strategic battle simulations.
    A. U.S.S. *Kirk*
    B. U.S.S. *Mandela*
    C. U.S.S. *Hathaway*

26. This *Excelsior*-class starship, named for a former Klingon leader, was Admiral Nechayev's flagship during the expected Borg invasion in "Descent, Part I."
    A. U.S.S. *Gowron*
    B. U.S.S. *Gorkon*
    C. U.S.S. *K'mpec*

27. Starfleet propulsion specialist Kosinski and his assistant, the Traveler, tested an experimental warp drive on this starship.
    A. U.S.S. *Fearless*
    B. U.S.S. *Akagi*
    C. U.S.S. *Yosemite*

28. This Federation transport ship, *Sydney*-class, crashed into a Dyson sphere.
    A. U.S.S. *Defiant*
    B. U.S.S. *Jenolen*
    C. U.S.S. *Constitution*

29. In "Ethics," this Federation transport ship was carrying colonists to the Beloti Sector when the ship struck a gravitic mine left over from the Cardassian wars.
    A. U.S.S. *Oklahoma*
    B. U.S.S. *Kuan*
    C. U.S.S. *Denver*

30. Forty-seven crew members were killed when this *Ambassador*-class starship conducted a disastrous first contact with the planet Ghorusda.
    A. U.S.S. *Adelphi*
    B. U.S.S. *Surak*
    C. U.S.S. *Virginia*

31. In "Night Terrors," this starship was trapped in a Tyken's Rift where all but one crew member died from lack of REM sleep.
    A. U.S.S. *Dallas*
    B. U.S.S. *Brattain*
    C. U.S.S. *Lincoln*

32. This Federation starship, commanded by Captain Jellico, transported Vice Admiral Nechayev to rendezvous with the *Enterprise*-D when it was feared the Cardassians were developing a new weapon.
    A. U.S.S. *Berlin*
    B. U.S.S. *Moscow*
    C. U.S.S. *Cairo*

33. In "The Neutral Zone," this *Excelsior*-class starship transported three revived 20th-century cryonic survivors back to Earth.
    A. U.S.S. *Naiskos*
    B. U.S.S. *Charleston*
    C. U.S.S. *Yeltsin*

34. This Federation starship, named for a famous Native American Indian leader, was part of task force 3, under Picard's indirect command during an expected Borg invasion.
    A. U.S.S. *Crazy Horse*
    B. U.S.S. *Sitting Bull*
    C. U.S.S. *Geronimo*

35. Future *Enterprise*-D crew member Miles O'Brien served aboard this starship as a tactical officer during the war between the Federation and Cardassians.
    A. U.S.S. *Zapata*
    B. U.S.S. *New Orleans*
    C. U.S.S. *Rutledge*

Prime Memory Bonus

Okay, so you know your Starfleet ships. How about Klingon Defense Forces spacecraft? What class was the attack cruiser first seen in the episode "Reunion"?

BEHIND THE SCENES

Part II

1. *Star Trek* creator Gene Roddenberry actually journeyed to the final frontier when his ashes flew round trip on a NASA space shuttle a year after his death. On which shuttle did the "Great Bird of the Galaxy" travel to space?

2. Michael Berryman portrayed the Bolian captain Rixx in the "Conspiracy" episode. The tall, bald actor is best known for what cult horror film?

3. Name the episode Gates McFadden, a.k.a. Dr. Crusher, directed in the seventh and final season?

4. She played the Romulan commander Toreth in "Face of the Enemy," Subcommander Taris in "Contagion," and Mirasta in "First Contact." Who is this British actress?

5. In "The Big Goodbye" episode, what was private dick Dixon Hill's office number?

6. Why was "Night Terrors" not one of Marina Sirtis' favorite episodes?

7. Before Gates McFadden, she was *Trek's* first female director. Who was she?

8. Who made a special wake-up call (featuring *Trek* theme music and a variation of the "to boldly go . . ." narration) to the crew of the *Atlantis* during a 1991 shuttle mission?

9. What was the name of the seventh season episode directed by LeVar Burton?

10. Who played Worf's foster brother, Nikolai Rozhenko?

11. She played a Vulcan in *Star Trek III* and *IV* and a Romulan named Tallera in *TNG* episodes "Gambit, Part I and II." Who is she?

12. Which cast member directed the episodes "Reunion," "The Drumhead," "Quality of Life," and "The Offspring"?

13. Which former regular cast member was in the movies *Toy Soldiers, December,* and *Liars' Club,* and an episode of HBO's *Tales from the Crypt*?

14. This actor played a recurring character on *TNG* and a perverted doctor who kills himself in the hit thriller *The Hand that Rocks the Cradle.* Who is he?

15. For the episode "Relics," engineers had to rebuild the original *Enterprise* bridge from blueprints. Where did they get the captain's chair?

16. Where did the name *Enterprise* come from?

17. What do the three colors of Starfleet uniforms represent?

18. Erik Menyuk, who portrayed the Traveler, co-starred with Kevin Bacon in what Disney comedy/drama?

19. Before his death in 1992, this costume designer won an Emmy for his *TNG* designs. Who was he?

20. Patrick Stewart hosted which T.V. comedy show on February 5, 1994?

21. What was the name of the episode in which Worf disguised himself as a Boraalan, enabling fans to see Michael Dorn without his Klingon makeup?

22. In which episode was a shuttlecraft shown on *TNG* for the first time?

23. The cable movie *Death Train* (re-named *Detonator* when released on video) featured which *TNG* cast member?

24. Who was the former cast member who guest-starred in the episodes "Parallels," "The Game," and "Journey's End"?

25. Who was the co-producer who began with *TNG* in 1990 as an intern with the show's writing staff and went on to write many of *TNG*'s most highly praised episodes?

26. Colm Meaney, who portrayed Miles O'Brien, was nominated for a Golden Globe best lead actor award for what critically acclaimed theatrical movie in 1993?

27. What role did Patrick Stewart play in the Mel Brooks' movie *Robin Hood: Men in Tights*?

28. Teri Hatcher played *Enterprise*-D transporter officer B. G. Robinson in "The Outrageous Okona." In 1993 she became a regular on which ABC-TV series?

29. Which former cast member joined Juliette Lewis and Brad Pitt in the film *Kalifornia*?

30. Which regular *TNG* cast member appeared in *Star Trek VI: The Undiscovered Country*?

31. Which *Deep Space 9* character popped up on *TNG* via viewscreen in the seventh season episode "Firstborn"?

32. Who was the *TNG* makeup supervisor who won two Emmys for his creation of hundreds of futuristic humanoid and alien characters?

33. Which regular cast member directed the "Sub Rosa" episode?

34. Which regular cast member co-starred with Christopher Lambert and Mario Van Peebles in the 1993 film *Gunmen*?

35. Diana Muldaur portrayed Dr. Pulaski during the second season of *TNG*. She had previously played a psychologist and an astrobiologist in which two episodes of *TREK-classic*?

36. Clive Revill played Sir Guy of Gisborne in Q's Robin Hood fantasy. What role did Revill portray in the *Star Wars* film *The Empire Strikes Back*?

37. Which former *Cheers* star made an appearance at the end of the episode "Cause and Effect" as Captain Morgan Bateson, commanding officer of the U.S.S. *Bozeman*?

Prime Memory Bonus

He portrayed a Starfleet officer who was killed in Star Trek II: The Wrath of Kahn *and the Tamarian captain, Dathon, on* TNG. *Who is he?*

EAT, DRINK, AND BE MERRY

Part I

Match the food or beverage with the corresponding person, alien species, or place served.

1. ____ Banana split

2. ____ Arcturian fizz

3. ____ Andonian tea

4. ____ Caviar

5. ____ Chocolate

6. ____ Earl Grey

7. ____ Feline supplement 74

8. ____ Gagh

9. ____ Warnog

10. ____ Valerian root tea

11. ____ Prune juice

12. ____ Heart of *targ*

A. A weakness of Deanna Troi

B. Wesley Crusher's favorite dessert

C. Klingon ale

D. Traditional Klingon dish

E. Picard's favorite tea

F. A pleasure-enhancing beverage offered to DaiMon Tog by Lwaxana Troi

G. Favorite food of Picard

H. The drink of warriors

I. Cat food designed for Data's cat, Spot

J. Favorite beverage of Counselor Troi

K. Klingon serpent worms

L. Beverage served at Starfleet HQ

Prime Memory Bonus

A Samarian Sunset is a drink that initially appears clear, but becomes multicolored when the rim of the glass is tapped sharply. Which Enterprise-D officer prepared this specialty beverage for Deanna Troi in "Conundrum"?

EAT, DRINK, AND BE MERRY

Part II

1. ____ Tamarian frost

2. ____ Ginger tea

3. ____ Jestral tea

4. ____ Iced coffee

5. ____ Mint tea

6. ____ Owon eggs

7. ____ Rokeg blood pie

8. ____ Romulan ale

9. ____ Tarvokian pound cake

10. ____ Kanar

11. ____ Mareuvian tea

12. ____ Thalian chocolate mousse

A. A beverage favored by Cardassians

B. Traditional Klingon dish

C. Dessert that uses 400-year-old chocolate beans

D. A sweet beverage served in Ten Forward

E. Beverage enjoyed by Geordi La Forge

F. Delicacy prepared by Riker for some of the crew members

G. Picard's Aunt Adele's home remedy for a common cold

H. Beverage favored by Perrin, Ambassador Sarek's last wife

I. A beverage served in Ten Forward

J. Highly potent alcoholic beverage

K. Dessert baked by Worf

L. Favorite beverage of Lwaxana Troi

Prime Memory Bonus

Which humanoid race invented the alcoholic substitute "synthe-hol"?

STARFLEET INTELLIGENCE OFFICER DOSSIER

Lieutenant Commander Data

1. Data was a sophisticated humanoid android created by renowned cyberscieneticist Dr. Noonien Soong. In what year was Data built?

2. Was Data the first or second android constructed by Dr. Soong?

3. Just prior to the destruction of the Omicron Theta colony by the Crystalline Entity, what was stored in Data's brain for safe-keeping?
   A. All of Dr. Soong's cybernetic research
   B. The location of Dr. Soong's new secret laboratory
   C. Memories from all the colonists

4. In what year was Data discovered in a dormant condition in an underground storage facility on Omicron Theta by the crew of a Federation starship?

5. (Fill in the blank) Data was based on a complex _____ brain developed by Dr. Soong.

6. What was Data's ultimate storage capability?
   A. Six hundred quadrillion bits
   B. Eight hundred quadrillion bits
   C. Nine hundred quadrillion bits

7. What was located two centimeters below Data's right ear?

8. (True or false) Data's optics were not capable of producing tears.

9. (True or false) Data's upper spinal support was a polyalloy, while his skull was composed of cortenide and duranium.

10. What was the primary purpose for Data's functional respiratory system?
    A. Distribution of biochemical lubricants
    B. Thermal regulation
    C. Microhydraulic power regulation

11. Data's system did not require food. How often, though, did he have to ingest a semi-organic nutrient suspension?
    A. Once a month
    B. Bi-monthly
    C. Twice a year

12. (True or false) Data could utilize the sensors in his oral cavity to simulate human response to food?

13. Data's basic programming included a strong inhibition? What was it?

14. Prior to his assignment to the *Enterprise*-D, Data served aboard the U.S.S. *Trieste.* How long did Data serve as an ensign?
    A. Five years
    B. Four years
    C. Three years

15. As operations manager (Ops) aboard the *Enterprise*-D, what was Data in charge of coordinating?

16. What was the nickname Commander Riker gave Data when he first met the android?

17. Name the *Enterprise*-D officer with whom Data became intimate while under the influence of the inhibition-stripping effects of a virus?

18. In gratitude for trying to save Q from an attack by the Calamarain, what was the gift the superbeing gave Data?

19. Data served as father of the bride for which two *Enterprise*-D crew members' wedding?

Prime Memory Bonus

What was the area of study in which Data excelled during his time spent at Starfleet Academy?

---

20. Who taught Data to dance on the holodeck?
    A. Riker
    B. Dr. Crusher
    C. Troi

21. (True or false) Data's first opportunity to command a starship came during the Federation blockade of the Vulcan civil war.

22. Who was the Romulan officer Data defeated while commanding the U.S.S. *Sutherland* in Captain Picard's blockade?
    A. Tebok
    B. Tomalak
    C. Sela

23. What was the name of Commander Data's favorite recreational holodeck program which re-created the world of 19th-century London?

24. What caused a holodeck malfunction to trap Alexander, Worf, and Troi in the American old West where everyone else was a replica of Data?

25. In 2368, Data traveled back in time to old San Francisco when his severed head was unearthed, suggesting he had died some 500 years earlier. Under the remains of what ancient fort and 20th-century military installation was Data's head discovered?

26. Who was successful in reattaching Data's head and body?

27. Data attempted to understand the concept of human humor with the help of a holodeck-created comedian and which *Enterprise*-D crew member?
    A. Guinan
    B. Troi
    C. La Forge

28. (True or false) Even though Data's hair was capable of growing at a controllable rate, he could not grow a beard.

29. Data shared his living quarters with a cat that he named Spot. What was the title of the poem he wrote about Spot?

30. Who was the *Enterprise*-D security officer with whom Data attempted to pursue a romantic relationship?

Prime Memory Bonus

Dr. Soong went to extraordinary lengths to create a naturalistic human appearance in Data. During the early years of his development, what did Data like to do which offended the Omicron Theta IV colonists?

---

31. What did Data begin to experience in 2369 as a result of an accidental plasma shock?

32. Which *Enterprise*-D officer attempted to introduce Data to the art of painting?
    A. Wesley
    B. La Forge
    C. Troi

33. What new technology did Data employ to allow his own neural pathways to be duplicated in his constructed daughter Lal's brain?

34. What does *Lal* mean in Hindi?
    A. Offspring
    B. God's gift
    C. Beloved

35. (Fill in the blank) Lal developed at a remarkable rate and showed evidence of growth potential beyond that of her father, even experiencing _____.

36. Lal became the focus of a heated custody battle between Starfleet and Data when he was ordered to release Lal to the

Daystrom Institute Annex on Galor IV. Who was the Starfleet admiral sent to gain custody of Lal?
  A. Haftel
  B. Quinn
  C. Styles

37. Lal died after having lived little more than two weeks. What was the cause of her death?

38. Upon returning to the Omicron Theta IV colony site in 2364, Data participated in the discovery and activation of his twin android brother, Lore. Upon reactivation, however, Lore exhibited sadistic behavior and attempted to commandeer the *Enterprise*-D. How was Lore forcibly removed from the starship?

39. Who gained control remotely of Data in 2367 and commanded him to pirate the *Enterprise*-D?

40. What did Dr. Soong attempt to install in Data's positronic brain?

41. (True or false) Dr. Soong admitted to Data before he died that he created the android as much for art's sake as any other reason.

42. Even though Data found both the drink and the symbolism enjoyable, why was Data slightly wary of champagne?

43. Why did Data begin to experience emotions in 2369?

44. Lore was dismantled while attempting to lead the Borg on a new campaign of conquest. What did Data remove from Lore's body after he was dismantled?

45. What was unique about Data's "mother," whom he didn't even know existed until she contacted him on the *Enterprise*-D?

46. Name the judge advocate who ruled that Data was indeed a sentient being and therefore entitled to civil rights, including the right to resign from Starfleet if he chose?
  A. Henry Thomas
  B. Aaron Satie
  C. Philipa Louvois

47.   As of stardate 42527, how many times had Data been decorated for gallantry?

Prime Memory Bonus

Name the software incorporated into Data's positronic network that kept him physically healthy and rarely in need of Dr. Crusher's professional services.

STARFLEET INTELLIGENCE OFFICER DOSSIER

Counselor Deanna Troi

1. What was the full name of Troi's human father?

2. How old was Troi when her father died?

3. What was the name of the Betazoid male Troi was betrothed to when they were both children?

4. Why did they never marry?

5. What kind of heroic stories from ancient Earth history did Troi's father read to her when she was a young girl?
   A. Vikings
   B. Westerns
   C. 1930s–1940s G-men crime-busters

6. Where did Troi study psychology prior to her joining Starfleet?

7. After a relationship with then-Lieutenant William T. Riker ended, Troi continued her studies at Starfleet Academy. In what year did she graduate?
   A. 2359
   B. 2356
   C. 2369

8. While aboard the *Enterprise*-D, Troi was once involuntarily impregnated by an unknown noncorporeal life form. What was the name Troi gave to her alien child?

9. Troi's proximity to what type of newly discovered life forms caused her to suffer a brief loss of her empathic powers?
   A. Solanagen-based aliens
   B. Submicroscopic robots
   C. Two-dimensional creatures

10. (Fill in the blank) Counselor Troi assumed temporary command of the *Enterprise*-D when the ship was disabled from collision with two _____ filaments.

11. Troi took command of the *Enterprise*-D because she was the senior officer on the bridge at the time. What Starfleet rank did Troi hold?

12. In 2369 Troi was kidnapped at a neuropsychology seminar on Borka VI by Romulan underground operatives who used her in an elaborate plot to help the Romulan vice proconsul defect to the Federation. What was his name?
    A. N'Vek
    B. M'Ret
    C. Rakal

13. A famous empathic mediator for the Federation almost killed Troi in 2369 when he surreptitiously tried to transfer his negative emotions into her, causing her to age rapidly. What was this Lumerian ambassador's name?
    A. Ves Alkar
    B. Q'Maire Endar
    C. Selin Peers

14. As the ship's counselor, Troi was in the habit of not wearing the standard Starfleet uniform. Who was the ranking officer who ordered her to dress in the same attire as the rest of the crew members?

15. (Fill in the blank) Troi once said she never met a _____ she didn't like.

16. What was the irritating pet name used by Troi's mother, Lwaxana, when addressing her daughter?

Prime Memory Bonus

Name the shuttlecraft pilot who was transporting Counselor Troi back to the Enterprise-D when the shuttle crashed on Vagra II, trapping both the pilot and Troi in the wreckage.

LOOK WHO'S TALKING

1. What were the first words out of Q's mouth in the episode "Déjà Q"?
    A. "Jean-Luc, give Q a great big hug."
    B. "Red alert."
    C. "Where's that de-evolved, Mr. Worf?"

2. Who said in "Remember Me" the words, "If there's nothing wrong with me, maybe there's something wrong with the universe"?
    A. Worf
    B. Data
    C. Dr. Crusher

3. To whom did Worf give the dating advice, "It is the scent that first speaks of love"?
    A. Wesley
    B. La Forge
    C. Riker

4. In "Sins of the Father," whom did Worf challenge by saying, "It is a good day to die and the day is not over yet"?
    A. Duras
    B. Toral
    C. Lursa

5. In "Cost of Living," who said, "Nothing would please me more than to give away Mrs. Troi"?
    A. Mr. Homn
    B. Riker
    C. Picard

6. Who issued a veiled threat to Ramussen in "A Matter of Time" by uttering the words, "I assume your handprint will open the door, whether you are conscious or not"?
    A. Picard
    B. Data
    C. Worf

7. Who saw a couple kissing in Ten-Forward and said, "He's biting that female"?
    A. Data
    B. Lal
    C. Worf

8. Which Klingon in "Redemption, Part I" asked, "Do you hear the cry of the warrior calling you to battle, calling you to glory?"
    A. Gowron
    B. Kurn
    C. Worf

9. In the episode "Haven," who asked Lwaxana Troi and the Millers, "Could you please continue the 'petty bickering'?"
    A. Counselor Troi
    B. Worf
    C. Data

10. When faced with a war with the Romulans, who quoted Shakespeare: "Now if these men do not die well, it will be a black matter for the king who led them to it"?
    A. Captain Picard
    B. Q
    C. Ambassador Spock

11. After Romulan operative Sela complained that she liked to write, but had little time to do it, who said, "Perhaps you would be happier in another job"?
    A. Picard
    B. Data
    C. Ambassador Spock

12. In "Fistful of Datas," who said, "I'm beginning to see the appeal of this program"?
     A. Alexander
     B. Data
     C. Worf

13. In the Dixon Hill episode, "The Big Goodbye," who imitated Humphrey Bogart's voice and said, "It was raining in the city by the bay . . . a hard rain, hard enough to wash the slime . . ."?
     A. Data
     B. Picard
     C. Guinan

14. Which *Enterprise*-D officer before a game asked, "If winning is not important, then, Commander, why keep score?"
     A. Data
     B. Worf
     C. Tasha Yar

15. Who said in "When the Bough Breaks" episode, "Things are only impossible until they are not"?
     A. Guinan
     B. Troi
     C. Picard

16. To whom was Worf describing Klingon love when he said, "Men do not roar; women roar. Then they hurl heavy objects and claw at you"?
     A. Riker
     B. Wesley
     C. La Forge

17. While trapped at The Royale, a casino-hotel, who said "Baby needs a new pair of shoes" before starting a phenomenal run at craps?
     A. Data
     B. Worf
     C. Riker

18. To whom did Q lecture, "If you can't take a little bloody nose, maybe you ought to go back home and crawl under your bed . . ."?

A. Riker
B. Worf
C. Picard

19. In "Manhunt," who asked after using the transporter, "Legs, where are the legs?"
    A. Barclay
    B. Lwaxana Troi
    C. The Antedian ambassador

20. Who asked in the "Reunion" episode, "Not even a bite on the cheek for old times' sake?"
    A. Worf
    B. K'Ehleyr
    C. K'mpec

21. The "Final Mission" episode was Wesley Crusher's last appearance before leaving the *Enterprise*-D for Starfleet Academy. Who said to him, "Oh, I envy you, Wesley Crusher. You're just at the beginning of the adventure"?
    A. Riker
    B. A holographic version of his father
    C. Picard

22. Who said to Ardra in the "Devil's Due" episode (after she made Picard vanish), "The advocate will refrain from making her opponent disappear"?
    A. Data
    B. A Ventaxian guard
    C. La Forge

23. In Q's Sherwood Forest fantasy, who said, "Sir, I protest. I am not a merry man"?
    A. La Forge
    B. Worf
    C. Data

24. Who congratulated Worf for killing Duras in "The Mind's Eye" by telling him, "Motives, who cares for motives"?
    A. The Klingon ambassador
    B. Gowron
    C. Kurn

25. Who told La Forge, "You've got a lot to learn if you want people to think of you as a miracle worker"?
  A. Barclay
  B. Guinan
  C. Scotty

Prime Memory Bonus

Who reassured a wary and stunned Picard in "The Child" by telling him, "Please don't worry. Everything is okay"?

OUT OF THIS WORLD

Part I

Match the name of the planet, star system, or other celestial object with the correct description or corresponding event in the right column.

1. _____ Qo'noS

2. _____ Vagra II

3. _____ Tyken's Rift

4. _____ Wolf 359

5. _____ Ventax II

6. _____ Turkana IV

7. _____ Risa

8. _____ Omicron Theta IV

9. _____ Mars

10. _____ Jupiter Outpost 92

11. _____ Jaros II

12. _____ Bynaus

A. First to report Borg incursion

B. Home planet to the Bynars

C. Birthplace of Tasha Yar

D. Location of the Utopia Planitia Fleet yards and where *Enterprise*-D was constructed

E. Planet where Ensign Ro was imprisoned by the Cardassians

F. Klingon Homeworld

G. Star system that was site of devastating battle against Borg

H. Planet where Data was discovered

I. Location of Tasha Yar's death

J.   Rupture in the fabric of
     space *Enterprise*-D
     encountered

K.   Tropical resort planet
     where Picard first met Vash

L.   A planet whose population
     made a pact with devil-
     like Ardra

Prime Memory Bonus

Name the planet where Captain Picard covertly met Captain Rixx to discuss the infiltration of Starfleet Command by alien parasites in the episode "Conspiracy."

OUT OF THIS WORLD

Part II

1. ____ Alpha Onias III

2. ____ Angel One

3. ____ Haven

4. ____ Kavis Alpha IV

5. ____ Forlat III

6. ____ Galaxy M33

7. ____ Argus Array

8. ____ Gamma Eridon

9. ____ Dyson sphere

10. ____ Deneb IV

11. ____ Delos IV

12. ____ Saturn

A. Star system in Klingon space

B. Planet where Riker was abducted by an alien boy who wanted a playmate

C. Accidentally visited by *Enterprise*-D with help from the Traveler

D. Location of Starfleet Academy flight range

E. Huge subspace radio telescope located at the very edge of Federation space

F. Planet where males are treated as second-class citizens

G. Location of Farpoint Station

H. Beautiful planet reputed to have mystical healing powers

I.   Planet attacked by the
     Crystalline Entity

J.   Became home of newly
     evolved Nanites

K.   Planet where Dr. Crusher
     completed her internship

L.   Gigantic artificial structure
     designed to enclose a star
     completely

Prime Memory Bonus

*What was the name of the astronomical cloud where the
Enterprise-D hid from the Borg in the episode "The Best of Both
Worlds, Part I"?*

TO EVERYTHING THERE IS A SEASON

Part I

The original *Enterprise*'s mission was intended to last five years, but the Peacock Network had other plans and the ship was dry docked after only three seasons. The *Enterprise*-D, however, spent seven years exploring deep space on T.V. before heading to the interstellar vastness of a movie franchise. For seven seasons the *Enterprise*-D and its crew introduced us to thrilling adventures, memorable characters, and unforgettable stories.

Run a level-3 diagnostic and test your memory banks' retrieval system by accessing *TNG*'s seven seasons.

SEASON LEGEND

1st season (1987–1988)	5th season (1991–1992)
2nd season (1988–1989)	6th season (1992–1993)
3rd season (1989–1990)	7th season (1993–1994)
4th season (1990–1991)	

1. Wil Wheaton, as Wesley Crusher, departed *TNG* cast midway through which season?

2. Which season finale ended with the Romulans informing Captain Picard, "We're back"?

3. In the second half of which season did Data finally meet his "mother"?

4. In which season did Commander Riker begin sporting a beard?

5. *Enterprise*-D Transporter Chief Miles O'Brien was promoted and assigned chief of operations on station *Deep Space 9* midway through which season?

6. La Forge's mother was a Starfleet officer. During which season was she killed?

7. "Redemption, Part I" was *TNG*'s 100th episode. In which season was it originally shown?

8. During which season did Captain Picard serve as Arbiter of Succession to determine the new leader of the Klingon High Council?

9. Name the season in which an extragalactic conspiracy attempting to infiltrate Starfleet Command was uncovered by Picard and Riker?

10. *Enterprise*-C briefly entered the 24th-century from the past during which season?

11. In which season was a Federation-wide "speed limit" of warp 5 imposed after the discovery of evidence that excessive use of warp drive could damage the fabric of space?

12. Ambassador Spock was sighted on Romulus supporting reunification of the Romulan and Vulcan peoples in which season.

13. The Cardassians proved to be ruthless and merciless enemies of the Federation. During which season was Captain Picard captured and tortured by a vicious Cardassian officer?

14. Which season finale ended with Worf resigning his Starfleet commission?

15. Name the season in which Ambassador Sarek died at the age of 203?

16. In which season did Counselor Troi learn that she had had a sister who accidentally drowned when she was a child?

17. Worf's step-brother, Nikolai Rozhenko, was mentioned briefly in an earlier season's episode. In which season was "Homeward" shown, the episode in which he was finally seen?

18. In which season did the propulsion expert, Kosinski, warp the *Enterprise*-D over 350 million light years from the galaxy?

19. Whoopi Goldberg portrayed Guinan, the alien hostess who usually presided over Ten Forward, the *Enterprise*-D's main lounge and social club. In which season did she make her debut appearance in this recurring role?

20. The third season cliffhanger ended with Picard's capture and assimilation by the Borg. In which season did the crew of the *Enterprise*-D *first* encounter this powerful race?

21. In which season finale did the *Enterprise*-D crew time-travel back to the 19th century for a rendezvous in San Francisco with Samuel Clemens?

22. During which season were the Starfleet uniforms redesigned from the simple, straight lines of a one-piece jumpsuit to the short jacket uniform top?

23. Which season finale ended with the Klingon Empire on the verge of a bloody civil war?

24. During which season did the Cardassians withdraw from Bajoran space and abandon station *Deep Space 9*?

25. In "Relics," Captain Montgomery Scott was discovered alive, suspended in a beam aboard a crashed Federation transport ship. Name the season in which this popular *TNG* episode was aired?

26. During which season did Worf accept discommendation for acts his late father did *not* commit against the Klingon Empire?

27. The *Enterprise*-D crew captured an injured Borg, nursed him back to health, gave him a sense of individuality, and named him Hugh. In which season was this episode shown?

28. In which season was Ten-Forward shown for the first time?

29. Riker served aboard a Klingon ship as part of an officer exchange program during which season?

30. In which season did Q transport Captain Picard and other *Enterprise*-D senior officers into a Robin Hood fantasy?

31. In "The Loss," Counselor Troi considered resigning her Starfleet Commission when she lost her empathic powers. Name the season in which this episode was shown.

32. During which season did Captain Picard fall in love with a member of his crew?

33. In which season did the *Enterprise*-D investigate a living spacecraft that was dying of loneliness?

34. During which season did an *Enterprise*-D away team become trapped in a bizarre re-creation of a setting from the pulp novel *The Hotel Royale*?

35. A group of Klingon renegades tried to capture the *Enterprise*-D in "Heart of Glory." Name the season in which the episode first appeared.

36. In which season was Worf's holodeck Klingon exercise program seen for the first time?

37. During which season did Majel Barret make her first appearance in the recurring role of Lwaxana Troi?

38. Mark Lenard portrayed Spock's father, Ambassador Sarek, on *TREK-classic* and in the *Trek* movies. In which season did he travel aboard the *Enterprise*-D for a crucial diplomatic mission?

39. "The Game" featured Wesley Crusher's first appearance on *TNG* since "Final Mission." Name the season "The Game" was aired.

40. In "The Mind's Eye," La Forge was abducted and subjected to mental reprogramming by Romulan agents who intended to

use him to murder a Klingon official. In which season was this episode originally shown?

41. Data decided to become a parent and built an android daughter during which season?

42. In which season did Data's dream program become activated?

43. Worf found evidence that his father was still alive in a secret Romulan prison camp during a two-part episode in which season?

44. The Ferengi DaiMon Bok used an illegal Thought Maker in his attempt to exact revenge upon Captain Picard in "The Battle" episode from the first season. During which season did Bok return for round 2 of his grudge match with Picard?

45. The Traveler appeared in three episodes over the course of *TNG*'s seven years on T.V. Name the season in which he made his final appearance.

46. During which season did Wesley Crusher admit helping to cover up a fatal accident at Starfleet Academy?

47. The first known contact with the Ferengi occurred in which season?

48. In which season did Q make his first return since his initial appearance in "Encounter at Farpoint"?

49. Terrorists seized the *Enterprise*-D in an attempt to steal trilithium resin during which season?

50. Captain Edward Jellico was given temporary command of the *Enterprise*-D in a two-part episode during which season?

Prime Memory Bonus

In which season were the Enterprise-D's *shuttle bays' enclosed launch-control rooms seen for the first time?*

TO EVERYTHING THERE IS A SEASON

Part II

1. The episodes "The Naked Now" and "Where No One Has Gone Before" were almost direct spinoffs of *TREK-classic* episodes. In which season were the two *TNG* episodes televised?

2. During which season did the *Enterprise*-D return to Nervala IV and find a duplicate of Riker?

3. In "Devil's Due," Data portrayed Ebenezer Scrooge in a holodeck dramatization of Dickens' *A Christmas Carol*. Name the season this episode was televised.

4. In which season was Romulan espionage suspected aboard the *Enterprise*-D and Picard accused of acts against the Federation?

5. In "Pen Pals," Data rescued a little humanoid girl from her disintegrating planet after she contacted him by subspace radio. In which season was this episode shown?

6. During which season was the Ferengi *Marauder* spacecraft seen for the first time?

7. In which season were aliens from another time continuum kidnapping *Enterprise*-D crew members during their sleep?

8. In the episode "The Schizoid Man," a reclusive scientist implanted his consciousness into Data's brain just prior to his death. Name the season it was televised.

9. During which season did the *Enterprise*-D visit the late Tasha Yar's homeworld and find her sister still living among the gangs there?

10. In "Half a Life," a scientist had to decide between helping his people or conforming to his society's expectation of ritual suicide at age 60. In which season was this episode aired?

11. During which season did Data refuse to send robotic servo-mechanisms to do hazardous tasks because he believed them to be sentient life forms?

12. In the episode "The Price," a professional negotiator used his Betazoid senses in his business dealings, as well as in a relationship with Counselor Troi. In which season was this episode first shown?

13. In "The Perfect Mate," Picard delivered an incredibly attractive woman to her future husband, even though she had "bonded" with the *Enterprise*-D captain. During which season was this episode aired?

14. In which season did Riker command a starship in a wargame against the *Enterprise*-D's Captain Picard?

15. The irascible Captain Okona dragged the *Enterprise*-D into a love-war relationship between two planets in which season?

16. During which season did Riker fall in love with an androgynous humanoid who dared to call herself female?

17. In "11001001," a group of Bynars hijacked the *Enterprise*-D in hopes of using the ship's computer to restart their planetary computer system. In which season was this episode shown?

18. In "The Next Phase," La Forge and Ensign Ro were believed dead, but they had merely been made invisible by a new Romulan cloaking device. In which season was this episode originally aired?

19. During which season did the *Enterprise*-D crew suffer severe sleep deprivation due to proximity to Tyken's Rift?

20. In which season was "New Ground" shown, the episode in which Alexander returned to the *Enterprise*-D to live with his father?

21. The *Enterprise*-D revived a group of 20th-century humans who had been frozen some four centuries earlier in which season?

22. During which season did Troi bear a child, the offspring of a mysterious alien life form attempting to learn more about humanoid life?

23. In which season was La Forge promoted to chief engineer?

24. Which season marked the first appearance of the mysterious Romulan Sela, although she was not identified until "Redemption, Part II"?

25. During which season was the surface of Troi's homeworld, Betazed, shown for the first time?

26. Following Tasha Yar's death, in which season was Worf promoted to security chief?

27. In which season did a time-traveling professor, apparently on a research project from the future, turn out to be a petty thief from the past?

28. In which season did Wesley Crusher become a regular bridge officer?

29. In "Manhunt," Lwaxana Troi returned to the *Enterprise*-D with the full intent of finding a husband. During which season were the men of the *Enterprise*-D the hunted and Lwaxana Troi the hunter?

30. The "Man of the People" was a famous Federation mediator who maintained extraordinary equanimity in tough negotiations by transferring his negative thoughts to his female companions. In which season was this episode first televised?

31. In which season did Data first show his interest in Sherlock Holmes stories?

32. During which season did a mysterious cloud attempt to communicate with the *Enterprise*-D crew through the body of Captain Picard?

33. In which season was Wesley Crusher sentenced to death for a minor infraction on a planet of hedonistic pleasure?

34. In the award-winning episode "The Inner Light," an alien probe took over Picard's mind and he experienced a lifetime of memories on a dead planet in just a few minutes. During which season did this episode air?

35. In which season did Data try to experience a romantic relationship?

36. During which season did a little girl's "Imaginary Friend" turn out to be terrifyingly real?

37. In "Identity Crisis," La Forge and his former shipmates from the U.S.S. *Victory* were compelled to return to a planet they visited years before, where they were transformed into alien life forms. Name the season.

38. During which season did Commander Riker's estranged father, Kyle Riker, visit his son on the *Enterprise*-D?

39. In "The Hunted," the *Enterprise*-D captured a fugitive whose crime was the fact that his government would not return him to normal society after having converted him into the "perfect soldier." In which season was this episode shown?

40. In which season was the first episode shown featuring the Trill "joined species"?

41. During which season was Dr. Crusher captured by a terrorist who hoped to draw the Federation into his struggle for freedom?

42. In "Hero Worship," a young boy coped with his parents' deaths by deciding he was an android just like Data. Name the season.

43. The *Enterprise*-D accidentally killed a large spaceborn life-form, then had to care for the creature's unborn child. In which season did "Galaxy's Child" air?

44. Things were certainly not as they appeared to be in "Future Imperfect." Riker woke up, apparently suffering from amnesia, 16 years in the future. Can you remember the season this episode was shown?

45. In "Frame of Mind," Riker was captured and tortured on planet Tilonus IV and wasn't sure what was reality and what was a nightmare. Name the season.

46. During which season were Alexander, Worf, and Troi trapped on the holodeck with "A Fistful of Datas"?

47. In which season did Captain Picard return to his "Family" in France to recover from the Borg experience?

48. In "Ethics," Worf was seriously injured and the only hope for recovery was a dangerous experimental procedure. Name the season in which this episode was shown.

49. During which season did Ensign Ro join the *Enterprise*-D crew for a special mission to locate a Bajoran terrorist?

50. Name the season in which Data was first seen playing the violin.

51. La Forge and a Romulan officer had to cooperate in order to survive on a hostile planet in the episode "The Enemy." In which season was it shown?

52. During which season was K'Ehleyr, Worf's Klingon mate, seen for the first time?

53. In which season did Data's Sherlock Holmes holodeck adventure malfunction, causing the character of the evil Moriarty to take a life of his own? It's "Elementary, Dear Data."

54. The *Enterprise*-D crew coped with a shipboard "Disaster," wherein Picard was trapped in a turbolift and Troi was in command. Name the season.

55. Which season's finale ended with the *Enterprise*-D encountering a group of Borg who were followers of "the sons of Soong"?

56. In "Déjà Q," the capricious superbeing lost his powers and took refuge on the *Enterprise*-D. In which season did this episode originally air?

57. During which season did a Romulan defector cross the Neutral Zone with a terrifying report of a planned Romulan attack on Federation space?

58. In which season was Data's cat, Spot, seen for the first time?

59. In "Darmok," an alien ship captain strands himself and Picard on a planet in hope of helping Picard understand a language based entirely on metaphors. During which season did this very popular *TNG* episode air?

60. Captain Picard, vacationing on a resort planet, became involved in archaeological intrigue with Vash. Name the season "Captain's Holiday" was first televised.

61. In which season was the *Enterprise*-D caught in a time loop, doomed to explode again and again?

62. "The Chase" episode was in part intended to answer the question of why *TNG* showed so many aliens that were humanoid. During which season was this landmark episode shown?

63. In which season did Wesley Crusher fail in his first attempt to gain entry into Starfleet Academy?

64. During which season did Captain Picard first order, "Tea, Earl Grey, hot" in that precise and commanding voice of his?

Prime Memory Bonus

During which season was the 79th episode of TNG *shown, equaling the total episode count of* TREK-*classic?*

THE NAME IS THE GAME

Part I

We hope you are one of those unique people who has a talent for never forgetting a name.

1. What was the name of Ambassador Sarek's personal assistant during the Legaran conference?
   A. Sortek
   B. Skon
   C. Sakkath

2. At the time of his death, Sarek was married to another human woman. What was her name?
   A. Perone
   B. Perrin
   C. Pearl

3. Who was the Vulcan Starfleet officer who presided over the inquiry into a cadet's death at the Academy Flight Range?
   A. Captain Selak
   B. Captain Satelk
   C. Captain Satok

4. What was the name of the terrorist who was killed by a baryon sweep during his pursuit of Captain Picard down a Jefferies tube?
   A. Satler
   B. Lefler
   C. Azeem

5. Who was the nurse at the Sikla Medical Facility who agreed to help Riker escape in exchange for a sexual favor?
   A. Deela
   B. Marva
   C. Lanel

6. What was the name of the Starfleet admiral and brilliant investigator who was largely responsible for exposing the alien conspiracy against Starfleet in 2364?
   A. Satie
   B. Mauldin
   C. O'Larney

7. What was the name of the professional gambler in "Time's Arrow, Part I" who welcomed Data to his poker game and provided the android with a stake in exchange for his communicator?
   A. Teddy Kuan
   B. Faubus "Five Card" Jenkins
   C. Frederick La Rouque

8. Name the rare historical object reported to be in the personal collection of Zibalian trader Kivas Fajo in "The Most Toys."
   A. Lawmim Galactopedia
   B. Rectyne Monopad
   C. Parrot's claw

9. What was the name of the hit man for gangster Cyrus Redblock in Picard's Dixon Hill holodeck program?
   A. Richard Swann
   B. Felix Leech
   C. Tom "Tommy Gun" Decker

10. What was the name of the Starfleet officer (a Vulcan) who was taken over by a parasitic alien intelligence that attempted to infiltrate Starfleet Command in "Conspiracy"?
    A. Setok
    B. Syvok
    C. Savar

11. Name the mission specialist who befriended Wesley Crusher and with whom was instrumental in helping the crew repel an attempted takeover in "The Game."
    A. Ensign Robin Behan
    B. Ensign Robin Lefler
    C. Ensign Janice Buchanan

12. Who was the *Enterprise*-D officer who played the role of Will Scarlett in Q's Robin Hood fantasy?
    A. Worf
    B. Data
    C. La Forge

13. What was the name of the Romulan science station destroyed, apparently scooped from the surface of the planet by the Borg?
    A. Delta Zero Five
    B. Alpha Zero Six
    C. Station Double M

14. Who was the Starfleet officer who earned the command of a starship at a younger age than any previous captain?
    A. Barbara Bair
    B. Brenda Traylor
    C. Tryla Scott

15. Name the Romulan admiral who stole a scoutship and defected to the Federation.
    A. Jarok
    B. Setal
    C. Neral

16. What was the name of the large set of documents that outlined all details of an arrangement between the devil-like Ardra and the people of Ventax II?
    A. Oath of Ardra
    B. Contract of Ardra
    C. Scrolls of Ardra

17. Who was the Vulcan physician, part of the *Enterprise*-D medical staff, who answered a distress call from Graves' World and was present when cyberneticist Dr. Ira Graves died?
   A. Dr. Selar
   B. Dr. Seleya
   C. Dr. Selor

18. Following Picard's capture by the Cardassians, the *Enterprise*-D captain was tortured in violation of the interstellar treaty governing treatment of prisoners of war. What was the name of the treaty?
   A. Artus II Accord
   B. Seldonis IV Convention
   C. Klaxius II Declaration

19. In "Identity Crisis," who was the Starfleet officer and former crew member with La Forge aboard the U.S.S. *Victory* who narrowly escaped transforming into another life form?
   A. Leah Johnson
   B. Theresa Braxton
   C. Susanna Leijten

20. He was the captain of the Cardassian warship *Reklar* in "Chain of Command, Part I." What was his name?
   A. Gul Damac
   B. Gul Lemec
   C. Gul Madak

21. Who was the Klingon captain loyal to the Duras family during the Klingon civil war?
   A. Larg
   B. Krax
   C. Kargan

22. Name the 19th-century Scotland Yard inspector in Data's Sherlock Holmes holodeck program?
   A. Welby
   B. Bannon
   C. Lestrade

23. What was the name of the Romulan warbird that, along with the *Enterprise*-D, was nearly destroyed by the Iconian software weapon in "Contagion"?
    A. *Devoras*
    B. *Haakona*
    C. *Prakal*

24. Who was the only crew member of the U.S.S. *Brattain* still alive when the *Enterprise*-D arrived on a rescue mission?
    A. Sam Bishop
    B. Andrus Hagen
    C. B. G. Graham

25. What was the name of the Romulan senator who betrayed Spock, Captain Picard, and Data to the Romulan authorities?
    A. Parem
    B. Paqu
    C. Pardek

26. Name the ancient city on Earth in which was located the office of the President of the Federation Council.
    A. Paris
    B. San Francisco
    C. Berlin

27. What was the name of the outdoor cafe in Paris where Picard once broke a date with the future Mrs. Janice Manheim?
    A. Le Ambiance
    B. Le Petit
    C. Cafe des Artistes

28. *Enterprise*-D personnel enjoyed an athletic game involving competition between two teams of four players. What was the game's name?
    A. Parrises Squares
    B. Dom-Jot
    C. Qa'vak

29. What was the true Romulan identity of Federation Ambassador T'Pel in "Data's Day"?
    A. Commander Badar
    B. Subcommander Selok
    C. Subcommander Toketh

30. What were the names of the two renegade Klingons who tried to recruit Worf in their cause in "Heart of Glory"?
    A. Kohman and K'Vort
    B. Klaget and Klav
    C. Korris and Konmel

31. What was the name of the celestial object that Samuel Clemens hoped to see from the *Enterprise*-D?
    A. Earth's moon
    B. Mars
    C. Halley's comet

32. Who was the commander of the Starship *Repulse* who once said he would have given Dr. Pulaski a shuttlecraft if it would have kept her aboard his ship?
    A. Captain Taggert
    B. Captain Grayson
    C. Captain Murphy

33. What was the name of the elite Romulan Imperial intelligence service?
    A. Rak'tal
    B. Tal Shiar
    C. Tai'Bak

34. Miles O'Brien, who was afraid of spiders, had to get past 23 of these creatures when he made repairs at a starbase in "Realm of Fear." Name this arachnid with half-meter-long legs.
    A. Talarian hook spider
    B. Markoffian wolf spider
    C. Denebian slime spider

35. Name the Starfleet Academy cadet who was killed in a flight accident while attempting a prohibited maneuver in "The First Duty."
    A. Peter Miller
    B. Joshua Albert
    C. Janie Cockrell

36. What was Worf's favorite Klingon opera?
    A. *Kerel and Humuh*
    B. *Saltah and Muktok*
    C. *Akthu and Melota*

37. Name the Klingon rite of passage marking an elevated level of spirituality.
    A. Dawn of Datjaj
    B. Age of Ascension
    C. Age of Decision

38. What was the name of the loud and discordant contemporary music form favored by young Talarians?
    A. Alba Ra
    B. Akagai Ke
    C. Nehi Ta

39. What was the name of the holodeck computer file, a virtual reality within which lived the computer intelligences Professor Moriarty and Countess Bartholomew?
    A. Holmes Alpha 2
    B. Moriarty Plus One
    C. Picard Delta One

40. What was the name of the Klingon ritual of marriage?
    A. The Bond
    B. The Oath
    C. The *K'Elah*

41. Who was the Starfleet officer who mounted an unauthorized offensive against the Cardassians, destroying one of their outposts and two ships?
    A. Captain Maxwell
    B. Admiral M'Benga
    C. Captain Maune

42. Name the alien race whose parting phrase was, "May you die well."
    A. Cardassian
    B. Klingon
    C. Romulan

43. According to Captain Picard, this appellation was not to be this large, spaceborne life form's official name, but it was nevertheless. Who was this "Galaxy's Child"?
    A. Little One
    B. Caboose
    C. Junior

44. What was the identity created for Riker when he participated in a covert surveillance mission on planet Malcoria III?
    A. Rivas Jakara
    B. Jek Jaeger
    C. Janar Ja'Dar

45. What was the name of the song from *The Wizard of Oz* that Dr. Graves whistled in Data's presence just prior to his death?
    A. "Somewhere Over the Rainbow"
    B. "Ding Dong the Witch Is Dead"
    C. "If I Only Had a Brain"

46. What was the psychological term describing the condition for holodeck addiction?
    A. Holoreality Denial
    B. Holodiction
    C. Holoholism

47. What was the name of the molecular cyberneticist and former teacher to Dr. Soong, who thus considered himself to be Data's "grandfather"?
    A. Dr. Ira Graves
    B. Dr. Zee Darnay
    C. Dr. Neil Cohagen

48. What was the name of the traditional Klingon dish that Riker tasted in an effort to acquaint himself with Klingon culture prior to his temporary assignment aboard a Klingon ship?
    A. T'Kec eggs
    B. Pipius claw
    C. Klarc shellfish

49. Name the Betazoid relaxation technique that Troi taught Barclay when she tried to help him overcome his fear of being transported.
    A. Plexing
    B. Phasing
    C. Prakalling

50. What was the name of the inhibition-stripping virus that infected the *Enterprise*-D crew in "The Naked Now"?
    A. Zetar 150
    B. PXK 36
    C. Psi 2000

51. What was the name of the traditional Klingon game involving a half-meter hoop and a spear?
    A. *Qa'vak*
    B. *Qol*
    C. *Qab K'tho*

52. Name the Starfleet officer who ordered Inspector General Remmick to investigate the *Enterprise*-D for possible infestation by parasitic aliens.
    A. Admiral Gregory
    B. Admiral Quinn
    C. Admiral Ryan

Prime Memory Bonus

According to Klingon mythology, what is the name of the creator?

STARFLEET INTELLIGENCE OFFICER DOSSIER

Lieutenant Worf Rozhenko

1. Worf was the first Klingon warrior to serve in Starfleet and was influential in Klingon politics. On which planet in the Klingon Empire was Worf born in 2340?

2. Worf's father was Mogh. What was the name of Mogh's father?

3. Worf was orphaned after his parents were killed in the brutal Khitomer Massacre. What were the first names of the Rozhenkos, the humans who adopted the Klingon?

4. What was the name of the farm world where young Worf spent his formative years, cared for by his adoptive parents?
    A. Philana
    B. Gault
    C. Genome

5. (True or false) Worf found it difficult to fit into the world of humans and was a bit of a hellraiser.

6. Worf was raised along with an adoptive brother. What was his name?

7. (True or false) Worf's adoptive brother entered Starfleet Academy at the same time as Worf, but graduated a year before Worf.

8. What was Worf's hobby when he was growing up?
    A. Writing Klingon love poetry
    B. Studying the battle strategies of great Klingon warriors
    C. Building ancient Klingon ocean-sailing vessels in bottles

9. In which year did Worf graduate from Starfleet Academy?
   A. 2361
   B. 2362
   C. 2363

10. What rank and grade did Worf hold when he was first assigned to the *Enterprise*-D as flight control officer?

11. (Fill in the blank) There was a _____ year period between Worf's graduation and his posting aboard the *Enterprise*-D that was unaccounted for.

12. In late 2364, what happened to the *Enterprise*-D Chief of Security that resulted in Worf's promotion to full lieutenant?

13. Who was the *Enterprise*-D officer whose accidental death on an away mission caused Worf to feel intense guilt?
    A. Marla Aster
    B. Dana Hawkings
    C. Joy Bianco

14. Worf, who understood the loneliness of being an orphan, took the dead officer's young son, Jeremy, into his family through *R'ustai* the Klingon bonding ceremony. The rite involved the lighting of ceremonial candles and the wearing of warrior's sashes. Who was honored at the conclusion of Worf's and Jeremy's *R'ustai*?

15. Worf's adoptive parents remained close to him over the years and made it a point to visit him in 2367 when the *Enterprise*-D was docked at Earth Station McKinley. Why was the starship being repaired?

16. (True or false) Worf's adoptive father had been a chief petty officer, serving as a warp field specialist aboard the U.S.S. *Intrepid*, the starship that rendered aid to the Klingons following the Khitomer Massacre.

17. Worf's adoptive mother mastered the technique of making a traditional Klingon dish. When she visited Worf aboard the *Enterprise*-D, Worf asked her to make the delicacy. What was this ancient Klingon food?

18. Worf had a son, Alexander, with ambassador K'Ehleyr. After K'Ehleyr was murdered (and Worf avenged her death), Alexander moved to Earth to be cared for by Worf's adoptive parents. How many years did Alexander remain in the Rozhenko's custody before returning to the care of Worf aboard the *Enterprise*-D?

19. (True or false) Alexander was fond of ancient American westerns.

20. When Worf tried to prepare Alexander for the Klingon Age of Ascension, the young Klingon told his father that he did not want to be a warrior. Who was the old Klingon who tried to convince Alexander that it was vitally important that he underwent the Age of Ascension?

21. Worf himself underwent his Age of Ascension ritual at age 15. How many years later did Worf celebrate the anniversary date with his *Enterprise*-D crewmates?
    A. 5
    B. 7
    C. 10

22. In accordance with Klingon tradition, Worf refused medical attention and opted for the Klingon suicide ritual when his spinal column was shattered in an accident. Name the dangerous experimental surgical procedure Worf underwent in which a new spinal cord was generated.
    A. Genetronic replication
    B. Spinal infusion
    C. Biogenerative replication

23. Worf once investigated a claim that his father had not died at Khitomer, but was instead being held prisoner at a secret Romulan prison camp in the Carraya System. Identify the Federation space station where Worf obtained a guide to take him to the secret location of the prison.

24. Although the rumor of Worf's father being alive was false, Worf did indeed find a prison camp comprised of Khitomer survivors. Worf led some of the prisoners to freedom, but the majority chose to remain, including a half-Klingon, half-Romulan

woman Worf fell in love with. Why did she not return with him to the *Enterprise*-D?
  A. She was killed trying to escape.
  B. Because of racial intolerance she would experience.
  C. She was dying of a rare Klingon disease.

25. Worf was thrust into high-level Klingon politics when he discovered that he had a biological brother, Kurn. When did Kurn discover he was the son of Mogh?
  A. His adopted father, Lorgh, told him on his deathbed.
  B. Kahlest, Worf's nursemaid, sought him out.
  C. At his Age of Ascension

26. The Klingon High Council ruled that Worf's and Kurn's father, Mogh, had committed treason at Khitomer. Which powerful Klingon family had falsified the charges against Mogh?

27. (True or false) Although Worf was willing to die to protect his family's honor, he eventually chose to accept Klingon ritual shaming rather than allow Kurn to be killed.

28. Why did Worf resign his Starfleet commission during the Klingon civil war in late 2367 and early 2368?

29. In 2369, why did Worf request a leave of absence from the *Enterprise*-D?

30. What type of literature did Worf enjoy reading?
  A. The quotations of Kahless the Unforgettable
  B. Klingon love poetry
  C. Ancient novels by Earth author Harold Robbins

31. Worf was an aggressive competitor in athletic events and usually obtained champion standing in what kind of tournaments?
  A. Bat'leth
  B. HarOS
  C. Sohchlm

32. It looked more like a weapon with its large bow. Identify this stringed instrument that Worf enjoyed playing.
    A. Kobliad
    B. Veridium
    C. ChuS'ugh

33. What was the small, curious piece of statuary that Worf kept in his quarters aboard the *Enterprise*-D?
    A. Klingon erotica
    B. The Battle of HarOS
    C. An impression of Alexander's forehead ridges

34. What did Worf keep hidden in the large, silver sash he wore over his Starfleet uniform?

35. What was Worf's nickname at the *Enterprise*-D's weekly poker game?

Prime Memory Bonus

When Alexander traveled back 40 years from the future, he tried to warn his father that he would be assassinated on the Klingon Homeworld. In which Qo'noS structure did Alexander say Worf would die?

STARFLEET INTELLIGENCE
FEDERATION MEMBER DOSSIER
Klingons

1. (Fill in the blank) Klingon tradition held that "the son of a Klingon is a man the day he can first hold a _____."

2. What was the Klingon name for the bonding ceremony, a ritual in which two individuals joined families, becoming brothers and sisters?
    A. *Brak'lul*
    B. *R'uustai*
    C. *Ha'DIbah*

3. (Fill in the blanks) Klingons possessed _____ livers, an _____-chambered heart, and _____ ribs.

4. (True or false) Klingons had tear ducts.

5. What color was Klingon blood?
    A. Black
    B. Brown
    C. Lavender

6. (Fill in the blank) To a Klingon a beard was a sign of _____.

7. What was the spoken and written language of the Klingon Empire?

8. The *Hegh'bat* ceremony was a Klingon ritualized suicide. Who was charged with delivering the knife to the warrior?

9. What did Klingons call the afterlife?

10. Discommendation was a Klingon ritual shaming in which the recipient was treated as nonexistent in the eyes of Klingon society. How many generations of a shamed Klingon's family was also disgraced?
    A. Four
    B. Seven
    C. Ten

11. What was the name of the ritual Klingon martial-arts form resembling terrestrial tai chi?
    A. *Kon'mah*
    B. *Dolak*
    C. *Mok'bara*

12. What was the name of the traditional, three-bladed warrior's knife?
    A. *N'tokrey*
    B. *KoH-man-ara*
    C. *D'K tahg*

13. Name the bladed weapon used by Klingon assassins.

14. (Fill in the blank) The Klingon disruptor was a directed-energy weapon also known as a _____ disruptor.

15. The Klingon death ritual was a ceremony practiced by warriors upon the death of a comrade. What was the purpose of the powerful howl?

16. What was the traditional "sword of honor," resembling a meter-long, two-ended scimitar?
    A. *Bat'telh*
    B. *K'Vort*
    C. *Vor'cha*

17. What was the military service of the Klingon Empire called?

18. (True or false) Klingon attack cruisers were among the largest and most powerful vessels in the fleet.

19. These Klingon starships were originally established to be Romulan. They were capable of both atmospheric entry and land-

ing as well as warp-speed interstellar travel. What was the name of these ships?

20. What were the starships called that formed the backbone of the Klingon military for decades?

21. What was the name of the ruling body of the Klingon Empire?

22. (True or false) In the 24th century females were not allowed to be members of the Klingon government.

23. The Klingon nation, founded some 1,500 years ago by Kahless the Unforgettable, first united the Klingon people by killing a tyrant in power. Who was he?
    A. Korob
    B. Mogh
    C. Molor

24. First contact between the Klingon Empire and the Federation was a disastrous event that led to almost a century of hostilities. In which year was first contact made between the two races?

25. The Klingon Empire nearly plunged into civil war in 2367 when council leader K'mpec was murdered. What was the cause of death?

26. Who replaced K'mpec as leader of the Klingon Empire?
    A. Toral
    B. Gowron
    C. Duras

27. Name the class-M planet in Klingon space where legend was that the Klingon messiah, Kahless the Unforgettable, promised to return following his death.

28. In 2369 a clone of Kahless was installed as the ceremonial Emperor of the Klingon people. Who produced Kahless's clone?

29. Name the two sisters of Duras who conspired with the Romulans in attempting a military coup of the Klingon leadership.

30. Who was the member of the Klingon High Council who presided over the installation of Gowron as head of the council?
    A. Kreeko
    B. K'Tal
    C. K'Retok

31. He was a Klingon officer who had sworn loyalty to Gowron during the Klingon civil war, until Gowron suffered multiple defeats and then he began to question Gowron's leadership. Gowron later killed him in the High Council chambers. Who was this Klingon officer?
    A. Kulge
    B. K'Vada
    C. Kurlan

32. How many Klingons were massacred by Romulan forces on the Klingon outpost at Khitomer in 2346?
    A. 3,000
    B. 4,000
    C. 5,000

33. What was the name of the Klingon who provided secret defense access codes to the Romulans, making him responsible for the Khitomer Massacre?
    A. K'lgat
    B. Ja'rod
    C. Kirok

34. The only survivors of the massacre were believed to be a Klingon child named Worf (a future Starfleet security officer) and his nursemaid. What was her name?
    A. Krola
    B. Krite
    C. Kahlest

35. Name the Klingon governor of the Kriosian system who became the target of an assassination attempt by *Enterprise*-D officer Geordi La Forge acting under Romulan control.

36. Why were Klingon uniforms made of metal and leathers?

37. Who was the famous Klingon who developed many sayings that were the foundation of Klingon thought, including "Revenge is a dish best served cold"?

Prime Memory Bonus

Draw the symbol for the Klingon Empire.

KLINGON TO YOUR UNIVERSAL TRANSLATOR

Match the Klingonese on the left with the correct English translation on the right.

1. _____ Qapla'
2. _____ K'adlo
3. _____ Qab jIH nagil
4. _____ Ha'DIban
5. _____ TlhIngan jIH
6. _____ Hol
7. _____ JuH
8. _____ Vulqanganpu'
9. _____ Verenganpu'
10. _____ Juppu'
11. _____ Terra'nganpu'
12. _____ NuqneH
13. _____ BaH
14. _____ NIb'poH

A. Earthers
B. Language
C. What do you want?
D. Success
E. Insult meaning animal
F. Thank you
G. Fire (as in fire your weapon)
H. Home
I. Friends
J. Vulcans
K. Déjà vu
L. Ferengi
M. Face me if you dare!
N. I am a Klingon!

Prime Memory Bonus

Translate the following greeting from Klingonese to English: qa-jatlh.

STARFLEET INTELLIGENCE OFFICER DOSSIER

Lieutenant Commander Geordi La Forge

1. Born blind because of a birth defect, La Forge wore a remarkable piece of bioelectronic engineering called a VISOR that allowed him to see with greater clarity than other humans could. What did the acronym VISOR stand for?

2. (Fill in the blank) La Forge's VISOR permitted vision in not only visible light, but across much of the electromagnetic spectrum, including _____ and radio waves.

3. (True or false) The VISOR, while giving La Forge better-than-normal sight, also caused him continuous pain.

4. Which doctor once proposed to La Forge a surgical procedure which would have replaced his VISOR with optical implant devices offering nearly the same visual range?
    A. Dr. Crusher
    B. Dr. Pulaski
    C. Dr. Toby Russell

5. (True or false) La Forge's VISOR provided the Cardassians with a unique opportunity to use his neural implants to provide direct input to his visual cortex, giving them the ability to program La Forge's mind to commit criminal acts.

6. When La Forge and a young Romulan centurion were marooned on Galorndon core, they linked La Forge's VISOR with a tricorder to form a device capable of detecting neutrino emissions, saving both men's lives. What was the Romulan's name?
    A. Bochra
    B. Barak
    C. Tevor

7. What range of frequencies did La Forge's VISOR receive?
    A. One to one hundred thousand terrawatts
    B. One to two hundred thousand terrawatts
    C. One to three hundred thousand terrawatts

8. La Forge came from a family of Starfleet officers. His father was an exobiologist, and his mother was a command officer. Which Federation ship was Silva La Forge commanding at the time of her death in 2370?
    A. U.S.S. *Ramsey*
    B. U.S.S. *Kennedy*
    C. U.S.S. *Hera*

9. (True or false) Even though he moved around a great deal, La Forge considered his childhood a great adventure.

10. How old was La Forge when he received his VISOR?

11. La Forge was caught in a fire when he was five years old. Who rescued him?

12. La Forge fondly described a pet he had when he was eight as "funny looking." Identify this domestic animal.
    A. Chulian hamster
    B. Circassian cat
    C. Terran Doberman pincher dog

13. (True or false) Possibly because his parents traveled so much when he was a child, La Forge learned several languages, including Hahliian.

14. In which year did La Forge graduate from Starfleet Academy?
    A. 2357
    B. 2358
    C. 2359

15. One of La Forge's first Starfleet assignments was as a shuttle pilot. Which route did La Forge run daily?
    A. The Lacunar run between Earth Station 1 and Mars
    B. The Turot run between Earth and its moon
    C. The Jovian run between Jupiter and Saturn

16. La Forge later served as an ensign on the U.S.S. *Victory*. Who was the captain La Forge served under on the starship?
    A. Delaney
    B. Zimbata
    C. McGregor-Scott

17. In 2362, La Forge participated in an away mission to Tarchannen III. It was learned several years later that all members of that away team were infected by an alien DNA strand. Who was the doctor whose medical intervention helped save La Forge from transformation into a native Tarchannen life form?

18. (True or false) La Forge first met Commander Riker when La Forge piloted Riker's shuttle on an inspection tour.

19. Prior to his promotion to full lieutenant and assignment as the *Enterprise*-D's chief engineer, what was La Forge's first posting aboard the starship?

20. La Forge had difficulty building relationships with women. As a result, La Forge developed an attachment to a holographic representation of a noted member of the Theoretical Propulsion Group. What was her name?
    A. Dr. Tracy Lieberman
    B. Dr. Sue Edwards
    C. Dr. Leah Brahms

21. Identify the technique developed by La Forge in 2368 which served to reduce the tactical effectiveness of cloaked Romulan ships?
    A. Tachyon detection grid
    B. T-tauri detection beam
    C. Tachyon beam net

22. La Forge and *Enterprise*-D ensign Ro Laren were lost and believed dead in an apparent transporter malfunction, but it was later discovered they had merely been made invisible by a new Romulan cloaking device. What was the name of this experimental cloaking technology?
    A. Molecular phase inverter
    B. Interphase generator
    C. Anyon spatial emitter

23. What was La Forge's favorite chilled beverage?

Prime Memory Bonus

What was the name of the Enterprise-D *crew member La Forge tried to impress with his unsuccessful "moonlight on the beach" holodeck program?*

Prime Memory Bonus

(Fill in the blanks) During the weekly poker game, La Forge's VISOR gave him "_____ _____" into the cards held by his shipmates, courtesy of infrared light.

STARFLEET INTELLIGENCE OFFICER DOSSIER

Chief Medical Officer Beverly Crusher

1. What was Dr. Crusher's maiden name?
   A. Edwards
   B. Howard
   C. Buchanan

2. In which year did she graduate from medical school?
   A. 2350
   B. 2351
   C. 2352

3. A terrible tragedy on Arvada III, in which many people died, was an important chapter in Dr. Crusher's life. Crusher and her grandmother were two of only a small number of survivors. What was the name of Dr. Crusher's grandmother?

4. Whom did Dr. Crusher credit for her knowledge of nontraditional pharmacopoeia?

5. Who introduced Dr. Crusher to her future husband, Starfleet officer Jack Crusher?
   A. Jean-Luc Picard
   B. Walker Keel
   C. Randall Rixx

6. (True or false) Jack Crusher proposed to Beverly by giving her a gag gift, a book entitled *How to Advance Your Career Through Marriage.*

7. The Crushers were married in 2348. In what year was their son Wesley born?

8. On which planet did Dr. Crusher complete her internship under the tutelage of Dr. Dalen Quaice?
    A. Bekel II
    B. Okuda III
    C. Delos IV

9. Lieutenant commander Jack Crusher was killed on an away mission while under the command of Captain Picard on the U.S.S. *Stargazer*. Following her husband's death in 2354, Dr. Crusher continued to pursue her Starfleet career. In which year did Dr. Crusher attain the position of Chief Medical Officer aboard the *Enterprise*-D?

10. (Fill in the blanks) During the second year of the *Enterprise*-D's mission, Dr. Crusher left the ship to accept a position as head of _____ _____, but returned to the *Enterprise*-D a year later.

11. Dr. Crusher became involved romantically with one of her patients, John Doe, who became the first of his race to transmute into a noncorporeal being. Identify John Doe's humanoid species.
    A. Zalkonian
    B. Betonian
    C. Dalteenian

12. The following year, Dr. Crusher fell in love with a Trill named Odan, a highly respected Federation ambassador. Why did Crusher end the relationship?

13. Dr. Crusher was quite an accomplished dancer. What was the nickname her colleagues gave her?
    A. "Dr. Nimble Toes"
    B. "The Dancing Doctor"
    C. "Dr. Dancer"

14. In which American city did Dr. Crusher win first place in a dance competition?
    A. Los Angeles
    B. Dallas
    C. St. Louis

15. Dr. Crusher also had a strong interest in amateur theatrics and was director of a successful theatre company aboard the *Enterprise*-D. Among the productions performed was a French play by Edmond Rostand. Name this play, which was first performed on Earth in 1897.

16. What was the name of the play Dr. Crusher wrote for her troupe that named a meal in the title?
    A. *Something for Breakfast*
    B. *Dinner with Three Men and a Woman*
    C. *The Future of Love After Lunch*

17. Another play written by Dr. Crusher was entitled *Frame of Mind*. Which *Enterprise*-D crew member played the lead role?

Prime Memory Bonus

In 2370, Dr. Crusher made a mistake that caused a dormant gene in an Enterprise-D *crew member to activate, triggering a de-evolving mutation process in all ship personnel. Name the crew member who Dr. Crusher originally misdiagnosed.*

HOUSE CALLS

A Federation starship officer with aspirations of promotion within the ranks of Starfleet must be knowledgeable of all onboard ship operations—including sickbay and medical services.

1. On *Galaxy*-class starships, what was the minimum number of medical personnel designated to be on duty at all times?
   A. Three
   B. Four
   C. Five

2. Which area of the *Enterprise*-D was converted into an emergency triage and treatment center during large-scale disasters?
   A. Shuttlebay
   B. Ten-Forward
   C. Gymnasium

3. This medical instrument was used aboard the *Enterprise*-D when wounds needed closure. Identify the instrument.
   A. Suture stimulator
   B. Sonicsuture
   C. Autosuture

4. What was the powerful neurostimulant administered by Dr. Pulaski to stimulate neural activity in Commander Riker when he had suffered a near-fatal injury on an away mission?
   A. Tricordrazine
   B. Tricyanate
   C. Trillium

5. Dr. Crusher used this device on Zalkonian patient John Doe to stabilize his immune system. Name this medical instrument.
    A. Trilaser connector
    B. Physiostimulator
    C. Protodynoplaser

6. What was the surgical instrument used by Starfleet medical personnel to incise the skin and expose underlying tissue?
    A. Bioscalpel
    B. Exoscalpel
    C. Sonicscalpel

7. Identify the surgical device used to sever neural connections.
    A. Drechtal beams
    B. Justinian beams
    C. Neural transducers

8. What was the emergency medical resuscitative measure used on Captain Picard following his exposure to the Kataan probe?
    A. Cardiac induction
    B. Cardiac stimulator
    C. Cardiac calibrator

9. These straplike devices were used to provide electrical stimulation to the limbs of neurologically damaged patients. Identify these four-centimeter-wide bands.
    A. Sonic-neurostimulation bands
    B. Neurostimulation bands
    C. Motor assist bands

10. What was the name of the small neural pad Dr. Crusher prescribed for La Forge when a possible malfunction of his VISOR was suspected of causing insomnia?
    A. REM inducer
    B. Somnetic inducer
    C. Somnetictricorder

11. This device increased the production of T cells, a type of lymphocyte which enabled humanoid bodies to fight infection. What was this medical device?
   A. T-cell infusion unit
   B. T-cell bioregenerator
   C. T-cell stimulator

12. What was the experimental medical device designed to translate the genetic code into a specific set of replication instructions?
   A. DNA replicator
   B. Biogenetic stimulator
   C. Genetronic replicator

13. This medication was used to treat the crew of the *Enterprise*-D when the ship was exposed to hazardous levels of radiation. Name this medication.
   A. Hyronalyn
   B. Sproxine
   C. Tulibiam

14. What was the medical instrument that completely eliminated the need for a needle to physically penetrate the skin?
   A. Aerosuspension injector
   B. Hypospray
   C. Hypoinjector

15. This emergency medical device could hold a patient in a state of suspended animation until medical treatment could be rendered. Identify this device.
   A. Cryostasis
   B. Stasis unit
   C. Cryogenic stasis unit

16. Dr. Pulaski's greatest medical skill was her empathy with her patients, evidenced by the use of PCS in treating the flu virus. What did the acronym PCS stand for?
   A. Pulaski's Crew Sick-reducer
   B. Prototype Sickbay Cleanser
   C. Pulaski's Chicken Soup

17. Name the emergency medical technique used for the stabilization of patients with brainstem injuries.
    A. Neurostabilizer
    B. Neurolink
    C. Neurodynoplaser

18. Dr. Crusher used this medical instrument to increase neural activity in the central nervous system of Tasha Yar's brain after she had been gravely injured by Armus. Identify this medical equipment.
    A. Neural stimulator
    B. Neural tranducer
    C. Neural paralyzer

19. These medical instruments were used in cases of severe spinal cord damage to give the patient some control over the affected extremities. What were these implantable bioelectric devices called?
    A. Neural scan interfaces
    B. Neural neutralizers
    C. Neural transducers

20. Identify the medical instrument which was used by Starfleet medical personnel to read and encode the DNA patterns of living tissue.
    A. Detronal scanner
    B. Physioscanner
    C. Fabrini DNA imaging monitor

21. This medical equipment was used aboard Federation starships to dispense fluid and electrolytes. What was the equipment called?
    A. Nenebek IV infusion unit
    B. Plasma infusion unit
    C. Electrolinks

22. What was the name of the emergency cardiopulmonary support unit in use aboard Federation starships?
    A. Special pulmonary react unit
    B. Pulmonary support unit
    C. Cardiopulmonary support and react team

Prime Memory Bonus

This Enterprise-D *nurse was first seen in "Future Imperfect," got a first name in "Clues," and a last name in "Identity Crisis." Who was she?*

THE NAME IS THE GAME

Part II

1. Name the Starfleet officer who had been in charge of the team that assembled the *Enterprise*-D at the Utopia Planetia Fleet Yards on Mars.
   A. Captain David Burton
   B. Captain Gary Sparks
   C. Commander Orfil Quinteros

2. Name the Romulan Tal Shiar agent who was murdered so that Deanna Troi could be coerced into assuming her identity as part of a defection plot.
   A. Commander Tomed
   B. Major Rakal
   C. Subcommander Garok

3. He was one of four survivors of the wreck of the Federation freighter *Odin* who drifted to Angel One in an escape pod. What was his name?
   A. Tarver
   B. McManus
   C. Ramsey

4. What was the name of the rare illness that sometimes affected Vulcans over the age of 200?
   A. Bendii Syndrome
   B. Bonventre Disease
   C. Vek'tal Virus

5. Who was the 22nd-century con artist from New Jersey who appeared on the *Enterprise*-D claiming to be a historian from the 26th century?
   A. Bencini Zarcone
   B. Belingoff Rasmussen
   C. Alexander Sareyan

6. What was the name of the team of elite cadet pilots at Starfleet Academy who were involved in a collision that destroyed all five craft and resulted in the death of a cadet?
   A. Nova Squadron
   B. Alpha Squadron
   C. Starburst Squadron

7. He was the officer in charge of Starfleet Academy entrance exams at the annex facility on Relva VII and supervised Wesley Crusher's first attempt to gain entrance to the Academy. What was his name?
   A. Tac Officer Kuan
   B. Tac Officer Chang
   C. Tac Officer Chen

8. What was the term designating a Starfleet subspace communique of extremely high sensitivity or secrecy, intended only for the eyes of a starship captain, for which voiceprint identification was required?
   A. Code 47
   B. Code 1
   C. Code Factor 1 Priority

9. What was the Starfleet signal indicating the discovery of a space vehicle in distress?
   A. Code Priority One Alpha
   B. Code One Alpha Zero
   C. Code One Alpha Omega

10. Name Picard's friend during their Academy days who was challenged to a game of dom-jot by a Nausicaan, leading to a fight in which Picard's heart was impaled?
    A. Marta Batanides
    B. Corey Zweller
    C. Darrell O'Toole

11. What was the name of Lwaxana Troi's valet before Mr. Homn?
    A. Xendi
    B. Xandu
    C. Xelo

12. Who was the leader of the Bandi who participated in the capture of a spaceborne shape-shifting life form, coercing it to assume the form of Farpoint Station?
    A. Groppler Zek
    B. Groppler Zorn
    C. Groppler Zeon

13. In Romulan mythology, what was the name of the creator?
    A. Sho Ka Ree
    B. V'sal Uthet
    C. Vorta Vor

14. What was the name of the small device that permitted the short-range transmission of visual images recorded by La Forge's VISOR?
    A. Visual Acuity Transmitter
    B. Visual Transit Conductor
    C. Visual Instrument Video

15. La Forge presented his former starship commander with the model of an ancient British sailing ship. What was the name of the vessel?
    A. H.M.S. *Victory*
    B. H.M.S. *Reliant*
    C. H.M.S. *Endeavour*

16. He was possibly the greatest archaeologist of the 24th century, who spent the last decade of his life trying to confirm a theory that numerous humanoid species in the galaxy had a common genetic heritage. What was his name?
    A. Dr. Galloway
    B. Professor Galor
    C. Professor Galen

17. While at Starfleet Academy, Picard carved the initials of an old friend into a prized elm tree on the parade grounds. What were the initials?
    A. A.F.
    B. T.K.
    C. T.C.

18. This Federation starship was named for the Greek mythological figure who was commander of the Greek forces during the Trojan War. What was the name of the ship?
    A. U.S.S. *Ajax*
    B. U.S.S. *Archon*
    C. U.S.S. *Agamemnon*

19. During this Klingon ritual, the celebrant proclaimed, "Today I am a Warrior. I must show you my heart. I travel the river of blood." What was the name of this Klingon rite of passage?
    A. Age of Ascension
    B. Oath of *R'uustai*
    C. Age of Decision

20. She was one of two 27th-century Vorgon criminals who traveled backward in time to locate Captain Picard and the *Tox Uthat*. What was her name?
    A. Erko
    B. Ajur
    C. Benar

21. From which Shakespearean play did Captain Picard quote in an effort to convince Q of the worthiness of human beings?
    A. *Hamlet*
    B. *Romeo and Juliet*
    C. *A Midsummer Night's Dream*

22. Who was the extradimensional life form who threatened the lives of one-third to one-half of the *Enterprise*-D crew in an effort to understand the human concept of life and death?
    A. Q
    B. Mundahla
    C. Nagilum

23. It was the planet where archaeologist Vash was wanted for stealing the Crown of the First Mother. Name the planet.
    A. PasKlun II
    B. Myrmidon
    C. Nutara

24. Name the leader of the Ferengi landing party at Delphi Ardu that made contact with the *Enterprise*-D in "The Last Outpost."
    A. Zek
    B. Letek
    C. Quor

25. What was the name of Miles and Keiko O'Brien's daughter?
    A. Obachan
    B. Michelle
    C. Molly

26. What was the name of the Klingon *Bird-of-Prey* on which Riker served as First Officer during an officer exchange program?
    A. *Pagh*
    B. *T'Acog*
    C. *K'Vada*

27. Name the commander of the NASA ship *Charybdis* who was the only survivor of a crew accidentally killed by an unknown alien intelligence in the episode "The Royale."
    A. Lieutenant Commander David Garrison
    B. Captain Ben Irvin
    C. Colonel Stephen Richey

28. Who was the author of the badly written *Hotel Royale*?
    A. Bryan Grayson
    B. Todd Matthews
    C. Raymond Edwards

29. Name the young and ambitious Starfleet officer who was placed in charge of planning for defense against the Borg in "The Best of Both Worlds, Parts I and II"?
    A. Commander Remmick
    B. Lieutenant Commander Shakaar
    C. Lieutenant Commander Shelby

30. Name the young Klingon who left the secret Romulan prison camp with Worf in order to join mainstream Klingon society.
    A. Toq
    B. L'Kor
    C. K'Tak

31. Who was the head of the Barzan government who asked to use the *Enterprise*-D as a place to hold negotiations for rights to the Barzan wormhole in "The Price"?
    A. Chancellor Vorg
    B. Premier Bhavani
    C. Minister Spax

32. Name the Hekaran female who killed herself in "Force of Nature," to prove her theory that the use of warp drive was causing irreparable damage to her home system.
    A. Serova
    B. Lateera
    C. Corbetta

33. Who was the child of mixed Klingon-Romulan heritage who became romantically involved with Worf while incarcerated at the Romulan prison camp in the Carraya system?
    A. Gatt'i
    B. Azetbur
    C. Ba'el

34. What was the racist term used for Cardassians in the episode "The Wounded"?
    A. Card-carrying assholes
    B. Cardies
    C. Cardasses

35. Name the colony engineer and friend of Riker who was killed by the Crystalline Entity in "Silicon Avatar."
    A. Carmen Davila
    B. Roxanne Debux
    C. Stacey Wyman

36. Who was the Zalkonian male who became romantically involved with Dr. Crusher, but was last seen flying off into space after transforming into a being of pure energy?
    A. Devos
    B. John Doe
    C. Barvis Telok

37. Name the Betazoid specialist in first contact with new life forms who found the living spacecraft "Tin Man" to be a kindred spirit.
    A. Tam Elbrun
    B. Jax Eminar
    C. Thrak Betor

38. Who was the young follower of the Klingon messiah Kahless the Unforgettable who received a vision of Kahless and was present on Boreth when the Klingon who claimed to be Kahless returned?
    A. Tahg
    B. K'Dreg
    C. Divok

39. Name the Starfleet shipbuilding and repair facility in Earth orbit where the *Enterprise*-D was in dock for six weeks following the defeat of the Borg.
    A. Earth 2 Station
    B. Earth Station Bobruisk
    C. Earth Station McKinley

40. She was a native of the long-dead planet Kataan and beloved wife of the ironweaver Kamin. What was her name?
    A. Eline
    B. Margot
    C. Rose

41. Name the charismatic leader of the Ansata terrorists who was responsible for the abduction of both Dr. Crusher and Captain Picard.
    A. Simeon Gerris
    B. Kyril Finn
    C. Fermi Croix

42. Located on the Klingon Homeworld, this was the seat of government for the empire, and location of the Great Hall. Name the city.
   A. Krull
   B. H'ghot
   C. First City

43. Raised from childhood to fulfill her role as an instrument of peace, the empathic metamorph, Kamala, was fated to wed which V.I.P. in "The Perfect Mate"?
   A. Chancellor Alrik
   B. President Kareel
   C. Premier Nohra

44. Name the father of Worf and his brother, Kurn.
   A. T'Ong
   B. Mogh
   C. Kutlac

45. Who was the Benzite who competed with Wesley Crusher for a single opening to Starfleet Academy in the episode "Coming of Age"?
   A. Mendon
   B. Mordock
   C. Mardeck

46. Name the Bolian barber aboard the *Enterprise*-D who was fond of giving useful tactical advice to the ship's senior officers, whether they wanted it or not.
   A. Tharp
   B. Adob
   C. Mot

47. Who was the most celebrated admiral in British maritime history whose courage Captain Picard drew inspiration from on the eve of battle with the Borg?
   A. Lord Nelson
   B. Admiral Wainwright
   C. Lord Marcus

48. Name the famed mediator from Ramatis III who, although deaf, negotiated several treaties between the Klingon Empire and the Federation.
    A. Sego
    B. Riva
    C. Sonchi

49. What was the process whereby a new leader was chosen for the Klingon High Council following the death of the previous ruler?
    A. Ritual of Decision
    B. *K'roc* Rite of Challenge
    C. Rite of Succession

50. Name the neurogeneticist in "Ethics" whose genetronic technique saved Worf's life.
    A. Dr. David Nerenburg
    B. Dr. Toby Russell
    C. Dr. Nickolaus Morrison

51. Who was the J'naii pilot who became romantically involved with Commander Riker, thereby exhibiting female sexual behavior in "The Outcast"?
    A. Toren
    B. Cretay
    C. Soren

52. Name the nonexistent physician who was projected into Riker's mind by political interrogation officers in the "Frame of Mind" episode.
    A. Dr. Syrus
    B. Dr. Talbot
    C. Dr. Shearer

53. Name the *Enterprise*-D crewman assigned as a medical technician who was accused in "The Drumhead" of conspiring in the Romulan theft of the starship's technical data.
    A. Peter Beagle
    B. Jeremy Tarcher
    C. Simon Tarses

54. What was the name of the Klingon ritual in which two friends shared a poisoned tea as a reminder that death was an experience best shared?
    A. Klingon *K'bok* tea ritual
    B. Klingon tea ceremony
    C. *T'Koguushi*

55. He was a Romulan officer who was reluctant to execute nearly a hundred Klingon prisoners after the infamous Khitomer Massacre. Who was he?
    A. Tokath
    B. Tomec
    C. T'Pak

56. Name the illegitimate son of Klingon High Council member Duras.
    A. Toral
    B. Toran
    C. Torigan

57. In "The Most Toys," this female humanoid assistant to Zibalian trader Kivas Fajo attempted to help Data escape, but was murdered instead by Fajo. What was her name?
    A. Mida
    B. Varria
    C. Sybo

58. What was the name of Tasha Yar's younger sister?
    A. Marissa Yar
    B. Jennifer Yar
    C. Ishara Yar

59. Name the sophisticated computer system built and programmed hundreds of centuries earlier by the Progenitors of planet Aldea, which provided for virtually all the needs of its citizens.
    A. The Provider
    B. The Custodian
    C. The Protector

60. In "The Hunted," this native of Angosia III became a leader of a veterans' uprising that forced the government to reconsider the plight of its ex-soldiers. What was his name?
    A. Bo Lozoff
    B. Dakar Glinn
    C. Roga Danar

61. During the "Darmok" episode, the story was told of a wild man in ancient Earth mythology who was raised among animals, but became the friend of a warrior king. What was the name of this mythical figure?
    A. Enkidu
    B. Ankarod
    C. Udek

62. What was the name of the gothic novel enjoyed by Lieutenant Aquiel Uhnari in "Aquiel"?
    A. *Passion's Fiery Flames*
    B. *The Fatal Revenge*
    C. *Loveswept in Summer*

63. Name the old French folksong that was a favorite of Captain Picard.
    A. "Frère Jacques"
    B. "Jacques Nouveau"
    C. "LaBarre Marie"

64. Connoisseurs of this Klingon cuisine claimed the culinary delicacy was best served live. Name this dish.
    A. *N'Nroc*
    B. *K'Hoth*
    C. *Gagh*

Prime Memory Bonus

What was the name of the 20th-century comic re-created on the holodeck by Data when he tried to learn the concept of human humor?

TREK TECH SPECS

From tractor beams to tricorders, from saucer separation to subspace communications, test your working knowledge of the *Enterprise-D's* technical specifications. (WARNING: Immediate disqualification will result if you sneak a peek at *ST:TNG Technical Manual*.)

1. How thick was the hull of the *Enterprise-D*?
   A. 2 meters
   B. 4 meters
   C. 6 meters

2. The ship's hull was constructed of what type of alloys?

3. (Fill in the blank) Saucer separation was a starship emergency maneuver generally employed so that the saucer module, containing most of the crew, could remain behind while the _____ section could go into battle or other hazardous situations.

4. What type of deflector did the *Enterprise-D* use to push aside debris, meteoroids, and other objects that could possibly collide with the ship?

5. (True or false) The saucer module of the *Enterprise-D* was also known as the secondary hull.

6. (True or false) Federation starships sometimes had odd numbers of warp drive nacelles.

7. What were the large electromagnetic devices located at the front of the nacelles of some Federation starships?

8. Impulse drive propulsion employed what kind of fuel to yield helium plasma (and a whole lot of power)?
   A. Deuterium
   B. Illium 629
   C. Arcytitium

9. What was the scientific term used to describe space-normal speeds, slower than the speed of light?

10. (Fill in the blanks) Warp drive systems used by Federation starships employed the controlled annihilation of _____ and _____, regulated by dilithium crystals.

11. (True or false) A starship at warp speeds existed within a warp bubble, or an enclosed subspace field, essentially its own universe.

12. Who was the noted scientist who invented warp drive?
    A. Dr. Sortok
    B. Zefram Cochrane
    C. Talo Muuchatokin

13. What was the vessel of the warp drive system within which matter and antimatter were allowed to intermix in a controlled fashion?

14. It was the unit of measurement used to measure faster-than-light velocities. What was it called?

15. At the cruising speed of warp factor 5, how many times the speed of light would a starship be travelling?
    A. 106
    B. 187
    C. 214

16. (Fill in the blank) Subspace field _____ were phenomena that generally indicated the presence of a warp propulsion system.

17. It was a focused linear graviton force beam used to physically manipulate objects across short distances. What was it?

18. (Fill in the blank) Large ship-mounted phaser weapons were often called phaser _____.

19. How many photon torpedoes could a starship simultaneously launch from a single tube?
    A. 4
    B. 7
    C. 10

20. What was usually the weapon of choice when a starship was at warp drive?

21. How many known substances could not be detected by standard internal scans on the *Enterprise*-D?
    A. 9,264
    B. 15,525
    C. 19,912

22. Where was the Operations Manager's freestanding console located on the bridge of Federation starships?

23. What was the abbreviation for flight controller or pilot of a starship?

24. What was another name for the verbally controlled turbolift system aboard Federation starships?

25. How many shuttlebays did *Galaxy*-class starships have on board for the launching and recovering of shuttles?
    A. 2
    B. 3
    C. 4

26. What was the mathematical expression describing a direction in space with relationship to a space vehicle?

27. What was the name of the systems access crawlway aboard Federation starships?

28. (Fill in the blank) A replicator used _____ technology to dematerialize a quantity of matter, then to rematerialize it in another form.

29. The holodeck permitted the simulation of virtually any environment or person with a degree of fidelity almost indistinguishable from reality. The holodeck was also known by another name. What was it?

30. How many transporters were on the *Enterprise*-D?
    A. 20
    B. 25
    C. 30

31. What was the safe distance for transport?
    A. 20,000 kilometers
    B. 40,000 kilometers
    C. 46,000 kilometers

32. (True or false) Ninety percent of the *Enterprise*-D's systems were automated.

33. How many power systems did the *Enterprise*-D contain?
    A. 2,000
    B. 3,000
    C. 4,000

34. How many independent safety interlocks ensured life support on the main bridge of the *Enterprise*-D?
    A. 6
    B. 7
    C. 12

35. (True or false) The transporter could safely beam through a thickness of 400 meters of solid granite.

36. How many phaser banks did the *Enterprise*-D have?
    A. 10
    B. 12
    C. 17

37. What was the most acoustically perfect spot on the *Enterprise*-D?
    A. Seven centimeters right of table 14 in Ten-Forward
    B. Fourth intersection of Jefferies Tube 25
    C. Shuttlebay 2

38. (Fill in the blank) Multiplex-pattern _____ were a technological breakthrough that stopped the illness "transporter psychosis."

39. Pattern enhancers were used by Starfleet transport systems to amplify a transport signal and lock on any object contained in their triangular formation. How many pattern enhancers were generally used?

40. (True or false) Subspace radio was invented over two centuries after the development of the warp drive.

41. What was the technical name for a huge swirling anomaly that drew surrounding matter into its central vortex?
    A. Subspace resonator
    B. Subspace transition rebound
    C. Subspace rupture

42. (True or false) The universal translator operated by sensing and comparing brainwave frequencies, then selected comparable concepts to use as a basis for translation.

43. It was one of three large cylindrical chambers aboard a *Galaxy*-class starship, housing the ship's primary computer hardware. What was it?

44. The observation lounge on the *Enterprise*-D was located directly behind the Main Bridge. What was the lounge's other name?

45. These portable devices were used aboard Federation starships for handling cargo and other items too large for a single crew member to carry. What were these devices?

46. The collapse of this device was thought to be the cause of dilithium chamber explosion aboard the *Enterprise*-D in 2367. What was it?
    A. Dilithium crystal articulation frame
    B. Dilithium chamber hatch
    C. Dilithium vector calibrator

47. What was the sophisticated information storage and processing device used aboard Federation starships called?

    A.   Isolinear coprocessor
    B.   Isolinear optical chip
    C.   Isolinear rod

48. (True or false) A particle stream was an energetic by-product of the *Enterprise*-D's impulse drive.

49. PADD was a handheld information unit used by Starfleet personnel aboard Federation starships. What does the acronym stand for?

50. ODN was a system of fiber-optic data-transmission conduits used aboard starships like the *Enterprise*-D. What did ODN stand for?

51. What was the small data-storage buoy designed to be ejected from a spacecraft when destruction of that vessel was believed imminent?
    A.   Flight marker
    B.   Recorder data buoy
    C.   Recorder marker

52. (True or false) In interstellar mapping, a quadrant is one-fourth of the Milky Way Galaxy.

53. What was the Starfleet command code for an object to be dematerialized, then immediately rematerialized in a disassociated condition, effectively destroying the object?
    A.   Transporter Code 14
    B.   Transporter Code D-R
    C.   Transporter Code D6

54. What was the computer record called which provided the identity of all transport subjects?

55. This handheld device incorporated sensors, computers, and recorders in a convenient portable form. What was this multipurpose and technical instrument called?

56. What was the name of the destruct sequence command program in the main computer system of a *Galaxy*-class starship?

57. (Fill in the blank) The Starfleet insignia communicator had a _____ sensor that could be used to restrict usage to one authorized individual only.

58. (True or false) Hand phasers were capable of power settings as high as 12.

59. (Fill in the blank) When two participants were involved in training at the phaser range facility aboard the *Enterprise*-D, each player had to remain within a semicircular area, with both players' areas forming a full circle about _____ meters in diameter.

60. What was the name of the computer software on the *Enterprise*-D responsible for noncritical systems such as replicator selections and recreational programming.
    A. Submicron D-41
    B. Datamatrix 2267
    C. Subroutine C-47

61. These devices were used by Starfleet personnel for remote activation of the transporter in situations when there wasn't sufficient time to contact the ship for transport orders. Identify these devices.

62. Captain Picard suggested disengaging these transporter compensators as a possible means of giving physical reality to the computer intelligence version of Professor Moriarty. What were these components of the transporter system called?

63. (Fill in the blank) An annular _____ beam was a cylindrically shaped forcefield used to insure that a person being transported remained within the beam.

64. In 2369, a shuttlecraft from the *Enterprise*-D used what type of explosive charges to threaten a Cardassian fleet?
    A. Antimatter mines
    B. Photon grenades
    C. Antimatter spread

65. (True or false) The auto-phaser interlock was a computer control subroutine on board Federation starships that allowed for precise timing in the firing of ship-mounted phasers.

66. What was the alternate term for the stardrive section of a *Galaxy-*class starship?

67. Which class of instrumental sensor probes were similar to photon torpedoes and were designed for extended flight at high warp speeds?
    A. Class 1
    B. Class 5
    C. Class 8

68. What was the engineering term used in measuring a phaser beam's component electromagnetic wavelengths?
    A. EPS generator
    B. EM base frequency
    C. EHA compensator

69. What was the emergency protocol used aboard Federation starships which disengaged all shipboard computer control and placed ships' systems on manual override?
    A. Emergency Manual Omega
    B. Emergency Procedure Alpha 2
    C. EMP Alpha Code 1

70. What was the high-frequency plasma field called that removed baryon particle contamination from starships?

71. (True or false) Gravitic mines were free-floating weapons used against space vehicles.

72. What was the key component of forcefield and artificial-gravity generators?
    A. Graviton field generator
    B. Graviton sensor net
    C. Gravimetric injunction

73. This personal hygiene device used for bathing replaced the ineffective and unsanitary method of water aboard Federation starships. Identify the device.

74. What was the unit of measure of data storage and transmission in Federation computer systems?

75. It was the large wall-mounted display in Main Engineering of a *Galaxy*-class starship. It featured a large cutaway diagram of the ship used for monitoring the overall status of the ship and its departments. What was the official name for this Engineering display?
     A. Master systems display
     B. Master situation monitor
     C. Master engineering control

76. This sensing device on Federation escape pods monitored the bioelectric signatures of the pod's passengers and allowed them to be traced if they became separated from the pod after landing. Identify the device.
     A. Myographic scanner
     B. Myographic transponder
     C. Bio-myo locater

77. Shuttlepods, unlike shuttlecraft, were limited to sublight travel across relatively short interplanetary distances. What was the maximum passenger complement of these small shuttle vehicles?

Prime Memory Bonus

Identify the components of a Federation starship's warp drive system used to divert a small amount of the drive plasma so that it could be used to generate electrical power for shipboard use.

STACKED DECK
Saucer Module

Could you find your way around within the maze of corridors aboard the *Enterprise*-D? Could you likewise instruct the voice-activated turbolifts to deposit you on the correct deck? Time to see if you're bluffing. Match the major features of the starship with their accurate deck locations listed below.

1. _____ Ten-Forward

2. _____ Transporter rooms 1–4

3. _____ Main shuttlebay

4. _____ Captain's yacht docking port

5. _____ Main bridge

6. _____ Residential apartments

7. _____ Junior officers quarters

8. _____ Captain's quarters

9. _____ Holodecks

10. _____ Science labs

11. _____ Maintenance

12. _____ Sickbay

A. Deck 1

B. Deck 2

C. Deck 4

D. Deck 5

E. Deck 6

F. Deck 7

G. Deck 8

H. Deck 10

I. Deck 11

J. Deck 12

K. Deck 15

L. Deck 16

Prime Memory Bonus

It's two minutes until the autodestruct sequence is completed. On which deck of the saucer module would you find the escape pods?

STACKED DECK

Stardrive Section

1. _____ Brig

2. _____ Battle bridge

3. _____ Shuttlebays 2 and 3

4. _____ Main Engineering

5. _____ Aft photon torpedo launcher

6. _____ Life support systems

7. _____ Personnel transporters 5 and 6

8. _____ Main impulse engines

9. _____ Forward photon torpedo launcher

10. _____ Phaser bank systems

11. _____ Antimatter injection reactors

12. _____ Docking latches

13. _____ Power distribution

14. _____ Deuterium fuel pumps

15. _____ Waste management

A. Deck 8

B. Deck 9

C. Deck 10

D. Deck 11

E. Deck 13

F. Deck 14

G. Deck 21

H. Deck 23

I. Deck 25

J. Deck 27

K. Deck 35

L. Deck 36

M. Deck 37

N. Deck 38

O. Deck 40

Prime Memory Bonus

On which deck of the Enterprise-D's *stardrive section would you find the dorsal docking port?*

IT'S ABOUT TIME

Part II

The series' two-hour finale was the all-time, hands-down, ultimate time travel episode. "All Good Things ..." found Captain Picard leap-frogging through the past, present, and future, eventually "charting the unknown possibilities of existence."

1. At the beginning of the episode, Troi and Worf had just returned from the holodeck. Who had chosen the romantic "Black Sea at night" simulation program?

2. Who interrupted Troi and Worf as they leaned close to kiss?
    A. Riker
    B. Data
    C. Picard

3. (True or false) While telling Troi about his time-shifting, Picard suddenly appeared in the past.

4. When La Forge approached Picard in his vineyard in France, he was no longer wearing his VISOR. What color were La Forge's eyes?

5. How long had it been since Picard and La Forge had last seen each other?
    A. 5 years
    B. 9 years
    C. 25 years

6. Who was La Forge's wife?
   A. The former Leah Brahms
   B. The former Christy Henshaw
   C. The former Aquiel Uhnari

7. (True or false) La Forge was the father of two children.

8. (Fill in the blank) La Forge had become a best-selling author. During his critique of his former comrade's latest literary endeavor, Picard said "the antagonist was a little too _____."
   A. Arrogant
   B. Underdeveloped
   C. Flamboyant

9. How did La Forge find out about Picard's debilitating illness?

10. (True or false) When La Forge asked Picard if he wanted to be called Captain, Ambassador, or Mr. Picard, the elderly Starfleet legend simply said Jean-Luc would be just fine.

11. Who were the mysterious people who kept trying to get Picard's attention while he was visiting with La Forge in the vineyard?
    A. His dead mother and father
    B. Post-atomic mutants
    C. Federation personnel killed when he was Locutus

12. While Picard was talking to La Forge, he shifted in time to the past, appearing in a shuttlecraft with Tasha Yar. Name the shuttle.

13. (True or false) Before taking command of the *Enterprise*-D, Captain Picard had been on a *Galaxy*-class starship before.

14. Where was the *Enterprise*-D in dock prior to Picard and Yar's arrival by shuttle?
    A. Earth Station McKinley
    B. Earth Station Nogura
    C. San Francisco Yards

15. As the shuttle approached the *Enterprise*-D, Picard shifted in time again. Where did he re-materialize?
    A. In the future with La Forge in the vineyard
    B. In the future aboard the *Enterprise*
    C. In the present with Troi in his quarters

16. (Fill in the blank) After subjecting Picard to a battery of tests, Dr. Crusher informed him that he had not undergone any temporal
    _____.
    A. Narcosis
    B. Displacement
    C. Distortion

17. (True or false) Worf stated that sensor readings showed that Captain Picard had never left the *Enterprise*-D.

18. Captain Picard received a message from Starfleet that a large spatial anomaly had been discovered in the Devron System of the Neutral Zone. How many *Warbirds* had the Romulans dispatched to the Devron System?
    A. 20
    B. 30
    C. 40

19. (True or false) Starfleet suspected that the spatial anomaly was a Romulan trick and deployed 10 starships to the Federation side of the Neutral Zone.

20. After Picard quantum-leaped to the vineyard in France, he told La Forge that he was in the wrong time and wanted to enlist Data's assistance. At which university had Data inherited the mathematics chair?
    A. Cambridge
    B. Harvard
    C. Oxford

21. Why had Data added a shock of gray to his hair?

22. (Fill in the blank) Data said he kept his plain-spoken house-keeper employed because she made him _____.
    A. Responsible
    B. Laugh
    C. Happy

23. (True or false) La Forge did not believe his former captain's claims that history seemed to be changing itself nor that the problem with time was caused by trouble in deep space.

24. When Picard time-shifted back to the past, he was addressing his new crew aboard the *Enterprise*-D. What type of Starfleet uniform was Troi wearing?

25. Why did Captain Picard order a Red Alert in the middle of his inaugural address to the crew?
    A. He saw Q in the crowd.
    B. He realized Tasha Yar was already dead.
    C. He saw the post-atomic mutants.

26. Why did Picard not tell the *Enterprise*-D crew of the past about his constant time-shifting?
    A. He tried, but none of them believed him.
    B. Q warned him not to do so.
    C. He did not want to give them the knowledge of the future.

27. (Fill in the blanks) The *Enterprise*-D was originally ordered by Starfleet Command to set a course for Deneb IV to investigate the mystery of _____ _____.

28. (True or false) After Picard shifted in time from the past to the present, Dr. Crusher told him that medical tests showed his brain had gathered two days' worth of memories in a matter of only minutes.

29. Captain Picard confided to Commander Riker that each time shift caused him momentary confusion. But why was Riker confused?
    A. Troi had turned him down for a date.
    B. He saw Troi and Worf kissing.
    C. He found out Troi and Worf had spent the night together on the holodeck.

30. What were the "Doctor's Orders" that Crusher gave Captain Picard when they were alone in his ready room?
    A. A mild sedative and a good night's sleep
    B. Warm milk and eight hours sleep
    C. A nap on the couch in his ready room

31. (True or false) Picard took Crusher by the hand and led her to the couch, where they shared an intimate kiss.

32. In which lab at the university did Professor Data want to run tests on the elderly Picard?
    A. Cryogenic
    B. Biometric
    C. Neurogenic

33. (True or false) The spatial anomaly had appeared in the Devron System in Picard's past and present.

34. In 25 years in the future, which humanoid race had taken over the Romulan Star Empire and closed the borders to the Federation?

35. When Picard said it was time to call in favors owed him, at which starbase did he contact Admiral Riker?
    A. Starbase 12
    B. Starbase 36
    C. Starbase 247

36. In an attempt to get to the Devron System, Data, La Forge, and Picard hitch a ride on a medical ship captained by Dr. Beverly Picard, divorced wife of Jean-Luc. What was the name of Beverly's ship?
    A. U.S.S. *Pasteur*
    B. U.S.S. *McCoy*
    C. U.S.S. *Salk*

37. Picard decided to ask for Worf's assistance in guiding them across the Klingon border and on to the Devron System. What political position did Worf hold at a lowly Klingon colony on the border?

38. When Picard time-shifted back to the past, he was standing on the bridge of the *Enterprise*-D. Who was he rather impatiently waiting on to make his appearance?
    A. Riker
    B. Q
    C. Worf

39. (Fill in the blank) Once again, Picard was on trial, the representative of what Q deemed a "dangerous, savage, _____ race."

40. Q said he was responsible for Picard's shifting in time. Who was the reason mankind was being pushed to the brink of annihilation?

41. Q found Picard guilty of barbaric behavior as the representative of humanity and adjourned court. What did Q say it was time to put an end to?
    A. Humanity's "grievously savage" history
    B. "All good things"
    C. Picard's "trek through the stars"

42. When Q sent Picard forward in time to the present, the captain conferred with his senior crew members in the ship's observation lounge. What was the analogy Data used in reference to the relationship between Q and Picard?
    A. A master and his pet
    B. A parent and its child
    C. A master and his slave

43. How many Romulan Warbirds were at the Neutral Zone when the present-time *Enterprise*-D arrived?
    A. 4
    B. 10
    C. 12

44. (Fill in the blanks) Picard hailed the Romulan flagship and he shifted in time to the future aboard the Pasteur. When Worf appeared on the viewscreen and informed Picard he could not violate Klingon regulations by allowing the medical ship to cross the border, Picard said the Worf he "used to know cared more

about _____ and _____ than rules and regulations."
  A. Pride, honor
  B. Honor, loyalty
  C. Duty, honor

45. Worf not only agreed to allow the Federation ship to cross the border, but offered to guide them to the Devron System. Once Worf beamed over to the Pasteur, at what warp speed did the ship engage?

46. When Picard traveled back in time to the past, he ordered the helm to set a course for the Devron System. Which command had not been programmed yet according to the computer?

47. Name the Romulan commander who appeared on the *Enterprise*-D's viewscreen in present time.
  A. Tokath
  B. Toreth
  C. Tomalak

48. Although the spatial anomaly appeared on the *Enterprise*-D's main viewscreen, nothing but vast, empty space appeared on the *Pasteur*'s viewscreen. What technique did Data devise to detect the spatial anomaly?
  A. Reverse tachyon beam
  B. Inverse tachyon pulse
  C. Subspace tachyon resonator

49. Who told Picard that it was possible that "all of this is happening in your mind"?

50. (True or false) Picard leapfrogged from the future to the present and then to the past, ordering the ship's crew in each time period to send out an inverse tachyon pulse.

51. According to Data, what was the spatial anomaly?
  A. An eruption of anti-time
  B. An interphase of time–space
  C. Temporal distortion

52. Even though it was a medical ship, Klingon warships opened fire on the *Pasteur*. How many Klingon vessels were involved in the attack?
    A. Two
    B. Four
    C. Six

53. Who did Beverly order to signal the *Pasteur*'s surrender?

54. What was the name of the cloaked starship that rescued the crew of the Pasteur before it exploded?

55. (True or false) In the future, Admiral Riker and Governor Worf did not speak to each other because Worf and Troi had taken the Oath, the Klingon marriage ritual.

56. What was the cause of Troi's death?

57. In the present time period, La Forge began growing new eyes due to the spontaneous regeneration of organs, but another crew member suffered a tragic miscarriage. Who was she?

58. Back on the *Enterprise* in the future, what happened to Picard when he insisted that the ship stay in the Devron System?
    A. Admiral Riker had Picard confined to quarters.
    B. Picard shifted in time again.
    C. Beverly administered a hypospray that rendered Picard unconscious.

59. Q transported Picard from the present to a time in ancient Earth history when life was just beginning to form. What was the status of the temporal anomaly?
    A. It was bigger.
    B. It was smaller.
    C. It did not exist.

60. (Fill in the blank) As Q and Picard witnessed the attempts of life to form, Q told Picard it was a shame he didn't bring his _____.

61. (True or false) Q revealed to Picard that his inverse tachyon pulses were the cause of the anomaly and if not stopped the anomaly would wipe out all of history.

62. How old was the temporal anomaly when Picard finally convinced Admiral Riker to take the *Enterprise* back to the Devron System?
    A. Twenty-five years old
    B. Five or six hours old
    C. A week old

63. (True or false) In a desperate race to save humanity from obliteration, Picard ordered *Enterprise* crews of the past, present, and future to stop the pulses.

64. When Picard ordered the *Enterprise* of the past to set a course for the center of the anomaly, which officer on the bridge demanded an explanation from Picard to the crew?
    A. Worf
    B. O'Brien
    C. Yar

65. (Fill in the blank) In a desperate attempt to repair the rupture and collapse the anomaly, Picard ordered all three *Enterprises* into the void at warp speed as he tried to create a _____ warp shell.

66. As the starships warped into the center of the anomaly, the tear in time repaired itself and the three *Enterprises* passed through each other. Which two ships exploded first?

67. (True or false) When Picard recovered in Q's court, the captain told Q he hoped it was the last time he found himself in Q's courtroom, but Q said the trial was just beginning.

68. Whose idea was it for Q to offer a "helping hand" to Picard as he traveled back and forth through three time periods?

69. Where did Q say he would see Picard next time?
    A. "Out there"
    B. "In the courtroom"
    C. "In the next life"

70. When the proper time was restored, Worf and Troi were about to kiss again in the *Enterprise*-D corridor. Where did Picard go after he found out the correct date from Worf and Troi?
    A. To the bridge
    B. To Dr. Crusher's quarters
    C. Back to sleep

71. Which members of the senior crew retained knowledge of everything that had transpired?

72. Who said the future in 25 years would be different than the one Picard experienced?

73. (Fill in the blank) When Captain Picard took a seat at the senior crew's regular Thursday night poker game, he established the rules as "Five card _____, nothing wild, and the sky's the limit."

Prime Memory Bonus

According to Professor Data, who had once resided in his gothic house at Cambridge University?

Prime Memory Bonus

(Fill in the blank) Governor Worf said Picard always used his knowledge of Klingon _____ to get what he wanted from Worf.

Prime Memory Bonus

In which year did Picard's future time period take place?

BATTLESTATIONS!

Romulans

The Romulans were a warrior race from the planets Romulus and Remus. Believed to be an offshoot of the humanoid Vulcan race that left Vulcan over a thousand years ago, the Romulans were a passionate, aggressive, but highly honorable people. Yet, the Romulans had been avowed enemies of the Federation for centuries.

1. The Romulan Star Empire consisted of two homeworlds: Romulus and Remus. What was the name given to Remus on Federation star charts?
    A. Remii
    B. Romii
    C. Remulus

2. (Fill in the blanks) Romulan admiral Jarok described Romulus as being a world of awesome beauty and spoke glowingly of such sights as the firefalls of Gal Gath'thong, the _____ of Chula, and the Apnex _____.

3. In which year did Ambassador Spock travel to Romulus on a personal mission to promote peaceful reunification between the Romulans and the Vulcans?
    A. 2364
    B. 2367
    C. 2368

4. (True or false) The Romulan Neutral Zone, a region of space dividing the Romulan Star Empire from the Federation, was approximately two light-years across.

5. The Neutral Zone was established around 2160 after a conflict between Earth and the Romulans. What type of weapons were used in that conflict?
    A. Metagenic
    B. Atomic
    C. Photon

6. What was the name of the peace accord that concluded the Romulan Wars and also forbade the Federation from developing or using cloaking devices on its spacecraft?
    A. Treaty of Algeron
    B. Treaty of Alliance
    C. Treaty of Sampalo Gandor

7. (True or false) The mysterious destruction of several Federation and Romulan outposts in 2364 triggered the end of Romulan isolationism when a *Warbird* crossed the Neutral Zone to investigate.

8. Name the commanding officer of the U.S.S. *Yamato* who violated the Neutral Zone in a successful effort to locate an ancient planet's legendary weapons technology.
    A. Captain Richard Stocker
    B. Captain John Langan
    C. Captain Donald Varley

9. Which Federation outpost detected a Romulan scoutship in the Neutral Zone in 2366?
    A. Kranus II
    B. Sierra VI
    C. Beto I

10. A Romulan defector, Admiral Jarok, convinced Captain Picard that planet Nelvana III was being prepared as a staging base for a massive assault against the Federation. Why did the Romulan High Command provide Jarok with this disinformation?

11. Name the Romulan commander who violated the Neutral Zone when his *Warbird* tried to rescue a scout ship?
    A. Toketh
    B. Sela
    C. Tomalak

12. What was the formal name of the Romulan nation?

13. What was the title of the leader of the Romulan empire?
    A. Praetor
    B. Pardek
    C. Proconsul

14. What was the title of the head of the Romulan Senate, one of the government's highest leaders?

15. (True or false) The Romulans pursued a long-term policy of using covert means to destabilize the Klingon government.

16. What was the name of the encounter between the Romulans and the Federation in 2311, which resulted in the loss of thousands of Federation lives?
    A. Neral Battle
    B. Tomed Incident
    C. Encounter at Sector 213

17. (True or false) When the Romulan government became aware of an underground movement in 2368, they tried to use it as a cover for an attempted invasion of the Klingon homeworld.

18. What was the site of an ill-fated Klingon outpost that was brutally attacked by the Romulans in 2344?
    A. Neela II
    B. Vedek 52
    C. Narendra III

19. What was the class designation of a massive and powerful Romulan *Warbird*?
    A. *T'Polair*
    B. *V'taxx*
    C. *D'deridex*

20. (Fill in the blank) A *Warbird* was nearly twice the overall length of a _____-class Federation starship.

21. What did a *Warbird* utilize as a power source for its warp drive system?
    - A. An artificial quantum singularity
    - B. An artificial multiphase inverter
    - C. A molecular MK-12 phase tracer

22. (True or false) Starfleet at one time designated the Romulan *Warbird* as a B-Type *Warbird*.

23. What was the crew complement of a Romulan science vessel?
    - A. 42
    - B. 56
    - C. 73

24. What was the color of the powerfully intoxicating beverage, Romulan Ale?

25. (True or false) Romulans were characterized as having great curiosity, while maintaining a tremendous self-confidence that bordered on arrogance.

26. How many years did the Neutral Zone remain unviolated?
    - A. 95
    - B. 106
    - C. 147

Prime Memory Bonus

How many Warbirds *were waiting on the* Enterprise-D *when Admiral Jarok persuaded Captain Picard to violate the Neutral Zone?*

Prime Memory Bonus

What were the two objects the giant predatory bird held in its talons on the emblem of the Romulan Star Empire?

BATTLESTATIONS!

Cardassians

Starfleet Intelligence records indicated that hostilities between the Cardassians and the Federation went back to at least the 2350s. A great commander once said, "Keep your friends close, but your enemies even closer." How well do you know the Cardassians, bitter enemies of the United Federation of Planets?

1. What was the formal name of the Cardassian government?
    A. Cardassian Alliance
    B. Cardassian Empire
    C. Cardassian Union

2. (True or false) Cardassia was a planet poor in natural resources, but in ancient times was home to a splendid civilization whose legendary ruins were considered some of the most remarkable in the galaxy.

3. What did the Cardassian military use to fund their war against the Federation?
    A. Stolen treasury accounts
    B. Archaeological treasures
    C. Religious artifacts

4. What was the name for the ancient people of Cardassia?
    A. First Cardassian Miarecki
    B. First Hebitian civilization
    C. First Galor Guernican

5. (True or false) After a bitter, extended conflict, an uneasy truce between Cardassia and the Federation was finally reached in 2368.

6. During negotiations on the treaty, with whom did Ambassador Spock publicly disagree?

7. Later that year, the treaty was violated by Starfleet Captain Benjamin Maxwell, who believed the Cardassian military was engaged in illicit activities. Name the Federation starship Maxwell commanded.
    A. U.S.S. *Phoenix*
    B. U.S.S. *Arizona*
    C. U.S.S. *Richmond*

8. During which year did Captain Picard and the crew of the U.S.S. *Stargazer* flee from a Cardassian warship, barely escaping with the *Stargazer* and its crew intact.
    A. 2355
    B. 2360
    C. 2362

9. (True or false) In the past, the Cardassians were a peaceful and spiritual people, but because their planet was resource-poor, starvation and disease were rampant, and people died by the millions.

10. (True or false) With the rise of the military to power, new territories and planets were taken by force at the cost of hundreds of thousands of lives sacrificed to the war effort.

11. Name the Starfleet captain who was partially credited for a historic peace treaty established between the Federation and Cardassia.
    A. Manuel DeLuna
    B. Gregory Quinn
    C. Edward Jellico

12. Which planet did the Cardassians annex in 2328, forcing most of its population to resettle on other worlds?

13. Name the commanding officer of the Cardassian warship *Trager* who came aboard the *Enterprise*-D in 2367 as an observer during a mission to locate the renegade Federation starship *Phoenix*.
    A. Gul Badar
    B. Gul Macet
    C. Gul Mukot

14. (True or false) Cardassians became very adept at physical and psychological torture.

15. What was the title given to Cardassian officers approximately equivalent to a Starfleet captain?

16. What was the class of Cardassian warship dispatched to the border to destroy a Bajoran *Antares*-class carrier in 2368?
    A. *Galis*
    B. *Darhe'el*
    C. *Galor*

17. Name the infamous labor camp on planet Bajor during the Cardassian occupation.

18. Prior to being designated *Deep Space 9* by Starfleet, what had the Cardassians called the old mining station in orbit around Bajor?
    A. *Terek Nor*
    B. *Cordan-Bu*
    C. *Ardana Cale*

19. In which year did the Cardassians abandon *Deep Space 9*?
    A. 2368
    B. 2369
    C. 2370

Prime Memory Bonus

(Fill in the blank) In 2369, Starfleet Intelligence believed that the Cardassians had discovered a new method to deliver deadly metagenic toxins in a dormant state on a _____ subspace carrier wave.

"WANNA BUY A USED STARSHIP?"
The Ferengi

1. (Fill in the blanks) The Ferengi were a technologically sophisticated humanoid race that was long a complete mystery to the Federation prior to first contact at planet _____ _____ in 2364.
    A. Delphi Ardu
    B. Alpha Fermi
    C. Fesarius Marglet

2. Name the pearls of wisdom in the Ferengi culture that children were expected to memorize and repeat on command.

3. (True or false) Considered the consummate capitalists, Ferengi entrepreneurs saw new opportunities shortly after first contact with the Federation and quickly assimilated themselves into Federation commerce.

4. Which race of humanoid telepaths were incapable of empathically reading Ferengi minds?

5. Which species' brains were structurally similar to those of the Ferengi?
    A. Legarans
    B. Rigelians
    C. Dopterians

6. Name the type of starship vessels the Ferengi used that were equipped with the ability to fire a powerful plasma energy?
    A. *D'Kora*
    B. *Marauder*
    C. *Ficus*

7. What did the Ferengi call their set of ethical guidelines governing behavior by Ferengi citizens?
    A. Words to Live By
    B. Ferengi Code
    C. The Grand Nagus' Rules of Commerce

8. In late 2369, one of these Ferengi vessels was mistaken for an attacking Borg ship when it entered the New Berlin system. What was this starship?
    A. Ferengi trading vessel
    B. Ferengi *Marauder*
    C. Ferengi *Probert*

9. (True or false) A Ferengi shuttle was a small four-person vessel used for short-range transport.

10. Which Ferengi code stated that anything found abandoned was open to claim by those who found it?

11. What type of Ferengi spacecraft, piloted by Dr. Arridor and Kol into the Barzan wormhole, was lost when the wormhole's terminus unexpectedly moved?

12. (True or false) Among the provisions of the Ferengi Code was a clause requiring the lives of subordinates be offered in payment for dishonorable deeds.

13. (True or false) When a Ferengi cargo shuttle crashed in the Hanolin asteroid belt in early 2368, the remains of the Vulcan ship *T'Pau*'s navigational deflector was found amid the debris in crates marked "Medical Supplies."

14. What was the formal name for the Ferengi government?
    A. Ferengi Federation
    B. Ferengi Trade Union
    C. Ferengi Alliance

15. What was the name of the Ferengi diplomatic enclave intended to further Ferengi business interests?
    A. Ferengi Trade Mission
    B. Ferengi Commerce Commission
    C. Ferengi Trade Council

16. (Fill in the blank) Ferengi were sexist in the extreme, and did not allow their females the honor of _____, although Ferengi males often found human females very attractive.

17. What was the name of the Ferengi weapon used to fire high-energy plasma discharges at a target?
    A. Ferengi disruptor
    B. Ferengi whip
    C. Ferengi exophaser

18. What was the crew complement of a Ferengi Marauder?
    A. 325
    B. 400
    C. 450

19. What was strictly forbidden according to the Ferengi death rituals?
    A. Funerals
    B. Autopsies
    C. Mourning

20. What was the title given to Ferengi leaders, approximately equivalent in rank to a Starfleet captain?

21. What was the title of the Ferengi master of commerce?

22. Name the emissary from the Ferengi Trade Commission who hoped to negotiate an exclusive trade agreement with Kriosian ambassador Briam in "The Perfect Mate" episode.
    A. Par Lenor
    B. Rom
    C. Zek

Prime Memory Bonus

How many Rules of Acquisition were there?

STARFLEET INTELLIGENCE
OFFICER DOSSIER
Ensign Wesley Crusher

1. Crusher was raised by his mother following the death of his father in 2354, when Crusher was five years old. Which sport did Crusher's father teach him to play before his untimely death?
   A. Baseball
   B. Krak'nuball
   C. Soccer

2. (True or false) Crusher showed a keen interest in science and music and had an extraordinary ability to visualize complex mathematical concepts, an ability that the Traveler once urged Captain Picard to nurture.

3. (Fill in the blank) The Traveler called Crusher a _____, like young Mozart.

4. (True or false) Picard commissioned Crusher an acting ensign in recognition of Crusher's key role in returning the *Enterprise*-D to Federation space after it was stranded by Kosinski's failed warp drive experiments.

5. As a member of an away team to Rubicun III, Crusher inadvertently broke a local law and was sentenced to the death penalty by the planetary government. Which *Enterprise*-D officer violated the Prime Directive in a successful attempt to free Crusher?
   A. Picard
   B. Beverly
   C. Riker

6. (Fill in the blanks) Crusher's first experience with command was when Riker assigned him the task of supervising geological surveys in the _____ _____ Sector in 2365.
    A. Maura Penthara
    B. Pentarus Paz
    C. Selcundi Drema

7. Name the legitimate life forms Crusher accidentally created during medical experiments.

8. These self-replicating, sentient beings interfered with the *Enterprise*-D onboard systems and nearly destroyed a landmark astrophysics experiment. Name the eminent scientist who was conducting the neutronium decay experiment aboard the starship.
    A. Dr. Jeanette Mentzel
    B. Dr. Paul Stubbs
    C. Dr. Harold Skidmore

9. Name the lovely young leader of Daled IV, who became Crusher's first romantic interest.
    A. Seelay
    B. Sahndara
    C. Salia

10. (Fill in the blank) The Daled IV leader, although not human, was a shape-shifting _____ who appeared as a teenaged human girl whose keen intelligence and wit captured Crusher's interest.
    A. Chameloid
    B. Allasomorph
    C. Horath

11. How old was Crusher when he first tried to gain entrance to Starfleet Academy?

12. Name the frightening animal Crusher considered re-creating on the holodeck to prepare himself for the Psych Test portion of the Starfleet Academy entrance exam?
    A. Bulgallian rat
    B. Klingon *targ*
    C. Wanoni tracehound

13.   Which incident involving Crusher's father did Wesley Crusher's Psych Test parallel?

14.   (True or false) Although Crusher did not win admission to Starfleet Academy at that time, he continued his studies and Starfleet granted him academic credit for his work aboard the *Enterprise*-D.

15.   Crusher was accepted to Starfleet Academy in 2366, but missed his transport to the Academy because he was participating in a rescue mission. Who had been kidnapped by the Ferengi?

16.   What was Crusher's reward in recognition of his personal sacrifice shortly after the rescue mission?

17.   (True or false) Crusher finally entered Starfleet Academy in 2368 when a position opened up mid-term in the current class.

18.   Crusher's final assignment as an *Enterprise*-D crew member was to accompany Captain Picard on a diplomatic mission to planet Pentarus V, but the mission was interrupted when their transport shuttle crashed. Name the shuttle's pilot whose impulsive actions (and constant reluctance to accept Crusher's leadership) caused his own death.
      A.   Captain Dimorus
      B.   Captain Kajada
      C.   Captain Dirgo

19.   Crusher's freshman year at Starfleet Academy was marred by a serious incident at the Academy Flight Range in which a cadet was killed. Although Crusher later came forward with the truth, he was severely punished by the Academy. Describe Crusher's disciplinary action.

20.   Crusher became disenchanted with his studies at the Academy and resigned his commission. Name the planet on which he chose to live among the American Indians, a world under Cardassian jurisdiction.
      A.   Utalando II
      B.   Dorvan V
      C.   Tekara II

21.   (True or false) Crusher discovered (with the assistance of the Traveler) that he possessed the ability to manipulate a previously unsuspected relationship between space, time, and thought.

Prime Memory Bonus

What was the required course Crusher had difficulty mastering at Starfleet Academy?

STARFLEET INTELLIGENCE
OFFICER DOSSIER
Lieutenant Commander Natasha Yar

1. Which nationality from ancient Earth was Yar descended from?
   A. Swede
   B. Ukranian
   C. German

2. Yar was born on a failed Federation colony on Turkana IV. How old was she when her parents were killed?
   A. Four
   B. Five
   C. Six

3. Yar spent much of her childhood in a bitter struggle for survival, evading marauding rape gangs and caring for her younger sister. What was her name?
   A. Yanara
   B. Thea
   C. Ishara

4. When Natasha left Turkana IV, her sister regarded her as a coward. What was the name of the faction that fought for control of the planet, of which the younger Yar became a loyal member?
   A. The Alliance
   B. The Coalition
   C. The Rebel Cadre

5. What kind of pet did Yar have as a child?
   A. Kitten
   B. Tarantula
   C. Puppy

6. How old was Yar when she escaped from Turkana IV, choosing
   to join Starfleet?
   A. 15
   B. 16
   C. 18

7. Captain Picard requested Yar's transfer to the *Enterprise*-D after
   she demonstrated her courage in rescuing a wounded colonist.
   Be more specific and choose Yar's exact act of heroism.
   A. She rescued the colonist and then tried to save a child.
   B. She fought six Argolian soldiers without a weapon.
   C. She made her way through a Carnellian minefield.

8. What was Yar's first position aboard the *Enterprise*-D?
   A. Assistant Security Chief
   B. Ops
   C. Security Chief

9. Yar was killed while participating in a rescue mission on Vagra
   II to save Counselor Troi. In what year did she die?
   A. 2363
   B. 2364
   C. 2365

10. Why did the malevolent life form kill Yar?
    A. For its amusement
    B. To keep Yar away from Troi's crashed shuttle
    C. In retaliation for Yar firing a phaser

11. What did Yar leave for her *Enterprise*-D comrades after her
    death?
    A. A holographic scrapbook of her life on Turkana IV
    B. A holographic farewell
    C. Something personal for each of them (including chocolates
    for Counselor Troi)

12. Who kept a small holographic portrait of Yar as one of his most
    precious possessions?
    A. Picard
    B. Worf
    C. Data

13. In the alternate time created when the *Enterprise*-C vanished from its "proper" place into a temporal rift, *Enterprise*-D security chief Yar did not die on Vagra II. When it was learned that the *Enterprise*-C had to return to the past, the alternate Yar volunteered to return with that ship. What happened to Yar after Romulans captured the *Enterprise*-C bridge crew at Narendra III?
    A. She was executed.
    B. She became a consort to a Romulan general.
    C. She was sold to a group of Andorian slave owners.

14. How old was Sela, the alternate Yar's daughter, when her mother tried to escape and was killed?
    A. Four
    B. Six
    C. Eight

Prime Memory Bonus

Name the Turkana IV drink that was so scarce it became a prized beverage worth stealing from opposing cadres.

STARFLEET INTELLIGENCE
OFFICER DOSSIER
Lieutenant Ro Laren

1. Born in 2340 and raised during the Cardassian occupation of her homeworld, Ro spent most of her childhood where?
   A. Cardassian child labor and reformatory on Claudus XI
   B. Cardassian re-education plant
   C. Bajoran resettlement camps

2. How old was Ro when she was forced to watch Cardassians torture her father to death?
   A. Five years old
   B. Seven years old
   C. Nine years old

3. What was Bajoran custom in regards to the order of speaking or writing a person's name?
   A. Given name first, followed by family name
   B. Family name first, followed by given name
   C. Each family decided order of listing for three generations

4. Why did most Bajorans, including Ro, wear an ornamental earring on their right ear?
   A. It was customary.
   B. It was an outward display of their inward spirituality.
   C. It was a sign of courage and bravery.

5. As a Starfleet ensign, Ro had numerous reprimands on her record, and she was court-martialed after a disastrous mission to Garon II in which she disobeyed orders. How many members

of her U.S.S. *Wellington* away team were killed because of her irresponsibility?
A. Four
B. Six
C. Eight

6. Name the planet on which Ro was imprisoned in a Federation stockade.
A. Jaya III
B. Rochani IV
C. Jaros II

7. Name the admiral who engineered Ro's release from prison.
A. Connally
B. Kennelly
C. Cokesburg

8. Ro was released in exchange for her participation in a covert mission aboard the *Enterprise*-D intended to apprehend Bajoran terrorists believed to have attacked Federation interests. Whom did Ro discover was really behind the attacks?
A. Cardassians
B. Federation double agents
C. Romulan operative Sela

9. Ro agreed to remain aboard the *Enterprise*-D. Which senior crew member did she share a brief romantic liaison?
A. Riker
B. La Forge
C. Worf

10. Which *Enterprise*-D senior officer was Ro frequently at odds with over her performance as a crew member?
A. Picard
B. Troi
C. Riker

11. The Bajorans were a deeply religious people, although Ro was never sure about her individual faith. What did Ro attempt to do when a Romulan interphase generator led her to believe she was dead?

A. Persuaded La Forge to give her the last celestial rites

B. Make peace with herself in accordance with Bajoran religious beliefs

C. Asked La Forge to grant her absolution of her sins

12. In 2368, Ro left the *Enterprise*-D for two years. Where was she during this time period?

A. Bajoran Shakaar Resistance Training Camp

B. Starfleet Advanced Tactical Training

C. Starfleet Academy

13. In 2370, when Ro returned to duty aboard the *Enterprise*-D as a lieutenant, she was once again chosen to participate in a covert mission. Name the Federation citizens who were waging a guerilla war against the Cardassians and whom Ro was instructed to infiltrate.

A. Maquis

B. Maqu

C. Navot

14. Which two *Enterprise*-D officers were sent planetside to help establish Ro's cover as a fugitive Starfleet officer wanted in the death of a Cardassian officer?

A. Picard and Data

B. Riker and Worf

C. Worf and Data

15. Who threatened to bring Ro before a Board of Inquiry and have her court-martialed if she sabotaged her covert mission?

A. Picard

B. Riker

C. Admiral Nortino

16. Whom did Ro pull a phaser on when she decided to leave Starfleet and join the freedom fighters in their war against the Cardassians?
     A. Picard
     B. Riker
     C. Data

Prime Memory Bonus

When Lieutenant Ro returned to duty aboard the Enterprise-D *in 2370, which deck housed her living quarters?*

Prime Memory Bonus

When the Maquis attacked the Cardassians in the demilitarized zone, which type of phaser did they use in conjunction with pho-ton torpedoes?

STARFLEET INTELLIGENCE
AMBASSADOR DOSSIER

Lwaxana Troi

1. (Fill in the blanks) Lwaxana Troi was never bashful in proclaiming her rather lengthy title of Daughter of the _____ House, Holder of the Sacred _____ of Rixx, Heir to the Holy _____ of Betazed.

2. Lwaxana, a full Betazoid, married a Starfleet officer and the couple had two children, Deanna and Kestra. Deanna, of course, grew up to be a Starfleet officer. Kestra, however, died at an early age. What was the cause of her death?

3. Ambassador Lwaxana represented her government at the Pacifica Conference and was credited for exposing an assassination plot at the conference. Who was the assassin?

4. When Lwaxana entered what was known in Betazoid culture as "the phase," a period in which a woman's sexuality matured and her sex drive quadrupled, Lwaxana hoped to marry either one or the other of two *Enterprise*-D officers. Who were they?

5. Who was the Ferengi who kidnapped Lwaxana in an attempt to use her empathic powers for his personal gain?
    A. DaiMon Zek
    B. DaiMon Tog
    C. DaiMon Nog

6. Lwaxana became engaged to marry Minister Campio of planet Kostolain. Why was the wedding cancelled?

7. Something of a free spirit, Lwaxana enjoyed vacationing at the colorful Parallax Colony on planet Shiralea VI. What did she find so appealing about the colony?
   A. The young, muscular lifeguards
   B. The nude beaches
   C. The mud baths

8. Lwaxana, in her latter years, suffered the Betazoid equivalent of a nervous breakdown. What was the root cause of her emotional problems?

9. What was the name of Lwaxana's tall and silent humanoid attendant?

Prime Memory Bonus

What was the name of the bartender whom Lwaxana became attracted to in Picard's Dixon Hill holodeck program, unaware that he was merely a simulation?

BEHIND THE SCENES

The Final Chapter

1. How many Emmys did *TNG* win during its first six years on the air?
   - A. 12
   - B. 16
   - C. 20

2. Name the only episode not to feature a single scene on the *Enterprise*-D bridge.

3. In how many fifth season episodes did John de Lancie appear as Q?
   - A. None
   - B. One
   - C. Two

4. What did Patrick Stewart do for the first time during the sixth season?

5. In seven years, how many episodes of *TNG* did Jonathan Frakes direct?
   - A. Five
   - B. Six
   - C. Seven

6. What do Majel Barrett, John de Lancie, Michelle Phillips, DeForest Kelley, and Carel Struycken have in common?

7. What was the name of the hour-long series retrospective hosted by Jonathan Frakes, which aired the week of *TNG*'s finale?

A. "Fond Farewell"
B. "Journey's End"
C. "Such Sweet Sorrow"

8. How many restrooms are on the *Enterprise*-D?

9. How many episodes did Patrick Stewart direct over the course of seven years?
   A. Four
   B. Five
   C. Six

10. What were the ceiling lights on the *Enterprise*-D's transporter room used for on the original *Enterprise*?

11. Where were all the outdoor scenes for "The Inner Light" episode filmed?

12. Marina Sirtis is a British expatriate. How many months after arriving in the U.S. did she land the role of Counselor Troi?
    A. 6
    B. 8
    C. 10

13. (True or false) Patrick Stewart, who was so sure he was going to get fired from *TNG* at its outset, didn't unpack his bags six weeks.

14. How much a year did *TNG* make for Paramount?
    A. $40 million
    B. $60 million
    C. $80 million

15. What was the name of the poorly received sequel to *North and South*, in which Jonathan Frakes starred with his wife, Genie Francis?

16. What did Michael Dorn consider his "crowning glory" in the role of Worf?
    A. Being the architect for all Klingons on the show
    B. The simmering romance between Worf and Troi
    C. Avenging K'Ehleyr's murder

17. Which *TNG* regular cast member was host of PBS's *Reading Rainbow*?

18. For which Charles Dickens story did Patrick Stewart win international success and various awards in his one-man stage version?
    A. *A Christmas Carol*
    B. *A Tale of Two Cities*
    C. *Oliver Twist*

19. How many episodes of *TNG* did LeVar Burton direct?
    A. One
    B. Two
    C. Three

20. Who told Denise Crosby (when she became disgruntled and decided to leave *TNG*), "If I was hungry and in my 20s, I'd probably have done the same thing"?
    A. Patrick Stewart
    B. Gene Roddenberry
    C. LeVar Burton

21. Name the director of "All Good Things . . ."
    A. Cliff Bole
    B. Winrich Kolbe
    C. David Carson

22. (True or false) Thanks to the holodeck, Data played Sherlock Holmes, Henry V, and Zorro.

23. Who played the tallest Klingon on record (he had to duck to get through the *Enterprise*-D portals)?

24. He only had two scenes in one episode, but he got to ask Captain Picard, "What happened to your hair?" Who was this T.V. veteran?

25. Mick Fleetwood's character, an Antedian dignitary, slurped vermicula. What did *TNG* tech wizards use to make this slimy Antedian delicacy?
    A. Silly Putty, kitty litter, and dye
    B. Egg yoke, pencil shavings, and dye
    C. Gelatin, sawdust, and food coloring

26. This renowed actor, who guest-starred on the "Interface" episode, has a framed set of Spock's ears given to him by Leonard Nimoy. Who is he?

27. Name the only person to appear on *TNG* who had actually been in space?

28. What was *TNG*'s cheapest and most effective special effect?

29. She actually got to say the line, "I've always wanted to make love to an alien." Who was this actress?
    A. Bebe Neuwirth
    B. Whoopi Goldberg
    C. Michelle Forbes

30. Name the *TNG* production designer who used to work as a designer for NASA.

31. What were the original Starfleet front-zipping jumpsuits made of?
    A. Rayon
    B. Spandex
    C. Cotton jersey

32. What did visual-effects technicians once use for the surface of a planet?
    A. Dog manure
    B. Alpo
    C. Vomit

33. She is considered the "First Lady of *Star Trek.*" Who is she?

34. What was the name of the seventh season episode in which Riker felt turmoil between old and present captains calling on his loyalty?

35. Who was Picard's fish, Livingston, named for?

36. What was *TNG*'s budget per show?
    A. $2 million
    B. $1.5 million
    C. $1 million

37. Which regular cast member guest-starred on HBO's *Dream On?*

38. (True or false) Gates McFadden tried to renegotiate her contract at the end of the first season and left when her requests were not met, but when she did return it was at a lower salary than the rest of her co-stars.

39. (True or false) Gates is McFadden's real name.

40. Initially Gene Roddenberry nixed the idea of Patrick Stewart as Captain Picard. What other *TNG* role was he considered for?

41. Only two actors read for the role of Data. Of course, Brent Spiner became Data, but the other actor went on to portray a recurring character on *TNG*. Who was he and what role did he play?

42. Originally the character of Wesley was supposed to be a female. What was her name?
     A. Sarah
     B. Robin
     C. Leslie

43. In the beginning the Tasha Yar character was meant to be a Latina, patterned after the feisty marine in *Aliens*. What was the character's name before it was changed to Tasha Yar?
     A. Maria Rodriguez
     B. Macha Hernandez
     C. Carmen Sanchez

44. Other than Marina Sirtis, who else read for the part of Counselor Troi?

45. Why did Marina Sirtis win the role of Troi?
     A. She had a more exotic look about her.
     B. Majel Barrett, a.k.a. Lwaxana Troi, made the final decision.
     C. The other actress had an accident.

46. (True or false) It was Gene Roddenberry's idea to have a Klingon on the bridge of the *Enterprise*-D.

47. (True or false) René Echevarria's first version of "The Offspring" was dramatically different from the episode produced: Data

mated with the ship's computer to create a unique android, making the ship's computer Lal's mother.

48. Which two episodes were Michael Dorn's personal favorites?
    A. "Firstborn" and "Parallels"
    B. "Birthright, Parts I and II"
    C. "The Offspring" and "The Drumhead"

49. What was the source of Dennis Bailey and David Bischoff's script for "Tin Man"?

50. Hallie Todd, who played Data's daughter, Lal, came from a family of Trekkers. What role did her stepfather, Guy Ramon, play in the popular *TREK-classic*, "The Trouble with Tribbles"?
    A. A Klingon
    B. An Enterprise crew member
    C. The bartender

51. In the episode "A Fistful of Datas," Alexander's holodeck simulation was set in the ancient west town of Deadwood. In which U.S. state did there once exist an actual town named Deadwood?
    A. Nevada
    B. South Dakota
    C. Texas

52. Marc Alaimo played the chief delegate of the Antican contingent in "Lonely Among Us," Commander Tebok in "The Neutral Zone," and Gul Macet in "The Wounded." What role did he play in "Time's Arrow, Part I"?
    A. The gambler Frederick LaRouque
    B. One of the Devidians
    C. Samuel Clemens

53. Name the martial-arts expert and *TNG* visual effects producer who designed the Klingon *bat'telh* and also helped develop the intricate dancelike movements associated with its use.

54. Which *TNG* episode was a "crossover," using elements from *TNG* and *Deep Space 9*?

55. The blue-skinned Bolians were named for a *TNG* director whose episode "Conspiracy" was the first episode in which these aliens were seen. Name the director.

56. Picard first mentioned Boothby, the groundskeeper at Starfleet Academy, in "Final Mission," then again in "The Game." In which episode did we finally get to see the character?

57. From which scientific term did writer Maurice Hurley derive the name Borg?

58. The U.S.S. *Bozeman* from the "Cause and Effect" episode was named for the hometown of writer Brannon Braga. Bozeman is located in which state?
     A.   Arkansas
     B.   Montana
     C.   Kentucky

59. What was the name of the unseen captain's yacht aboard the *Enterprise*-D?
     A.   *Newton*
     B.   *Hawking*
     C.   *Calypso*

60. Where were the exterior scenes of Mintaka III filmed for the episode "Who Watches the Watchers"?
     A.   Vasquez Rocks, near Los Angeles
     B.   A Paramount sound stage
     C.   On the Nevada side of Lake Tahoe

61. (True or false) One of the shuttlepods carried aboard the *Enterprise*-D was named for deceased Challenger astronaut Ellison Onizuka.

62. (Fill in the blanks) The second season episode "_____ _____" was originally written for the proposed *Star Trek II* television series in the late 1970s.

63. Name the book about time travel that Samuel Clemens described to the reporter in "Time's Arrow, Part II."

64. Who was Wesley Crusher named for?

65. Which episode marked the first appearance of the new midsized shuttlecraft?
    A. "Silicon Avatar"
    B. "Redemption, Part II"
    C. "Darmok"

66. Which episode was the last one to carry Gene Roddenberry's name in the writing credits?
    A. "Angel One"
    B. "Datalore"
    C. "Coming of Age"

67. (Fill in the blank) When the traditional Klingon warrior's knife, _____, was used for *TNG*, the original was not available, so the *Trek* techs duplicated the design for the show's prop makers, using a *Star Trek* trading card for reference.
    A. *d'K tahg*
    B. *V'Kag*
    C. *Ha'Keeth*

68. What did visual effects technicians use to build the miniature of the Echo Papa 607 automated weapons drone in "The Arsenal of Freedom"?
    A. L'Eggs pantyhose container and a shampoo bottle
    B. Silly Putty container and a peanut butter jar
    C. Plastic Easter egg and a glass Coke bottle

69. Which episode was the second episode filmed for the third season, but was the first episode aired for that season?

70. What was the origin of the term "Jefferies tube"?
    A. Named after Dr. Lionel Jefferies
    B. A fan in Dallas by the name of Stan Jefferies
    C. A gag among the *TREK-classic* production staff

71. The 14-year-old Talarian boy, Jono, used a dagger to stab Captain Picard in "Suddenly Human." Where had the knife originally come from?
    A. An archaeological dig on Icor IX
    B. It was Picard's Klingon *cha'Dlch* ceremonial knife.
    C. Riker gave it to Picard as a gift.

72. (True or false) The season premier episode "The Best of Both Worlds, Part II" was considered to be so secret that each copy of the script was covertly numbered, so that if unauthorized copies were made, it would be possible to trace whose copy it came from.

73. Executive producer Rick Berman named the *Enterprise*-D shuttlecraft *Justman* in honor of his colleague, a veteran of both *TREK-classic* and *TNG*. Who is he?

74. At the time "Heart of Glory" was written, what was the intended name for the Klingon homeworld?
    A. Kling
    B. Qo'noS
    C. Kligat

75. Patricia Tallman was a stunt person on several *TNG* episodes and played Kiros, one of the terrorists, in "Starship Mine." In which syndicated T.V. science-fiction series pilot episode did she have a role?
    A. *Time Trax*
    B. *Tek Wars*
    C. *Babylon 5*

76. (True or false) All the Klingon-language words on *TNG* came from linguist Marc Okrand's book, *The Klingon Dictionary*.

77. (True or false) The makeup differences between the *TREK-classic* Klingons and the *Trek* movies and *TNG* Klingons were never addressed?

78. Following the original airing of "The Chase," a small ceramic archaeological artifact was seen in later episodes adorning a corner table of Picard's ready room. What was the name of the statue?
    A. Tarquin Hill
    B. Kurlan Naikos
    C. K'Temoc

79. (True or false) The name of La Forge's mother was listed as Alvera K. La Forge on Geordi's death certificate as seen in "The Next Phase," but was established as Silva La Forge in "Interface."

80. He played Trent in "Angel One" and the initial, featureless Lal in "The Offspring." Who is he?
    A. Leonard J. Crowfoot
    B. Robert Running Bear
    C. Cecil Screaming Eagle

81. This Federation starship as seen in "Unnatural Selection," had been used earlier in *Star Trek II: The Wrath of Kahn* as the U.S.S. *Reliant*. What was its name designation in *TNG*?
    A. U.S.S. *Niagara*
    B. U.S.S. *Lantree*
    C. U.S.S. *Rigel*

82. He portrayed Romulan Senator Pardek in "Unification, Parts I and II" on *TNG* and Commodore Jose Mendez in "The Menagerie, Parts I and II" on *TREK-classic*. Who is this actor?
    A. Brooker Bradshaw
    B. Malachi Throne
    C. David Warner

83. An example of Mintakan tapestry was given to Captain Picard by Nuria, the Mintakan leader, in appreciation for his concern for her people in "Who Watches the Watchers." In later episodes, where in Picard's quarters was this tapestry seen?

84. Name the actor who played the Benzite Mendon in "A Matter of Honor" and the Benzite Mordock in "Coming of Age."
    A. John Putch
    B. Daniel Davis
    C. Marc Alaimo

85. Stock footage of this nebula from *Star Trek II: The Wrath of Kahn,* was re-used several times for other nebulae seen on *TNG*. What was the name of the nebula in *Star Trek II*?
    A. Netari
    B. Quincet
    C. Mutara

86. What did "A Matter of Time," "Birthright," and "Final Mission" have in common?

87. What was Keiko O'Brien's maiden name?
    A. Fuji
    B. Ishikawa
    C. Ogawa

88. In which episode did we finally learn Miles Edward O'Brien's first and middle names?
    A. "Family"
    B. "Legacy"
    C. "Birthright, Part I"

89. How did O'Brien order his coffee from the replicator?
    A. Irish, double-strong, black
    B. Jamaican, double-strong, double-sweet
    C. Irish, stout, one teaspoon of sugar

90. The Paris city skyline backdrop from "We'll Always Have Paris" was re-used in which *Trek* movie?

91. In which *TNG* episode were transporter pattern enhancers first seen?
    A. "Frame of Mind"
    B. "Ship in a Bottle"
    C. "Power Play"

92. He played the young Picard in "Rascals" and also René Picard, Jean-Luc's nephew, in "Family." Who is he?
    A. Jeremy Kemp
    B. David Tristen Burkin
    C. Clive Church

93. Matt Frewer was familiar to genre fans as T.V.'s Max Headroom. What role did he play in *TNG* episode "A Matter of Time"?

94. Cyrus Redblock, a fictional gangster character from the Dixon Hill detective stories, was a tip of the hat to a famous actor. Name him.

95. He was a Starfleet officer with the Inspector General's office and was seen in "Coming of Age" and "Conspiracy." Remmick was his last name. What was his first name?

    A. Dexter
    B. Robert
    C. Scott

96. (True or false) Actor Howie Sego, who portrayed the famed deaf mediator in "Loud as a Whisper," was also deaf in real life.

97. Which *TNG* episode did writer Tracy Torme intend to be an homage to the British series *The Prisoner*?
    A. "A Matter of Honor"
    B. "The Survivors"
    C. "The Schizoid Man"

98. Which episode was a "clip show," designed to use scenes from earlier episodes in an effort to save money?
    A. "Shades of Grey"
    B. "All Good Things . . ."
    C. "The Best of Both Worlds, Part II"

99. How many times was the huge main shuttlebay shown during *TNG*'s seven seasons?

100. Name the character who had the dubious distinction of being the first *Enterprise*-D crew member killed.
    A. Lieutenant Commander Raz
    B. Lieutenant Commander Kari
    C. Lieutenant Commander Singh

101. Actor Judson Scott portrayed Sobi in the episode "Symbiosis." In which *Star Trek* movie did he play a character called Joachim?

102. (True or false) The aliens in "Schisms" were given a formal name when Picard recorded his captain's log.

103. Why did Brent Spiner play the part of Dr. Noonien Soong?

104. (Fill in the blank) Data's pet, Spot, was a _____ cat in "Data's Day," but in later appearances he was just a common house cat.

105.   The matte painting cityscape from "Angel One" was re-used for the exterior of a starbase in "Samaritan Snare." Which starbase number was it?
    A.   515
    B.   343
    C.   440

106.   After this episode was shown, it was decided that starbase numbers shouldn't go much higher than 500. Name the episode in which Starbase 718 appeared.
    A.   "Violations"
    B.   "The Neutral Zone"
    C.   "The Emissary"

107.   Where were the Starfleet Academy grounds seen in "The First Duty" filmed?
    A.   TRW plant in Los Angeles
    B.   It was nothing but a matte painting
    C.   Tillman Water Reclamation plant in Van Nuys, California

108.   (Fill in the blanks) Professor _____ _____, when visiting the *Enterprise*-D engine room at Paramount Pictures in 1993, stated he was working on warp drive.

109.   The Tango Sierra Science Station was a re-use of a space station model seen in a *Star Trek* movie. Name the movie.

110.   Name the episode in which a furry piglike Klingon *targ* appeared on the bridge of the *Enterprise*.
    A.   "Q Who"
    B.   "True Q"
    C.   "Where No One Has Gone Before"

111.   The three-dimensional chess game in Ten-Forward used pieces replicated in the detail of a robot from another T.V. science-fiction series. Name the television show.

112.   The L.K.C. *T'Ong*, the Klingon deep-space exploratory cruiser seen in "The Emissary," was a re-use of a Klingon battle cruiser from a *Star Trek* movie. Which one?

113. (Fill in the blank) Landing a huge spaceship every week would have cost far too much for a television budget, but the _____ provided an ingenious means of getting the characters quickly (and inexpensively) into the midst of action.

114. How many stars were on the U.S. flag in "The Royale" episode?

115. The late Sam Rolfe wrote TNG's "The Vengeance Factor" episode. Which television series did he develop in the 1960s?
    A. The Man From U.N.C.L.E.
    B. Lost in Space
    C. The Outer Limits

116. (True or false) La Forge's VISOR was modeled on a hair clip donated to the show by a U.C.L.A. researcher.

117. (Fill in the blanks) The ancient sailing ship model of the H.M.S. Victory that La Forge gave his former captain still graces the home of _____ _____.
    A. LeVar Burton
    B. Majel Barrett
    C. Patrick Stewart

118. (True or false) Wolf 359, the site of a terrible battle with the Borg in which a majority of the Federation's starships were destroyed, is a real star located 7.8 light years away from Earth.

119. (True or false) Worf was originally intended to be nothing more than a costumed extra with elaborate makeup?

120. What was the name of the potent Klingon beverage that Worf ordered for the Bringloidi leader in "Up the Long Ladder"?
    A. H'teKoth
    B. Chech'tluth
    C. Leck'roth

121. What was the name of the Klingon beast that Ardra transformed into in "Devil's Due"? (Worf was not impressed.)
    A. Hokul'ar
    B. Ruk'let
    C. Fek'lhr

122.   What caused a two-day production delay in filming "Genesis," the episode that marked Gates McFadden's directorial debut?

Prime Memory Bonus

Which issue of "T.V. Guide" was hailed on the cover as a "Collector's Edition" because it saluted "seven seasons of success from the Star Trek *sequel"?*

Prime Memory Bonus

Whose writings did Patrick Stewart quote from at Gene Roddenberry's memorial and also to TNG cast when filming was completed on the series finale?

Prime Memory Bonus

How many square feet of living area did the Enterprise-D *reserve for its crew and family members?*

STAR SEARCH

From Starbases to stardates, from Starfleet Academy to Starfleet regulations, trek to the stars and search for the correct answers to this trivia test.

1. The *Enterprise*-D underwent a computer systems upgrade at this massive orbital facility in "11001001."
    A. Starbase 2
    B. Starbase 74
    C. Starbase 11

2. This starbase was evacuated for two days, apparently because key Starfleet officials were under the control of a parasitic intelligence.
    A. Starbase 12
    B. Starbase 220
    C. Starbase 512

3. Captain Picard and Wesley Crusher traveled to this Starfleet facility in the Scylla Sector when Picard underwent a cardiac replacement and Wesley took Academy tests.
    A. Starbase 128
    B. Starbase 515
    C. Starbase 520

4. This starbase was the location of an emergency conference that Picard attended to discuss the possibility of a new Romulan incursion.
    A. Starbase 301
    B. Starbase 343
    C. Starbase 718

5. This Starfleet facility was where a young Ensign Picard was nearly killed when he picked a fight with three Nausicaans.
    A. Starbase *Montgomery*
    B. Starbase G-6
    C. Starbase *Earhart*

6. The *Enterprise*-D picked up a shipment of scientific equipment and also Dr. Leah Brahms at this Federation starbase in 2367.
    A. Starbase 313
    B. Starbase 260
    C. Starbase 326

7. From this starbase Captain Picard launched his armada to blockade Romulan forces during the Klingon civil war.
    A. Starbase 301
    B. Starbase 234
    C. Starbase 29

8. This Starfleet facility, located near Khitomer, was where young Worf's nursemaid was taken for treatment of her injuries following the Romulan attack on Khitomer.
    A. Starbase 81
    B. Starbase 133
    C. Starbase 24

9. Worf delivered Alexander to this Starfleet facility, where his adoptive parents took custody of the boy after the murder of K'Ehleyr.
    A. Starfleet 73
    B. Starfleet 36
    C. Starfleet 29

10. Counselor Troi and La Forge were ordered by the Ktarians to travel to this starbase and distribute the addictive Ktarian game to all the starships docked there.
    A. Starbase 31
    B. Starbase 46
    C. Starbase 67

11. This planetside facility was where the *Enterprise*-D underwent engineering consultations in "The Icarus Factor."
    A. Starbase *Korolev*
    B. Starbase *Montgomery*
    C. Starbase *Merced*

12. Admiral J. P. Hanson returned to this Federation starbase after receiving confirmation of the encroachment of the Borg into Federation space.
    A. Starbase 7
    B. Starbase 12
    C. Starbase 324

13. The U.S.S. *Phoenix* was escorted by the *Enterprise*-D to this starbase following Captain Maxwell's unauthorized attack in Cardassian space.
    A. Starbase 211
    B. Starbase 96
    C. Starbase 123

14. The *Enterprise*-D traveled to this facility when Q returned the ship to Federation space after first contact with the Borg.
    A. Starbase 83
    B. Starbase 107
    C. Starbase 121

15. The *Enterprise*-D was en route to this starbase when it encountered the ancient Kataan probe in "The Inner Light."
    A. Starbase 16
    B. Starbase 93
    C. Starbase 218

16. The *Enterprise*-D visited this planetside facility for personnel rotation and to pick up Ensign Mendon as part of an Officer Exchange Program.
    A. Starbase 163
    B. Starbase 179
    C. Starbase 295

Prime Memory Bonus

Name the Starfleet facility near planet Betazed from which Counselor Troi was able to visit her home via shuttlecraft.

---

17. This was the stardate for Ambassador Sarek's visit aboard the *Enterprise*-D for a critical diplomatic mission.
    A. 42156.8
    B. 43917.4
    C. 44182.6

18. What was the stardate for the "I, Borg" episode, in which Hugh was given a sense of individuality?
    A. 45854.2
    B. 44326.1
    C. 45961.6

19. This was the stardate when the Romulans ended their isolationism and violated the Neutral Zone.
    A. 40923.0
    B. 41201.3
    C. 41986.0

20. What was the stardate for the "present" time period in the time-shifting series conclusion, "All Good Things . . ."?
    A. 46996.1
    B. 47316.6
    C. 47988.0

21. This was the stardate for the discovery of Scotty's crashed transport ship on a Dyson sphere.
    A. 45794.1
    B. 46125.3
    C. 47006.2

22. The *Enterprise*-C emerged from the past into the present on this stardate.
    A. 43625.2
    B. 44973.5
    C. 45106.9

23. What was the stardate for "Unification, Part I," when Ambassador Spock was spotted in Romulan territory?
    A. 44691.6
    B. 45233.1
    C. 46726.5

24. This was a stardate that would live in infamy—the Borg ship decimated a Starfleet armada and almost reached Earth.
    A. 42067.2
    B. 43911.6
    C. 44001.4

Prime Memory Bonus

What was the stardate for "The Offspring," the episode in which Data decided to build an android daughter?

---

25. What was the name of the 40-kilometer footrace held among Starfleet cadets in which Picard became the only freshman to win, passing four upperclassmen on the last hill on Danula II?
    A. Starfleet Academy Marathon
    B. Starfleet Academy 40-K
    C. Starfleet Academy Cadet Challenge

26. Where in San Francisco was Starfleet Academy located?
    A. At Starfleet Command
    B. On Alcatraz Island
    C. At the Presido

27. In which year was Starfleet Academy established as a four-year institution and training facility for Starfleet personnel?
    A. 2121
    B. 2150
    C. 2161

28. The motto for Starfleet Academy was *"ex astris, scientia."* What is the English translation?
    A. "There will be an answer, let it be."
    B. "From the stars, knowledge."
    C. "Eternal hostility against every form of ignorance."

29. Which NASA Apollo mission patch provided the basis of the Starfleet Academy motto?
     A.   Apollo 10
     B.   Apollo 13
     C.   Apollo 16

30. How did Starfleet Command stay in touch with its starships while they were in interstellar space?
     A.   Subspace radio
     B.   Subspace field inverters
     C.   Subspace matrix transmitters

31. Starfleet Command was the operating authority for the interstellar scientific, exploratory, and defensive agency of the United Federation of Planets. In which year was Starfleet Command founded?
     A.   2161
     B.   2176
     C.   2192

32. What type of large transit station was located at Starfleet Headquarters in San Francisco?
     A.   Docking facility for atmospheric entry and landing spacecraft
     B.   Air bus
     C.   Aerial tram

33. What was the name of the scientific publication on artificial intelligence and advanced computer systems?
     A.   *Starfleet Cybernetics Review*
     B.   *Starfleet Cybernetics Journal*
     C.   *Starfleet Cybernetics and Scientific Monthly*

34. Name the instructional class offered to Starfleet personnel to prepare them to render aid in many medical emergencies, including childbirth, should licensed personnel not be available.
     A.   Starfleet First Aid Course
     B.   Starfleet Emergency Medical Course
     C.   Starfleet Medical Promptness Instruction

35. What was the name for Starfleet's special projects division responsible for the construction of starbases and other Starfleet facilities?
    A. Starfleet Corps of Engineers
    B. Starfleet Facilities Department
    C. Starfleet Projects/Construction Division

36. Which General Order was the Starfleet Prime Directive?
    A. General Order 12
    B. General Order 7
    C. General Order 1

37. Who authored Starfleet Regulation 42/15, the engineering procedure relating to impulse engines?
    A. Dr. Leah Brahms
    B. Dr. Richard Daystrom
    C. Montgomery Scott

Prime Memory Bonus

Which Starfleet regulation stated that the chief medical officer could relieve a commander if he or she were mentally or physically unfit?

TRANSPORTER SCRAMBLE

The following *TNG* characters' transport patterns have degraded to dangerous levels. No wonder Bones, Barclay, Lwaxana Troi, Dr. Pulaski, and a host of others (including some Trills) were deathly afraid of the transporter. Your assignment is to reassemble these scrambled transport subjects back into their original forms before they are, well, before they are lost forever!

1. RKSAE

    — — — — —

2. KEIRR

    — — — — —

3. NEPIRR

    — — — — — —

4. RAY

    — — —

5. LAYRACB

    — — — — — — —

6. TOSCULU

    — — — — — — —

7. HEYBSL

    — — — — — —

8. NICIMIT

    — — — — — — —

9. KOB

    — — —

10. VSAH

    — — — —

11. CIOELJL

    — — — — — — —

12. TAWYT

    — — — — —

13. NEBRUL

    — — — — — —

14. SARDU

    — — — — —

15. TAAD

— — — —

16. LEIQUA

— — — — — —

17. QOT

— — —

18. RONWOG

— — — — — —

19. COMCY

— — — — —

20. NANAED

— — — — — —

21. SARNYB

— — — — — —

22. LEXDAAREN

— — — — — — — — —

23. EOLR

— — — —

24. UNKR

— — — —

25. RIDEOG

— — — — — —

26. LECSNEM

— — — — — — —

27. RICDAP

— — — — — —

28. MARSBH

— — — — — —

29. TOTYSC

— — — — — —

30. RRUSHEC

— — — — — — —

31. NAAXWAL

— — — — — — —

32. ROWF

— — — —

33. KISAPUL

— — — — — — —

34. GUHH

— — — —

35. ICEQAU

— — — — — —

36. NIQUN

— — — — —

37. KOKIE

— — — — —

38. RAIHAS

— — — — — —

39. FATLEH

— — — — — —

40. DENNOM

— — — — — —

41. TIAES   42. LIMES

___ ___ ___ ___ ___   ___ ___ ___ ___ ___

Prime Memory Bonus

Unscramble this actor's name (combined first and last). He played a character who used the transporter on the original Enterprise *and on the* Enterprise-D.

DARRKNEAML

___ ___ ___ ___ ___ ___ ___ ___ ___ ___ ___

TREKKERS' TOP TEN

The episodes in this section are almost always chosen at *Star Trek* conventions as the ten best *TNG* episodes out of a video library of 178 (excluding the two-hour pilot and time-tripping series finale). So keeping with the tradition of NASA's space launch procedures and, on a more contemporary level, David Letterman's Top Ten List, we will begin with Number Ten and count down to Number One.

Number Ten: "Attached"

1. On which planet did this episode take place?
   A. Shonar II
   B. Kesprytt III
   C. Laxon IV

2. With whom did Picard discuss the situation on the planet over breakfast?
   A. Riker
   B. Admiral Okuda
   C. Dr. Crusher

3. Which group made up the majority of the planet's population?
   A. The Kes
   B. The Prytt
   C. The Sho'

4. Which group on the planet was reclusive to the point of xenophobia?
   A. The Kes
   B. The Prytt
   C. The Sho'

5. To whose chambers did Picard and Crusher attempt to transport on the planet?
    A. Minister Mirek
    B. Vice-Consul Zenak
    C. Ambassador Mauric

6. Instead, Picard and Crusher awoke in a dank prison cell. What was attached to each of their cerebral cortexes?
    A. Transporter ID tracers
    B. Electronic implants
    C. Collars with motion detectors

7. Name the woman who entered Picard and Crusher's cell and accused them of conspiring with the Kes to establish a military alliance against the Prytt.
    A. Minister Lorin
    B. Council Leader Farrod
    C. Senator Eugenec

8. Back on the *Enterprise*-D, which two officers discovered that a tractor beam from the Prytt Alliance had interfered with the transporter beam?
    A. Data and La Forge
    B. La Forge and Worf
    C. Worf and Data

9. Why couldn't the *Enterprise*-D crew determine the beam's exact origin or the location of Picard and Crusher?
    A. Prytt territory was heavily shielded
    B. An ion storm was interfering with ship sensors
    C. The Prytt were using an interphase generator

10. A guard brought Picard and Crusher a tray with the doctor's tricorder on it. What had been programmed on the device?
    A. A tracking transponder
    B. An escape route and security access codes
    C. Coordinates to a Kes safe house

11. Where did the Kes ambassador offer to Riker to insert a hostage rescue team?
     A. The Prytt main prison compound
     B. The Prytt capital city
     C. The Prytt defense bunker

12. The ambassador happily announced to Riker that Kes operatives had freed Picard and Crusher and that they were en route to the Kes border. Where did the ambassador establish an ultra-secure command post?
     A. Deep within Prytt territory
     B. In the Kes–Prytt demilitarized zone
     C. On board the *Enterprise*-D

13. As Picard and Crusher fled from attacking Prytt troops, they discovered their neural implants were beginning to operate. What did the devices transmit?
     A. Each other's thoughts to one another
     B. Prytt propaganda
     C. Prytt secured communications

14. What happened when Picard and Crusher distanced themselves from each other?
     A. A microscopic pain-inducing implant became activated.
     B. They became sick with intense nausea.
     C. A high-pitched and painful signal was emitted in their ears.

15. Picard and Crusher realized that they could hear every thought, every daydream, and scattered minutiae the other had. What did Crusher discover about Picard?
     A. He still suffered from the Borg assimilation.
     B. He still suffered from the Cardassian torture.
     C. He wasn't as confident as he appeared.

16. What did Picard call their "sharing of thoughts and feelings"?
     A. "Compelling"
     B. "An invasion of privacy"
     C. "Mental voyeurism"

17. What was protecting the Kes border?
     A.   A force field
     B.   A cloaking device
     C.   10,000 troops

18. What happened on board the *Enterprise*-D when the Kes ambas-
     sador received word that Picard and Crusher had deviated from
     the escape plan?
     A.   The ambassador told Riker his two comrades were dead.
     B.   The ambassador went into a paranoiac rant.
     C.   The ambassador ordered a hostage rescue team to find Pi-
          card and Crusher.

19. After they made camp for the night, Picard and Crusher found
     that the intimacy caused by the neural implants was both fasci-
     nating and disturbing. What was the surprising thought of Pi-
     card that Crusher picked up on?
     A.   He always wondered if Wesley was his son.
     B.   He was extremely jealous when she took other lovers.
     C.   He had loved her *before* her husband died.

20. After summoning a suspicious Kes ambassador to the bridge,
     whom did Riker have Worf transport to the *Enterprise*-D against
     her will?
     A.   Minister Lorin
     B.   The captain of the Prisoner Retrieval Unit
     C.   The General-Secretary of the Kesprytt United Nations

21. Riker, who ran out of patience, told the Kes ambassador that
     their group would be denied Federation membership. How
     many starships did Riker threaten the Prytt leader with if Picard
     and Crusher were not returned?
     A.   10
     B.   14
     C.   25

22. Near the border, what did Crusher recalibrate her tricorder to
     emit in order to open the force field?
     A.   A molecular reversion field
     B.   A multiphase pulse
     C.   An inverse tractor beam

23. Aboard the *Enterprise*-D (and after the implants were removed), Picard hosted Crusher to a candlelight dinner in his quarters. What did they drink?
    A. Romulan ale
    B. Champagne
    C. Wine from his family's vineyard

24. What did Picard and Crusher do after discussing their newly discovered closeness?
    A. Share a passionate kiss
    B. Spend the night together
    C. Crusher kissed him on the cheek and left

Prime Memory Bonus

What did Dr. Crusher do to Picard after cracking open the border force field?

Number Nine: "Parallels"

1. The episode opened with Worf making his way back to the *Enterprise*-D aboard a shuttlecraft. On which planet had Worf won a huge trophy and champion standing at the *bat'leth* competition?
    A. Siloam II
    B. Forcas III
    C. Dedaevs IV

2. What did Worf fear was awaiting for him aboard the *Enterprise*-D?
    A. An evaluation by Starfleet Intelligence
    B. A security systems check
    C. A surprise birthday party

3. Worf's quarters were filled with crewmates, cake, and party hats. Name the party song his comrades sang in Klingon.
    A. "For He's A Jolly Good Fellow"
    B. "Happy Birthday"
    C. "H'Kblat d'eget R'uuKlat"

4. What was Data's birthday gift to Worf?
    A. A bottle of Klingon booze
    B. An abstract painting of a Klingon battle
    C. A clay sculpture of Kahless the Unforgettable

5. Where was Alexander during Worf's surprise birthday party?
    A. Attending Starfleet camp on Rigalius III
    B. Visiting Lwaxana Troi
    C. Visiting his grandparents

6. Worf asked Troi to serve as Alexander's foster mother and be responsible for him if anything ever happened to Worf. What was the Klingon word Worf used for "foster mother"?
    A. *Tok'let*
    B. *Sohchlm*
    C. *S'Keer*

7. What did the *Enterprise*-D discover was the real "malfunction" of the Argus Array?
    A. It was transmitting information outside Federation space.
    B. Cardassians had wired it with explosive devices.
    C. Romulans had secretly hidden troops on it.

8. What was the site of new Federation starship development?
    A. Lunar Two Shipyard
    B. Saturn Station Shipyard
    C. Utopia Plantia Shipyard

9. Which Federation enemy's warship was detected in the area of the Argus Array?
    A. Cardassian
    B. Romulan
    C. Borg

10. Disoriented and confused, Worf reported to Sickbay. What had Dr. Crusher discovered was wrong with Worf when he complained to her of a ringing in his ears earlier that morning?
    A. He had the first symptoms of Triaxleon Virus.
    B. He had a concussion.
    C. He was losing his eyesight.

11. What did Worf learn when he activated his personal log?
    A. He never participated in a tournament.
    B. Alexander had been killed.
    C. He placed ninth in the tournament.

12. Who told Worf that the Argus Array had not been tampered with?
    A. Data
    B. La Forge
    C. Riker

13. Worf once again became dizzy, and when he looked up the painting by Data had moved to another wall and was a completely different painting. Whose uniform also changed?
    A. Troi's
    B. La Forge's
    C. Data's

14. Worf again became dizzy and, in the blink of an eye, he was on the bridge. Why couldn't Worf raise the *Enterprise*-D's shields as Riker ordered?
    A. He became dizzy again.
    B. He woke up in his quarters.
    C. His console was foreign to him.

15. Name the race of beings who attacked the *Enterprise*-D and destroyed the Argus Array.
    A. Romulans
    B. Cardassians
    C. Bajorans

16. Worf discovered in his quarters that Troi was his mate. How many years had they been married?
    A. Three
    B. Five
    C. Seven

17. Who informed Worf that La Forge, his crewmate and friend, died during the Cardassian attack?
    A. Dr. Crusher
    B. Dr. Ogawa
    C. Captain Picard

18. Worf became dizzy, and when he came to he was a Commander. What position did he hold on the *Enterprise*-D?
    A. Ops
    B. Chief of Engineering
    C. First Officer

19. What did Data discover was in Worf's cellular RNA?
    A. Temporal flux
    B. Quantum flux
    C. Temporal rift

20. When had Captain Riker taken command of the *Enterprise*-D?
    A. After Picard was killed in the Borg incident
    B. After Picard was killed by Armus on Vagra II
    C. After Picard's cardiac replacement malfunctioned

21. What caused Worf to shift from one quantum reality to another?
    A. The shuttle's warp field
    B. The Argus Array
    C. La Forge's VISOR

22. Who suggested a scan of the fissure to locate the quantum state which matched Worf's subatomic signature to find a way to return Worf to his proper universe?
    A. Captain Riker
    B. Lieutenant Wesley Crusher
    C. Commander Data

23. What was the name of Worf and Troi's daughter?
    A. Kestra
    B. Kirsten
    C. Shannara

24. Who fired on the *Enterprise*-D, causing the quantum fissure to destabilize?
    A. Bajorans
    B. Cardassians
    C. Klingons

25. How many days, according to Data, would it have taken for the sector to be filled with *Enterprises*?
    A. Two
    B. Three
    C. Six

26. How many other *Enterprise*-Ds hailed the *Enterprise*-D in Worf's quantum reality?
    A. 150,000
    B. 285,000
    C. 435,000

27. When Worf re-entered the fissure in his original shuttle, what did he emit in an attempt to seal the fissure and stop additional realities from entering?
    A. Inverse tachyon pulse
    B. Anyon beam
    C. Broad-spectrum warp field

28. A badly crippled *Enterprise*-D opened fire on Worf's shuttle, refusing to return to its own universe. Who had destroyed the Federation in that quantum reality?
    A. Borg
    B. Bajorans
    C. Cardassians

29. Safely back on the *Enterprise*-D in his proper universe, how did Worf celebrate his birthday?
    A. Meditated
    B. Hit himself with a Klingon pain stick
    C. A quiet dinner with Troi

Prime Memory Bonus

What did Klingons prefer to do on their birthday?

Number Eight: "Inheritance"

1. The *Enterprise*-D assisted the government of Atrea to avert the planet's molten core from completely solidifying. How much time was estimated before the planet became uninhabitable?
   A. Six months
   B. Just over a year
   C. Less than three years

2. What was Data's permanent solution to the planet's natural disaster?
   A. Re-liquify the core
   B. Ferro-plasmic infusion
   C. Interphase spread field

3. La Forge and Data were assigned to work with two geologists, Dr. Pran Tainer and his human wife, Juliana, in an attempt to solve Atrea's problem. Who had Juliana been married to before?
   A. Lore
   B. Dr. Soong
   C. Dr. Graves

4. Juliana told Data she was essentially his mother and described his "childhood," when he began to develop motor skills and processed sensory information. What did Juliana and Dr. Soong do to Data after this phase?
   A. Dismantled and deactivated him
   B. Ran a level-5 diagnostic and deactivated him
   C. Wiped his memory processors clean and deactivated him

5. Why didn't Juliana and Dr. Soong reactivate Data?
   A. The Omicron Theta colonists threatened to destroy him.
   B. Lore wouldn't allow them.
   C. The Crystalline Entity attacked.

6. To where did Juliana and Dr. Soong elope to get married in secret?
   A. Mavala IV
   B. Sayers II
   C. Koeppel III

7. Why did Juliana leave Dr. Soong?
    A. He devoted his life solely to his work.
    B. She met and fell in love with Pran Tainer.
    C. He became too eccentric.

8. What did Juliana and Dr. Soong do to Data in his early days to get him to wear his clothes?
    A. Threaten to deactivate him
    B. Write a modesty subroutine
    C. Dress him themselves

9. What did Data show Juliana in his quarters?
    A. A painting of Dr. Soong
    B. His dream diary
    C. A painting of Lal

10. Why was Juliana originally against Data's creation?
    A. She was afraid she'd become attached to him.
    B. The Omicron Theta colonists were against the creation of another android.
    C. Because of her experience with Lore

11. Who made Dr. Soong leave Data behind on Omicron Theta when the Crystalline Entity attacked?
    A. Juliana
    B. Lore
    C. The colonists

12. What did Juliana and Data perform for the *Enterprise*-D crew in the concert hall?
    A. A poetry reading
    B. A violin duet
    C. A piano recital

13. Why did Data request Juliana's medical history from Dr. Crusher?
    A. He thought Juliana was suffering from a terminal illness.
    B. Juliana said she was dying.
    C. He believed Juliana wasn't who she claimed to be.

14. Who was injured on Atrea when pockets drilled by Juliana and Data caved in?
    A. Pran Trainer
    B. La Forge
    C. Juliana

15. What happened to Juliana when she fell to the floor of the cavern?
    A. Her left arm was torn off, revealing wiring and circuitry.
    B. Her right arm was torn off, revealing wiring and circuitry.
    C. Her right leg was torn off, revealing wiring and circuitry.

16. It was determined in Sickbay that Juliana was a Soong-type android, designed to fool others that she was human. What had Dr. Soong implanted in Juliana to send out a false bio-signal to medical scans?
    A. An interphase generator
    B. A feedback processor
    C. A bio-signal reverter

17. What was discovered within the information module inside Juliana?
    A. An information subroutine
    B. A glitch that would terminate Juliana
    C. A holographic interface

18. Where did Data activate Dr. Soong's holographic information module?
    A. On the holodeck
    B. In his quarters
    C. In Sickbay

19. The real Juliana was, indeed, Data's mother, having helped Dr. Soong create his first successful android. On which planet did Juliana die after being injured when the Crystalline Entity attacked?
    A. Terlina III
    B. Augustus II
    C. Bythana XI

20. Dr. Soong's Juliana android awakened to believe she had just re-covered from a terrible injury. According to Dr. Soong, why did she eventually leave him?
    A. She fell in love with Pran Trainer.
    B. He never told her he loved her.
    C. She could not return his love.

21. Dr. Soong urged Data to let Juliana live out her days believing she was human. Who did Data discuss his weighty decision with?
    A. Picard, La Forge, and Riker
    B. Picard, Riker, and Troi
    C. Picard, Crusher, and Troi

22. Data returned to Sickbay and woke Juliana, telling her she broke an arm, but Dr. Crusher repaired it. Which three words did Data say to Juliana before leaving her in Sickbay?
    A. "I love you."
    B. "Everything is fine."
    C. "Father loved you."

23. The geological mission to Atrea was a success, with the planet's core re-liquified. Before Juliana transported, from whom did she quote as she said her goodbyes to Data?
    A. The philosophers of Atrea
    B. Shakespeare
    C. Surak

24. What did Data say to Juliana as she de-materialized on the trans-porter?
    A. "Adieu, Mother"
    B. "Goodbye, Mother"
    C. He stood silently, looking after her for a moment.

Prime Memory Bonus

What technique did Dr. Soong perfect so that he could transfer the comatose Juliana's memories into the android Juliana's positronic matrix?

Number Seven: "Skin of Evil"

1. As Counselor Troi returned from a conference, her shuttle lost power and crashed on planet Vagra II. Name the region where this planet was located.
    A. Sector 21305
    B. Sector 39J
    C. Zed Lapis Sector

2. What was the name or number of Troi's shuttlecraft?
    A. *Shuttlecraft* 9
    B. *Magellan*
    C. *Shuttlecraft* 13

3. An assistant chief of engineering had been supervising routine servicing of the *Enterprise*-D's dilithium chamber when forced to quickly bring the warp drive back on line for a rescue mission to Vagra II. What was the engineering assistant chief's name?
    A. Leland T. Lynch
    B. David R. Golden
    C. Edward D. Reynolds

4. Who was the lieutenant Tasha Yar was scheduled to compete against in a martial-arts competition aboard the *Enterprise*-D?
    A. Drexler
    B. Minnerly
    C. Stefano

5. Although Yar was favored in the ship's pool, which of the lieutenant's martial-arts styles did Yar expect to be a formidable challenge?
    A. Jet Kwan-Do
    B. Kick-boxing
    C. Akido

6. Name the Science Officer who was also scheduled to participate against Yar in the martial-arts competition?
    A. Swenson
    B. Beecher
    C. Seurat

7. When the *Enterprise*-D arrived at Vagra II, an away team beamed down to rescue Troi and the pilot. Which officers comprised the away team?
    A. Riker, Data, Worf, and Yar
    B. Riker, Data, Crusher, and Yar
    C. Riker, Data, La Forge, and Yar

8. Armus, a malevolent life form, blocked the away team's path. How had Armus been formed?
    A. A Vagran gene-splitting experiment gone awry
    B. From the cast-off evils and intents of the Vagrans
    C. Vagran experimentation with a mutation weapon

9. What had Armus generated around the shuttle wreckage?
    A. An invisible deflector shield
    B. Shield inverters
    C. A force field

10. When Armus refused to listen to Riker's negotiations for Troi's release, Yar tried to force the issue, and Armus killed her. What reason did Armus give for murdering Yar?
    A. To teach her a lesson in manners
    B. She threatened him.
    C. For his own amusement

11. What did Armus do when the away team returned to the *Enterprise*-D?
    A. Enveloped the shuttle
    B. Began laughing hysterically
    C. Screamed for them to come back

12. Name the medication, a derivative of norepinephrine, which Dr. Crusher ordered administered to Tasha Yar in an unsuccessful attempt to revive her after she had been killed.
    A. Norep
    B. Nopin
    C. Nophrine

13. Who noticed that every time Armus enveloped the shuttle, his power diminished, as did the force field over the shuttle?
    A. Data
    B. Worf
    C. Riker

14. On the planet, Armus amused himself with another away team. Which officer did he envelope in his oil slick–like "skin of evil"?
    A. Data
    B. Dr. Crusher
    C. Riker

15. When Picard beamed down to the planet, he demanded to see Troi. Why did Armus agree to the captain's request?
    A. It amused him.
    B. He wanted Picard to take him off the planet.
    C. He planned to trap Picard in the shuttle with Troi.

16. What had caused Armus' malevolence to be compounded?
    A. The loneliness of having been abandoned
    B. The unrelenting boredom
    C. Sexual deprivation

17. What did Troi tell Picard caused Armus' energy drops?
    A. Angering him
    B. Calmly talking to him
    C. Forcing him to face his fears

18. How did Picard get Armus' force field to drop low enough to beam Troi, the shuttle pilot, and himself back to the *Enterprise*-D?
    A. He angered Armus to the point he was yelling.
    B. He tricked Armus into thinking he was taking him off the planet.
    C. He forced Armus to face his fears.

19. Tasha, knowing her line of work entailed considerable risk, left a holographic farewell to her comrades in which she thanked her shipmates for being part of her life. What was the setting for her computer-simulated goodbye?
    A. Atop a hill with clouds passing by
    B. In a forest with a stream running close by
    C. In a big, wide-open field with horses galloping by

Prime Memory Bonus

What was the martial-arts technique that Tasha Yar was trying to master for the competition aboard the Enterprise-D *just prior to her death?*

Prime Memory Bonus

Just after Armus engulfed Riker, the rest of the away team ran up to the edge of the oil slick. When they stopped, whose phaser plopped out onto the ground?

Number Six: "I, Borg"

1. While mapping a star system for possible colonization, the
   Enterprise-D intercepted an unknown transmission. What was the
   name of this star system?
   A. Argolis Cluster
   B. Regalais System
   C. Brachman Cluster

2. When an *Enterprise*-D away team investigated, they found a
   badly damaged Borg scout ship on the surface of a moon. How
   many dead Borg were discovered in the spacecraft?
   A. Three
   B. Four
   C. Six

3. Dr. Crusher immediately began resuscitation efforts on the one
   severely injured survivor. Who wanted to kill him?
   A. Picard
   B. Worf
   C. Riker

4. What was the mass of the small, cubical-shaped Borg scout ship?
   A. 1.5 million metric tons
   B. 2 million metric tons
   C. 2.5 million metric tons

5. After consideration, Picard allowed Dr. Crusher to beam the
   adolescent Borg into a detention cell on the *Enterprise*-D so she
   could continue her ministrations. Whom did Picard order to iso-
   late the Borg from all subspace signals?
   A. Data
   B. La Forge
   C. Worf

6. What was the Borg's designation?
   A. Second of Five
   B. Third of Five
   C. Fifth of Five

7. Dr. Crusher discovered that several of the Borg's biochips were damaged in the crash. What would have happened to the Borg if these cybernetic implants were removed?
   A. He would have died.
   B. His organic molecules would have de-synthesized.
   C. His physical abilities would have decreased.

8. What was the name of the basic computer programs that controlled the Borg collective, the group consciousness of the Borg civilization?
   A. Cybernetic command structure
   B. Subroutine command structure
   C. Root command structure

9. When Picard realized the Borg's biochips were damaged, the captain seized the opportunity and ordered La Forge to replicate new chips, complete with a computer software weapon to destroy the Borg collective when this Borg returned to his ship. What was the name of this computer "virus"?
   A. Invasive program
   B. Geometric reconstruct program
   C. Biodegenerative program

10. The computer virus was a paradoxical geometric construct that, when introduced into the Borg system, was expected to form a recursively insoluble puzzle, causing a fatal overload in the entire Borg system. Name the systems connector port used aboard Borg ships to allow individual Borg to link to their collective.
    A. Access connector
    B. Access terminal
    C. Cybernetic terminal

11. Which *Enterprise*-D officer became friends with the young Borg and named him "Hugh"?
    A. Dr. Crusher
    B. La Forge
    C. Data

12. Who asked for clarification on the term "total system failure," trying to make the point that they were contemplating destroying an entire race?

    A.   Dr. Crusher
    B.   La Forge
    C.   Data

13. Picard discovered that, removed from the Borg collective, Hugh
    had begun to exhibit signs of individuality. What did Picard
    offer Hugh after he vetoed the mass destruction computer
    virus?
    A.   An opportunity to become totally human
    B.   Asylum
    C.   A shuttlecraft to escape the Borg

14. Why did Hugh refuse Picard's offer?
    A.   He could not totally separate himself from the Borg.
    B.   He was scared to be on his own.
    C.   He knew the Borg would seek him out.

15. Hugh returned to the crash site and waited for another Borg
    ship to arrive and re-assimilate him into the collective. Where did
    the *Enterprise*-D position itself to obscure its presence from the
    Borg's sensors?
    A.   On the dark side of the moon
    B.   Close to the sun
    C.   In an interstellar dust cloud

16. In which episode was the story of Hugh later continued?
    A.   "The Quality of Life"
    B.   "The Next Phase"
    C.   "Descent, Parts I and II"

Prime Memory Bonus

Name the ancient Earth weapon Picard instructed Guinan in the use of during this episode.

Prime Memory Bonus

In which century were the Borg responsible for the near-extinction of Guinan's race?

Number Five: "Relics"

1. Responding to a distress call from a transporter ship, the U.S.S. *Jenolen*, Riker issued a signal indicating the discovery of a space vehicle in distress. What was the official Starfleet code for this signal?
    A. Two Delta One
    B. One Alpha Zero
    C. Factor One Delta

2. What scan did Data use to locate the *Jenolen*?
    A. FWD Navigational Scan 302
    B. DFW Navigational Scan 202
    C. FWD Doppler Scan 94-1

3. The *Enterprise*-D found the *Jenolen* crashed on the surface of a Dyson sphere. What did Data calculate to be the sphere's diameter?
    A. 187 million kilometers
    B. 200 million kilometers
    C. 287 million kilometers

4. Which Earth scientist first proposed the basic concept of a Dyson sphere, a gigantic artificial structure designed to completely enclose a star in a hollow sphere?
    A. Albert Einstein
    B. Edouard Dyson
    C. Freeman Dyson

5. Near which planet was the Dyson Sphere discovered?
    A. Durken II
    B. Norphin V
    C. Avel III

6. What type of spatial distortion phenomenon was partially responsible for the *Jenolen*'s crash into the surface of the Dyson Sphere?
    A. Gravimetric interference
    B. Gravitational constant
    C. Gravimetric fluctuations

7. What was the registry number of the *Jenolen*?

A. NCC-1657
B. NCC-2593
C. NCC-2010

8. What class designation was the *Jenolen*?
   A. *Ambassador*
   B. *Sydney*
   C. *Nebula*

9. When an *Enterprise*-D away team to the *Jenolen* found a jury-rigged transporter still functioning, they were surprised to have discovered a 75-year-old pattern in the pattern buffer. Whose transport pattern had degraded 53 percent, essentially beyond recovery?
   A. Lieutenant Ronald Moore
   B. Ensign Matt Franklin
   C. Commander Leslie Morris

10. What portion of the operation cycle of the transporter had Scotty disabled in an attempt to keep himself and his comrade suspended in the beam until help arrived?
   A. Autosequencers
   B. Heisenberg compensator
   C. Rematerialization subroutine

11. When Riker told Scotty the away team was from the *Enterprise*, whom did Scotty believe had sent a rescue team?
   A. Kirk
   B. Sulu
   C. Spock

12. Scotty had finally retired in 2294 at the age of 72. What was the location of the retirement community he was en route to when the *Jenolen* crashed?
   A. Norphin Colony
   B. Beimler XI
   C. Sorbax II

13. Name the injury Scotty had sustained in the *Jenolen*'s crash landing?
   A. Broken ankle
   B. Broken arm
   C. Broken leg

14. How many years had Scotty been a Starfleet engineer?
    A. 42
    B. 50
    C. 52

15. Who had given Guinan the green-colored Aldebaran whiskey that she kept behind the bar?
    A. Worf
    B. Picard
    C. Riker

16. How many ships had Scotty served on during the course of his Starfleet career?
    A. 4
    B. 7
    C. 11

17. How could Scotty tell the speed the original *Enterprise* was travelling?
    A. By the feel of the deck plates
    B. The steady rhythm of the warp engines
    C. The humming of the dilithium crystals

18. While La Forge and Scotty were back on the *Jenolen* extracting its records, Data located an opening in the Dyson sphere. What were the tractor beams that pulled the *Enterprise*-D into the sphere?
    A. Autosequencing navigational beams
    B. Automatic piloting beams
    C. Automatic confinement beams

19. On the *Jenolen*, La Forge discovered the *Enterprise*-D was missing and the two starship engineers got the transport ship spaceborn again. How did they trace the *Enterprise*-D to the sphere's opening?
    A. Followed the matter/antimatter trail
    B. Trailed the anionic particles emitted from the tractor beam
    C. Followed the starship's ion trail

20. What did Scotty want to bet with La Forge that the *Enterprise*-D was in the Dyson sphere?
    A. A case of Aldebaran whiskey
    B. Two cases of Saurian brandy
    C. Two cases of scotch

21. La Forge and Scotty held open the sphere's bay doors with their shields while the *Enterprise*-D made a dash for safety. Why did Picard have to transport La Forge and Scotty back to the *Enterprise*-D?
    A. The *Jenolen* was faced with a warp core breach.
    B. The *Jenolen*'s engines failed.
    C. The sphere's weapon system was re-activated.

22. In appreciation for his help, Picard "loaned" Scotty one of the *Enterprise*-D's shuttles so he could embark for parts unknown. What was the name of the shuttlecraft?
    A. *Bateman*
    B. *Goddard*
    C. *Virgo*

23. What was the last word Scotty spoke before heading to the cockpit of the shuttle?
    A. "Goodbye"
    B. "Farewell"
    C. "Aye"

Prime Memory Bonus

Which TNG *cast member's only scene in "Relics" came at the very end?*

Prime Memory Bonus

According to La Forge, what had taken the place of the older, less efficient duotronic enhancers aboard starships like the original En-terprise?

Number Four: "Yesterday's Enterprise"

1. At the beginning of the episode, who did Worf talk to about his need for "companionship" with a Klingon woman?
   A. Troi
   B. La Forge
   C. Guinan

2. What did Worf call Earth women?
   A. "Unresponsive"
   B. "Too fragile"
   C. "Boring and unimaginative"

3. A strange, swirling cloud, defying description, appeared in front of the *Enterprise*-D. Which class of sensor probe did the starship launch into the anomaly?
   A. Class-8
   B. Class-5
   C. Class-1

4. Vaguely resembling a wormhole, Data surmised the anomaly was a temporal rift, "a hole in time." What type of sensor readings accompanied the appearance of the rift?
   A. Gravimetric fluctuations
   B. Coherent graviton emissions
   C. Tachyon emissions

5. When the *Enterprise*-C emerged some 22 years in the future, suddenly everything on the *Enterprise*-D changed. How many years had the *Enterprise*-D been battling with the Klingons?
   A. 10
   B. 20
   C. 30

6. Worf disappeared and Tasha Yar was back once again as security chief. Which former *Enterprise*-D medical officer's name was heard being paged STAT to Sickbay?
   A. Dr. Pulaski
   B. Dr. Ogawa
   C. Dr. Selar

7. Who attacked the *Enterprise*-C when it responded to a distress call from a Klingon outpost?
   A. Romulans
   B. Renegade Klingons
   C. Cardassians

8. What was the site of the ill-fated Klingon outpost?
   A. Corillus Minor
   B. Narenda III
   C. Thedus II

9. How many survivors did the away teams find on the *Enterprise*-C?
   A. 125
   B. 150
   C. 165

10. Data noted that the temporal rift was not stable. How many hours did Picard give repair crews to complete their work on the *Enterprise*-C?
    A. Six hours
    B. Seven hours
    C. Nine hours

11. What class of starship was the *Enterprise*-C?
    A. *Excelsior*
    B. *Ambassador*
    C. *Nebula*

12. At the time the *Enterprise*-C shifted in time, the Klingons and the Federation were discussing a peace treaty. The disappearance of the *Enterprise*-C meant no Federation ship came to the aid of the Klingon outpost. When negotiations broke down, no symbolic act stopped the outbreak of war between the Federation and the Klingons. How many lives were lost in the next 22 years?
    A. 20 billion
    B. 30 billion
    C. 40 billion

13. Starfleet Command said the war was going badly and defeat was inevitable. How many more months before Federation surrender was expected?
    A. 6
    B. 9
    C. 12

14. Picard discussed the state of the war with the *Enterprise*-C captain, and she agreed to take her ship back to its proper time so that history would be restored. What was the captain's name?
    A. Denise Garrison
    B. Jill Ryan
    C. Rachel Garrett

15. What was the name for the standard meal pack used aboard the *Enterprise*-D when replicators were on minimum power?
    A. LTK ration
    B. TKL ration
    C. KLT ration

16. Which planet was the site of a significant Klingon defeat at the hands of the Federation?
    A. Sardana
    B. Archer IV
    C. Zarcos III

17. What did Guinan have that Picard learned to trust?
    A. Her "special wisdom"
    B. Her "uncanny insight"
    C. Her "special intuition"

18. Who told Tasha Yar that she had died an "empty death without purpose" in the other time-line?
    A. Troi
    B. Guinan
    C. Picard

19. When the *Enterprise*-C attempted to go back to its proper time, a Klingon ship attacked, and the captain of the *Enterprise*-C was killed. Name the helm officer who took command of the ship?

    A.   Commander James Wellman
    B.   Lieutenant Richard Sanchez
    C.   Lieutenant Richard Castillo

20.   Yar, who realized she died a meaningless death in the original time-line, received permission to go back with the *Enterprise*-C. As the starship headed back into the rift, how many Klingon warships attacked the *Enterprise*-D?
    A.   Two
    B.   Three
    C.   Four

21.   Which *Enterprise*-D officer was killed in the attack?
    A.   Riker
    B.   Dr. Crusher
    C.   La Forge

22.   What did Captain Picard say when the Klingons demanded his surrender?
    A.   "Go to hell."
    B.   "That'll be the day."
    C.   "It is a good day to die."

23.   Once the proper time-line was restored, whom did Guinan want to know more about?
    A.   Picard
    B.   Worf
    C.   Yar

Prime Memory Bonus

In the alternate time-line, what was the Captain's Log called instead?

Prime Memory Bonus

How many Romulan Warbirds attacked the Enterprise-C *at the Narenda III Klingon outpost?*

Number Three: "The Offspring"

1. What type of conference had Data attended when he returned to the *Enterprise*-D and cloistered himself in a lab?
   A. Pressure Variances in Impulse Reaction Chambers
   B. Xenobiology
   C. Cybernetics

2. Which three *Enterprise*-D officers did Data invite into his lab to view his new android creation?
   A. La Forge, Troi, and Wesley
   B. Dr. Crusher, Troi, and Guinan
   C. La Forge, Riker, and Wesley

3. What was the name of a new technique for replicating existing neural net pathways, which Data had learned at the conference and later used to transfer his programming to his android "offspring"?
   A. Neural transfer-link technology
   B. Positronic brain replication
   C. Submicron matrix transfer technology

4. What type of android did Starfleet classify Data's creation?
   A. Korby
   B. Soong
   C. Maddox

5. Initially built with a featureless humanoid body, Data's offspring became a daughter named Lal. Who chose the form of a human female for Lal?
   A. Troi
   B. Data
   C. Lal

6. Lal briefly attended the *Enterprise*-D's primary school. Name Lal's teacher.
   A. Lieutenant Ballard
   B. Lieutenant Wiseman
   C. Lieutenant Patterson

7. How many calculations could Lal perform in one second?
   A. More than sixty billion
   B. More than ninety billion
   C. More than sixty trillion

8. As Lal began to achieve sentience, she became very inquisitive and asked questions constantly. How did Data respond?
   A. He turned her off.
   B. He demonstrated fatherly pride.
   C. He tried to answer her every question.

9. What did Lal say to Guinan upon seeing a couple kiss in Ten Forward?
   A. "He's trying to eat that female."
   B. "He's biting that female."
   C. "Are they inseparatable?"

10. Picard wondered if Data was ready to accept responsibility for the new sentient life he had created. Starfleet reacted with distress and dispatched an admiral (who was also a cybernetics scientist) to interview Lal. What was the admiral's name?
    A. Haftel
    B. Coster
    C. Nicolas

11. The admiral believed it was imperative that Lal was studied in a controlled environment under the guidance of cybernetics specialists. What was the name of the major center for science and technology where the admiral wanted Lal observed?
    A. Decius Science Center on Borash II
    B. Starfleet Cybernetic Institute in San Francisco
    C. Daystrom Institute annex on Galor IV

12. Lal left the interview with the admiral confused and bewildered, realizing that he wanted to separate her from her father. Which genuine emotion did Lal begin experiencing at the thought of leaving the *Enterprise*-D?
    A. Sadness
    B. Fear
    C. Depression

13. Where did Lal retreat to on the *Enterprise*-D after she became the focus of the heated custody battle?
    A. Data's lab
    B. The holodeck
    C. Ten-Forward

14. By the time the admiral, Picard, and Data arrived at the lab, Lal was barely functioning. What type of major breakdown had she suffered?
    A. Innate systems overload
    B. Positronic brain termination
    C. A systemwide cascade failure

15. Data transferred Lal's entire process of existence and development (memories) into his own positronic brain. What was he forced to edit out of the transfer else risking potential self-destruction?
    A. Lal's decayed positrons
    B. Her submicron matrix technology
    C. Her emotional capacity

Prime Memory Bonus

What was the Enterprise-D's *destination following Lal's death?*

Prime Memory Bonus

Name the actress who portrayed Lal.

Number Two: "The Best of Both Worlds, Part I"

1. What was the name of the Federation colony on Jouret IV that disappeared after an attack by the Borg?
    A. New Manhattan
    B. New Providence
    C. Paradise II

2. What was left in place of the colony and all its buildings?
    A. A radioactive disaster area
    B. A gaping hole
    C. An inferno

3. How many colonists were missing and unaccounted for?
    A. 900
    B. 1,500
    C. 2,500

4. What was the "footprint" left behind in the remains of the colony, confirming that the Borg had encroached into Federation space?
    A. Magnetospheric emissions
    B. Transwarp residue
    C. Magnetic resonance traces

5. How many months had Commander Shelby headed the Borg tactical analysis team at Starfleet headquarters?
    A. Four
    B. Six
    C. Eight

6. Name the Federation freighter that was reported lost after encountering a Borg ship near Zeta Alpha II?
    A. U.S.S. *Lexington*
    B. U.S.S. *Gage*
    C. U.S.S. *Lalo*

7. What was the planetary destination of the freighter?
    A. Sentinel Minor IV
    B. Egalus II
    C. Lextron IV

8. Which starbase received a distress signal from the freighter after it suffered an attack from a Borg vessel?
   A. Starbase 324
   B. Starbase 157
   C. Starbase G-7

9. The *Enterprise*-D managed to escape after the starship encountered the Borg. What was the name of the sensor-obscuring nebula in which the *Enterprise*-D hid?
   A. Mutara Nebula
   B. Graham Nebula
   C. Paulson Nebula

10. During the respite, the *Enterprise*-D crew devised a new weapon to use against the Borg. How did the ship channel a high-energy beam, tuned to the Borg's most vulnerable frequency?
    A. Through a modified navigational deflector
    B. Using an inverse tractor beam
    C. Multiplexed all hailing frequencies

11. A Borg ship could remain operable up to what percentage of damage?
    A. Up to 86%
    B. Up to 78%
    C. Up to 72%

12. Picard compared the fate of the Federation at the hands of the Borg to the defeat of the Roman Empire under which emperor?
    A. Pilot
    B. Flavius
    C. Honorius

13. After the Borg kidnapped Picard, Riker gave chase and sent an away team to the Borg ship. Shelby stated that they would only be able to use the phasers a few times before the Borg adapted to each phaser's different frequency. What was the engineering term used in measuring a phaser beam's component electromagnetic wavelengths?
    A. Level-1 electromagnetic diagnostic
    B. EM base frequencies
    C. PHS component frequencies

14. After assimilating Picard into the cybernetic organism, Locutus, what sector of space did the Borg ship set a course for?
     A. Sector 001
     B. Sector 3-0
     C. Sector 39J

15. After Locutus hailed the *Enterprise*-D and told them "resistance is futile," to whom did Riker give the order to fire the high-energy beam on the Borg ship?
     A. Shelby
     B. La Forge
     C. Worf

Prime Memory Bonus

Who directed "The Best of Both Worlds, Part I"?

Prime Memory Bonus

Instead of using normal warp travel, what type of primary propulsion system did the Borg ship utilize?

Number One: "The Best of Both Worlds, Part II"

We've saved not only the best, but also the hardest for last. There are no multiple choice questions, no 50/50 odds with true or false, or anything else to give you a wee bit of help. As an old Texas college professor once said, "You either know it or you don't." Every question in this final section is a Prime Memory Bonus and each correct answer counts as five points. You've come to the end of your Trekial Pursuit and you alone sit in the Captain's chair. Your resistance is hopeless, Number One . . .

1. What did the *Enterprise*-D deploy to cover the departure of a shuttlecraft from the saucer section?

2. Name the ensign assigned to Battle Bridge Ops during the rescue attempt of Picard.

3. What were the devices used by the rescue away team for remote activation of the transporter?

4. It was a directed energy beam considered for possible use against the Borg, but the idea was abandoned when it was determined that local field distortion generation would prove ineffective against Borg defenses. What was the name of this weapon?

5. Which outpost was the first to report the entrance of the Borg ship into the Sol system?

6. What was the registry number for the U.S.S. *Kyushu,* the Federation starship destroyed at the battle of Wolf 359?

7. What class designation was the *Kyushu?*

8. Name the Starfleet defense border designed to protect the inner solar system.

9. What were the Borg devices implanted into Picard's healthy tissue which caused changes in the cellular DNA and made surgical removal impossible?

10. Name the advanced technique used to process subspace sensor data exchanged between Locutus and the Borg collective consciousness after Picard had been rescued.

11. How many weeks would it have taken the nanites to have had an effect on the Borg?

12. What was the name of the small, short-range personnel transporter built into the *Enterprise*-D shuttlecraft used by Worf and Data in their away mission to rescue Captain Picard?

13. How many fatalities were there at the battle of Wolf 359?

14. What did Locutus say would happen to Data in the New Order?

15. What did Worf consider the *Enterprise*-D's advantage in fighting the Borg?

16. After Data accessed the Borg consciousness, what mode did he place them in?

17. What were Picard's exact words when asked how he felt after the Borg assimilation was over?

18. What was Picard's answer when asked, "What do you remember?"

CREWS THROUGH TIME

Star Trek: Generations

Six months after *TNG* aired its series finale, *Star Trek: Generations* boldly went where no previous *Star Trek* film had gone before, earning almost $24 million at the box office on its opening weekend. *Generations*, the seventh *Trek* movie (although to emphasize the maiden voyage of *TNG*, there wasn't a number in the title) accomplished precisely what it was supposed to do: ease the transition from the veteran *Enterprise* crew to *The Next Generation*.

1. The first scene in the movie was of a Dom Perignon bottle tumbling toward the screen in slow motion. What year was the champagne's vintage?
    A. 2265
    B. 2286
    C. 2295

2. Who referred to Kirk, Scotty, and Chekov as "living legends"?
    A. Ensign Demora Sulu
    B. Captain Harriman
    C. A woman reporter

3. (True or false) When asked by a reporter, "What have you been doing since retiring?" Captain Kirk replied, "Having fun."

4. How many years had elapsed since Kirk had last seen Demora Sulu?
    A. 10
    B. 12
    C. 15

5. What did Kirk say when Captain Harriman asked him to "give the order to take us out"?
   A. "Take us out."
   B. "Let's take her for a quick run around the block."
   C. "Ensign Sulu, let's get her underway."

Prime Memory Bonus

Who asked Kirk, "How does it feel to be back on the Enterprise *bridge?"*

---

6. Name the furthestmost planet the *Enterprise*-B was going to cruise to on its "quick run around the block"?

7. How many light years away were the transport ships when the *Enterprise*-B received their distress call?
   A. Five
   B. Four
   C. Three

8. (True or false) The *Enterprise*-B's tractor beam and torpedoes were scheduled to be installed on the Tuesday following its launch.

9. (Fill the blank) The first maxim of a starship captain should be "Be prepared." An astonished Kirk asked Captain Harriman, "You left _____ without a tractor beam?"

10. (True or false) Starbase 27 was the intended destination of the transport ships ferrying the El-Aurian refugees.

11. How many refugees were killed when the effect of the temporal energy anomaly collapsed the hull of the first transport ship?
    A. 265
    B. 276
    C. 285

Prime Memory Bonus

Who said, "Their life signs are . . . are phasing in and out of our space–time continuum"?

---

12. How many refugees out of 150 was Scotty able to beam aboard the *Enterprise*-B before the energy distortion destroyed the second transport ship?
    - A. 37
    - B. 44
    - C. 47

13. Identify the correct deck number and section on the *Enterprise*-B where Captain Kirk died.
    - A. Deck 14, Section 20 Alpha
    - B. Deck 12, Section 22 Alpha
    - C. Deck 15, Section 21 Alpha

14. (True or false) 78 years passed between Kirk's death aboard the *Enterprise*-B and Worf's promotion "at sea" on a 19th-century sailing vessel.

15. Which *Enterprise*-D officer instructed Data, "Learn to be spontaneous. Live in the moment. Do something unexpected"?

Prime Memory Bonus

On which holodeck did Worf's promotion to commander aboard the seafaring S.S. Enterprise *take place?*

---

16. According to Riker, what was the personnel complement of the Amargosa Observatory before it was attacked?
    - A. 19
    - B. 24
    - C. 29

17. (Fill in the blank) During an away team investigation of the Amargosa Observatory, Worf stated that the "blast patterns are consistent with type _____ disrupters."

18. Which *Enterprise*-D officer discovered Dr. Soran alive in the internal wreckage of the observatory?

19. For how many years had Data told La Forge he had "endeavored to become more human"?
   A. 31
   B. 34
   C. 36

20. (True or false) Three dead Romulans were discovered by the *Enterprise*-D away team on the Amargosa Observatory.

21. Armed with an arsenal of uncontrollable emotions, Data went to Ten-Forward to try drinking. What was the planetary origin of the new alcoholic beverage Guinan encouraged Data to sample?
   A. Brudick IV
   B. Farrand II
   C. Forcas III

22. What ancient device did Dr. Soran carry in his pocket?

23. (Fill in the blank) Worf described trilithium, a potential super-explosive, as a nuclear _____.
   A. Stabilizer
   B. Trigger
   C. Inhibitor

24. (Fill in the blank) While investigating the Amargosa Observatory's solar probe, Data said that the emotion chip had "overloaded my positronic _____."
   A. Matrix
   B. Relay
   C. Processor

Prime Memory Bonus

(Fill in the blank) The implosion of the Amargosa star produced a level _____ shock wave, enough to destroy everything in the solar system.

---

25. Who did Picard describe as a "dreamer"?

26. At what warp speed did the *Enterprise* engage to escape the implosion of the Amargosa star?
    A. Warp 1
    B. Warp 5
    C. Warp 7

27. Who killed Dr. Soran's entire family?

28. (Fill in the blank) Guinan described the peaceful tranquility of the Nexus as like "being inside _____."
    A. Bliss
    B. Joy
    C. Heaven

29. Who was Soran referring to when he said, "Normal is what everybody else and you are not"?

30. (True or false) El-Aurians were known throughout the galaxy as a "race of listeners."

31. (Fill in the blanks) Captain Picard stated in his log that Data's emotion chip could not be removed because it had fused into the android's _____ _____.
    A. Neural net
    B. Neural matrix
    C. Positronic cascade

Prime Memory Bonus

(Fill in the blank) Data said research had shown that the Nexus traveled through the galaxy every _____ years.

---

32. Identify the Federation starship that was forced to make a course correction when the Amargosa star was destroyed.
    A. U.S.S. *Farragut*
    B. U.S.S. *Lantree*
    C. U.S.S. *Bozeman*

33. (True or false) Counselor Troi told Data, "Part of having feelings is learning to integrate them into your life."

34. Soran had been systematically destroying whole stars to reroute the energy ribbon to his location. Why couldn't the El-Aurian just navigate a spacecraft directly into the anomaly?

35. How many millions of humanoids on the preindustrial society of Veridian IV would have been killed if Soran was successful in destroying the Veridian star?
    A. 230
    B. 250
    C. 276

36. How old was Lursa and B'Etor's Klingon *Bird-of-Prey*?
    A. 12
    B. 17
    C. 20

37. How many years did Soran say he had been looking for a way to get back into the Nexus?
    A. 72
    B. 78
    C. 80

38. Who taught Soran that "if there is one constant in the universe, it is death"?

Prime Memory Bonus

What shield modulation was the Enterprise-D *operating on when the Duras sisters fired on the starship?*

---

39. Which decks experienced hull breach when the *Bird-of-Prey*'s torpedoes hit the *Enterprise*?
    A. 19 through 24
    B. 21 through 27
    C. 31 through 35

40. (True or false) Worf told Riker that the Duras sisters' *Bird-of-Prey* model had been retired from service because of defective plasma coils.

41. (Fill in the blank) As a last-ditch effort to survive in their battle with the Klingon vessel, the *Enterprise*-D targeted the *Bird-of-Prey*'s primary _____.
    A. Reactor
    B. Integrator
    C. Stabilizer

42. What was breached on the *Enterprise*-D that caused Riker to order the crew evacuated from the drive section to the saucer and have the ship separated?

43. Which *Enterprise*-D officer held Deanna in his arms when an explosive shock wave slammed the ship's saucer section into Veridian III's surface?

44. (Fill in the blank) When Picard encountered Guinan in the Nexus, she told him to "think of me as a(n) _____ of the person you know."
    A. Shadow
    B. Echo
    C. Copy

45. What was Kirk doing when Picard first met him in the Nexus?

46. Which former *Enterprise* officer had Kirk given the clock to that was sitting on the fireplace mantel in Kirk's cabin in the Nexus?

Prime Memory Bonus

According to Kirk, how many years had his dog, Butler, been dead when he walked through the cabin door in the Nexus?

---

47. Name Kirk's girlfriend who was waiting for him to bring breakfast to her upstairs in the bedroom.

48. To whose barn did Kirk and Picard suddenly transport when they passed through the doorway of the cabin's upstairs bedroom?

49. What were Kirk's last words before he died?
    A. "Least I could do . . . for the captain of the *Enterprise*."
    B. "It was fun."
    C. "Oh my."

50. What did Picard place atop Kirk's grave on Veridian III?

51. How many Starfleet vessels were in orbit to beam up *Enterprise-D* crash survivors?
    A. Two
    B. Three
    C. Four

Prime Memory Bonus

How many distinct emotions did Data tell Troi he had experienced since the installation of the chip?

---

52. Who said, "Time is a companion who goes with us on the journey"?

53. Who said, "I plan to live forever"?
    A. Soran
    B. Kirk
    C. Riker

54. Identify the last line in the movie.
    A. "Two to beam up."
    B. "Energize."
    C. "I doubt this will be the last ship to carry the name *Enterprise*."

55. Which Starfleet starship beamed up Picard and Riker from the *Enterprise-D*'s crash site on Veridian III?
    A. U.S.S. *Farragut*
    B. U.S.S. *Intrepid*
    C. U.S.S. *Bradshaw*

Prime Memory Bonus

What was the name of the transport ship that ferried Guinan, Soran, and other El-Aurian refugees before it was destroyed by the energy ribbon?

Prime Memory Bonus

Who told Kirk, Scotty, and Chekov, "I remember reading about your missions when I was in grade school"?

BEHIND THE SCENES

Star Trek: Generations

1. Alan Ruck, the captain of the *Enterprise*-B, also played a nervous tourist in which 1994 action-adventure thriller?
   A. *Speed*
   B. *The River Wild*
   C. *True Lies*

2. Identify the *Generations* cast member who admitted to the press that he had never seen a single episode of either *TNG* or *TREK-classic*.
   A. Tim Russ
   B. Alan Ruck
   C. Malcolm McDowell

3. On what date did *Generations* begin filming in Los Angeles?
   A. March 28, 1994
   B. April 15, 1994
   C. May 24, 1994

4. How many days after *TNG* wrapped up filming for the series finale did the cast move down the Paramount lot to Stage 7, where they began filming *Generations*?
   A. Three
   B. Four
   C. Five

5. Which *TNG* cast member negotiated an anti-typecasting clause in his new contract with Paramount that allowed him to do *Generations* only if the studio cast him in another film later on?
   A. Patrick Stewart
   B. Brent Spiner
   C. LeVar Burton

6. Which *Trek* star turned down an offer to direct *Generations*?
   A. Jonathan Frakes
   B. William Shatner
   C. Leonard Nimoy

7. Who was the first *TNG* actor to go before the *Generations* cameras?
   A. LeVar Burton
   B. Patrick Stewart
   C. Jonathan Frakes

8. Name the *Trek* actress who figured prominently in *Generations* but was not listed in the credits at her request.
   A. Majel Barrett
   B. Barbara March
   C. Whoopi Goldberg

9. Who was the only *TREK-classic* regular character not seen or at least mentioned in the film?
   A. McCoy
   B. Spock
   C. Uhura

10. John Alonzo, the film's director of photography, worked with Malcolm McDowell once before on another movie. Can you identify which film?
    A. *Time After Time*
    B. *Blue Thunder*
    C. *Cat People*

Prime Memory Bonus

On which date did Generations *premiere in movie theatres in the United States?*

Prime Memory Bonus

On which date did Paramount Home Video release Generations *on videocassette in America?*

---

11. Which *Generations* star later played an astronaut who encountered a Martian alien on Showtime's *The Outer Limits* cable series?
    A. Michael Dorn
    B. LeVar Burton
    C. Gates McFadden

12. How did Kirk die in the original filming of *Generations'* climax?
    A. Soran shot Kirk in the back with a phaser.
    B. Soran and Kirk were destroyed when the star-killer missile launcher exploded.
    C. Soran and Kirk fell to their deaths while fighting atop the Veridian III mountain.

13. Which *Trek* series was being filmed at the same time as *Generations* on neighboring Paramount lots?
    A. *Deep Space 9*
    B. *TNG*
    C. *Voyager*

14. The *Enterprise*-D's saucer crash sequence had originally been proposed for which *TNG* cliff-hanging episode?
    A. "The Best of Both Worlds, Part I"
    B. "Redemption, Part I"
    C. "All Good Things . . . Part I"

15. The Demora Sulu character aboard the *Enterprise*-B was originally scripted to be which *TREK-classic* regular's daughter?
    A. Chekov's
    B. McCoy's
    C. Uhura's

16. In *Generations,* the *Enterprise-*D's main bridge received a copper ceiling and darker brown walls and the ready room received a wider window and a bigger aquarium. Why was the construction of a new captain's chair an unintentional change to the ship?
    A. The first chair had been dismantled and given to the Smithsonian Institute.
    B. The original chair had been stolen.
    C. The original chair was "loaned" to *Voyager.*

17. Where was the dramatic climax between Picard, Kirk, and Soran filmed?
    A. Death Valley, California
    B. Santa Fe, New Mexico
    C. Valley of Fire, Nevada

18. Which character actor's ranch provided the on-location filming for Kirk's barn and horse jump sequence in the Nexus?
    A. Noah Beery Jr.'s
    B. Ben Johnson's
    C. John Putch's

19. In reality, what was the chair that Dr. Soran strapped La Forge in to torture him?
    A. A dentist chair
    B. A birthing chair
    C. Kirk's captain's chair from the original *Enterprise*

20. Where was the location of Guinan's quarters in *Generations?*
    A. Deck 7, Room 2150
    B. Deck 10, Room 1150
    C. Deck 8, Room 3150

Prime Memory Bonus

William Shatner rode his own mare in Generations. *What was her name?*

Prime Memory Bonus

Tasha Yar's character in the embryonic days of TNG was inspired by the tough space marine, Vasquez, in the movie Aliens. *What role did actress Jenette Goldstein (who played the Latino soldier in the* Alien *sequel) have in* Generations?

---

21. Kirk's dog, Butler, was originally named Jake. Which *Generations* actor changed the canine's name to honor his own dog which had recently died?
    A. Patrick Stewart
    B. William Shatner
    C. Malcolm McDowell

22. Dr. Soran's name was originally scripted to be "Moresh." Why was it changed?
    A. They wanted to avoid parallels with the late cult leader, David Koresh.
    B. Moresh is Hebrew for "saint."
    C. Moresh is Arabic for "godly."

23. How many different scripts were commissioned for *Generations*?
    A. Two
    B. Three
    C. Four

24. How many optical shots out of the 207 used in *Generations* came from previous *Trek* movies?
    A. Six
    B. Three
    C. One

25. *Generations* was not originally intended to have any *TREK-classic* characters in it. Who approached Paramount with the idea to integrate some of them into the film?
    A. William Shatner
    B. Producer Rick Berman
    C. Director David Carson

26. What did Shatner and Stewart wear under their Starfleet uniforms in the Nexus horseback scene?
    A. Thermal underwear
    B. Nothing
    C. Pantyhose

27. What was the refugee transport ship *Lakul*'s registry?
    A. NFT-7793
    B. NBT-2253
    C. BBI-0920

28. Journalists aboard the *Enterprise*-B's launch from spacedock at the beginning of *Generations* were from the EBC (Earth Broadcasting Co.), SFB (Starfleet Broadcasting), and the FNN. What news-gathering agency did the acronym FNN stand for?
    A. Federation Nightly News
    B. Federation News Network
    C. Federation Network News

29. The *Generations* shuttlecraft on Veridian III was new to *TNG*, but not *Star Trek*. In which movie was it used previously?
    A. *The Voyage Home*
    B. *The Wrath of Khan*
    C. *The Final Frontier*

30. In Kirk's Nexus cabin, there was a painting of a cowboy on horseback at night watching a shooting star in the background. Whose face did the cowboy have?
    A. William Shatner's
    B. Leonard Nimoy's
    C. DeForest Kelley's

31. On which national weekly newsmagazine's cover did William Shatner and Patrick Stewart appear in their *Star Trek* uniforms to coincide with the theatrical release of *Generations*?
    A. *Time*
    B. *Newsweek*
    C. *U.S. News*

Prime Memory Bonus

We learn in TNG episode "Relics" (written by Ronald D. Moore) that the events in Star Trek VI: The Undiscovered Country took place in 2293. Legendary engineer Montgomery Scott retired from Starfleet two years later and was missing for 75 years after his transport ship crashed on a Dyson sphere. An Enterprise-D away team discovered Scotty alive in 2369 after he had survived for 75 years by suspending himself inside a transporter beam. Scotty, unaware that over 70 years had passed, assumed that "James Kirk had gotten the old girl out of mothballs" and came to rescue him when Commander Riker told Scotty that the away team was from the Enterprise. Generations (also written by Ronald D. Moore) took place in the 24th century in the year 2371 and Kirk's death aboard the Enterprise-B in the early scenes of the movie occurs 78 years earlier in 2293. Why would Scotty, who was with Kirk aboard the Enterprise-B in 2293 when he died trying to save the ship from the energy ribbon, believe that his old starship captain would come to his aid when he crash landed his transport ship in 2295, two years after Kirk's death?

ANSWER KEY

Each correct answer is worth one point. For every Prime Memory Bonus answered correctly, add an additional 5 points.

Q and A

1. Riker
2. "Q Who"
3. 3
4. 7,000
5. Q Continuum
6. Picard
7. Calamarain
8. Data
9. Sakharov
10. La Forge
11. Lord High Sheriff of Nottingham

12. 2
13. Dr. Crusher
14. Amanda Rogers
15. 3
16. 2
17. 2,005
18. Still holding Picard on trial as the representative of "barbaric" humanity

Prime Memory Bonus: *Trelane*

MAXIMUM SCORE POTENTIAL: **23**
YOUR SCORE: _____

It's About Time, Part I

1. The Traveler
2. Picard's
3. Dr. Crusher
4. 2
5. Eric-Christopher
6. Photon torpedo

Prime Memory Bonus:
  La Forge

7. Guinan
8. "Redemption, Part I"
9. "Timescape"
10. "Time Squared"
11. U.S.S. *Bozeman*
12. Jack London
13. Devidians (No, not the ones from Waco)

14. *A Midsummer Night's Dream*
Prime Memory Bonus: *Mrs. Carmichael*
15. Riker
16. "A Matter of Time"
17. "Tapestry"

18. "Journey's End"
19. QE II
20. 25 minutes
21. U.S.S. *Jenolen*
Prime Memory Bonus: *Aldebaran whiskey*

MAXIMUM SCORE POTENTIAL: **36**
YOUR SCORE: _____

A Time to Play, Part I

1. C
2. K
3. D
4. J
5. I
6. L
7. F

8. G
9. B
10. H
11. A
12. E
Prime Memory Bonus: *"Booby Trap"*

MAXIMUM SCORE POTENTIAL: **17**
YOUR SCORE: _____

A Time to Play, Part II

1. G
2. I
3. H
4. F
5. J
6. A
7. L

8. C
9. K
10. D
11. B
12. E
Prime Memory Bonus: *"The Perfect Mate"*

MAXIMUM SCORE POTENTIAL: **17**
YOUR SCORE: _____

Behind the Scenes, Part I

1. Jonathan Frakes and Diana Muldaur
2. The mysterious one-armed man
3. "The Schizoid Man"
4. Lurch
5. "Half a Life"

6. La Forge's father
7. George La Forge
8. James Worthy
9. The Betazoid gift box face
10. *CHiPS*
11. Jonathan Frakes
12. 2 *TNG* Klingons had to wear

boots left over from *The Planet of the Apes*
13. Riker's
14. "Final Mission"
15. Mick Fleetwood
16. *2001: A Space Odyssey*
17. Dr. Isaac Asimov
18. *seaQuest DSV*
19. Daniel Stewart, Patrick's son
20. *My Favorite Martian*
21. *The A-Team*
22. Corbin Bernsen
23. 1
24. Leonard Nimoy's
25. *Hunt for Red October*
26. "Realm of Fear"
Prime Memory Bonus: *Gene Roddenberry*
27. Tasha Yar
28. Paris
29. Dr. Timicin was portrayed by David Ogden Stiers; the number was a salute to his work as Dr. Winchester on *M*A*S*H*
30. The false god image

MAXIMUM SCORE POTENTIAL: **60**
YOUR SCORE: _____

31. Chancellor Gorkon
32. The alien hunter
33. Majel Barrett, a.k.a. Lwaxana Troi
34. "Data's Day"
35. The Mamas and the Papas
36. KGB General Gogol (M's counterpart)
37. "The Measure of a Man"
Prime Memory Bonus: *"The Inner Light"*
38. Australian
39. General Koord
40. Scotty and La Forge beamed off the U.S.S. *Jenolen* while the ship's shields were still up
41. The distinctive arrowhead symbols were on a background of 4 lines instead of the usual oval shape
42. Mitchell Ryan
43. "Hero Worship"
44. Himself
45. Texas Guinan
Prime Memory Bonus: *Kurak*

To Seek Out New Life . . . , Part I

1. B
2. M
3. G
4. L
5. N
6. H
7. O
8. J
9. C
10. K
11. E
12. I
13. F
14. A
15. D
Prime Memory Bonus: *Glob fly*

MAXIMUM SCORE POTENTIAL: **20**
YOUR SCORE: _____

To Seek Out New Life . . . , Part II

1. B
2. A
3. B
4. C
5. A
6. C
7. B
8. B
9. C
10. A
11. A
12. B
13. A
14. C
15. A
16. C
17. B
18. A
19. B
20. C
21. A
22. B
23. A
24. C
25. C
Prime Memory Bonus: *A*

MAXIMUM SCORE POTENTIAL: **30**
YOUR SCORE: ____

Starfleet Intelligence Officer Dossier: Captain Jean-Luc Picard

1. B
2. His father
3. LaBarre
4. A
5. True
6. He was the only freshman to win the marathon.
7. C
8. Cardiac replacement
9. Sarek
10. The future Jenice Manheim
11. B
12. Constellation
Prime Memory Bonus: *Maurice*
13. C
14. A
15. The Picard Maneuver
16. Phillipa Louvois
17. Bok
18. False (2363)
19. Starfleet Academy
20. A
Prime Memory Bonus: *Dr. Pulaski*
21. Dr. Crusher
22. Locutus
23. 39
24. René
25. Louis
26. Arbiter of Succession
27. B
28. A
29. Metagenic
30. Counselor Troi
Prime Memory Bonus: *"There . . . are . . . four . . . lights!!!"*
31. Professor Richard Galen
32. Since his Academy days
33. San Francisco
34. Piano
35. 1000 years
36. A
37. Vash
38. Kamala
Prime Memory Bonus: *Amazing Detective Stories*
39. B

40. Tallera
41. By killing Picard's son
42. C
43. On a missile recovery mission with Data in
    a shuttlecraft
44. 2364
Prime Memory Bonus: *Omicron-omicron-alpha-yellow-daystar-2-7*

MAXIMUM SCORE POTENTIAL: **69**
YOUR SCORE: ____

Starfleet Intelligence Officer Dossier: Commander William Thomas Riker

1. Valdez
2. Two
3. 15
4. Eighth
5. C
6. Lieutenant
7. A
8. True
9. Back on the surface of Nervala IV
10. Thomas
11. B
12. A
Prime Memory Bonus: *Over a magnetic pole*

13. C
14. First officer
15. B
16. A
17. "Mr. Worf, fire!"
18. True
19. Trombone
20. Jazz
21. Cooking
22. A
Prime Memory Bonus: *Theta-alpha-2-7-3-7-blue (Later it was changed to Riker-omega-3.)*

MAXIMUM SCORE POTENTIAL: **33**
YOUR SCORE: ____

When the Starships Shine

1. B
2. C
3. B
4. A
5. B
6. B
7. C
8. A
9. B
10. A
11. B
12. C

13. C
14. A
15. B
16. A
17. C
18. B
19. A
20. B
21. C
22. B
23. A
24. A

25. C
26. B
27. A
28. B
29. C
30. A
31. B

32. C
33. B
34. A
35. C

Prime Memory Bonus: *Vor'cha class*

MAXIMUM SCORE POTENTIAL: 40
YOUR SCORE: ____

Behind-the-Scenes, Part II

1. *Columbia*
2. *The Hills Have Eyes*
3. "Genesis"
4. Carolyn Seymour
5. Room 312
6. She had lost some weight, but her stunt double had a bigger rear.
7. Gabrielle Beaumont
8. Patrick Stewart
9. "The Pegasus"
10. Paul Sorvino
11. Robin Curtis
12. Jonathan Frakes
13. Wil Wheaton
14. John de Lancie, a.k.a. Q
15. From a fan
16. Gene Roddenberry named the starship after the Navy aircraft carrier.
17. Burgundy signifies command; mustard for ship services; and teal for medical, science, and teaching fields.
18. *The Air Up There*
19. William Ware Theiss
20. *Saturday Night Live*
21. "Homeworld"
22. "Coming of Age"
23. Patrick Stewart
24. Wil Wheaton
25. Brannon Braga
26. *The Snapper*
27. King Richard
28. *Lois & Clark: The New Adventures of Superman*
29. Michelle Forbes
30. Michael Dorn
31. Quark
32. Michael Westmore
33. Jonathan Frakes
34. Patrick Stewart
35. "Is There in Truth No Beauty" and "Return to Tomorrow"
36. The galactic emperor
37. Kelsey Grammer

Prime Memory Bonus: *Paul Winfield*

MAXIMUM SCORE POTENTIAL: 47
YOUR SCORE: ____

Eat, Drink, and Be Merry, Part I

1. B
2. F
3. L
4. G
5. A
6. E
7. I

8. K
9. C
10. J
11. H
12. D

Prime Memory Bonus: *Data*

MAXIMUM SCORE POTENTIAL: **17**
YOUR SCORE: _____

Eat, Drink, and Be Merry, Part II

1. D
2. G
3. L
4. E
5. H
6. F
7. B

8. J
9. K
10. A
11. I
12. C

Prime Memory Bonus: *Ferengi*

MAXIMUM SCORE POTENTIAL: **17**
YOUR SCORE: _____

Starfleet Intelligence Officer Dossier: Lieutenant Commander Data

1. 2336
2. Second
3. C
4. 2338
5. Positronic
6. B
7. His ventral access panel
8. False
9. True
10. B
11. A
12. True
13. Harming living beings
14. C
15. The various departments of the ship
16. Pinocchio

17. Tasha Yar
18. The brief experience of human laughter
19. Miles O'Brien and Keiko

Prime Memory Bonus: *Exobiology*

20. B
21. False (It was the Klingon Civil war.)
22. C
23. Sherlock Holmes program 3A
24. La Forge's interface experiment on Data
25. Presidio
26. La Forge
27. A
28. False (He did once to the

amusement of his
shipmates.)

29. "Ode to Spot"
30. Jenna D'Sora
Prime Memory Bonus: *Walk around naked*
31. Dreams
32. B
33. Positronic matrix transfer
34. C
35. Emotions
36. A
37. A fatal systemwide cascade failure
38. He was beamed into space.
39. Dr. Soong
40. An emotion chip
41. True

42. Lore had used poison in a glass of champagne to subdue him.
43. Lore secretly bombarded Data with signals that triggered negative emotions in his positronic brain.
44. The emotion chip Lore stole from Data
45. She was an android who wasn't aware she was an android.
46. C
47. 3
Prime Memory Bonus: *Biomechanical maintenance program*

MAXIMUM SCORE POTENTIAL: **62**
YOUR SCORE: _____

Starfleet Intelligence Officer Dossier: Counselor Deanna Troi

1. Ian Andrew Troi
2. Seven
3. Wyatt Miller
4. Wyatt chose to join the last surviving Tarellians in search of a cure for their decimating plague.
5. B
6. University of Betazed
7. A
8. Ian Andrew Troi, Jr.

9. C
10. Quantum
11. Lieutenant Commander
12. B
13. A
14. Captain Edward Jellico
15. Chocolate
16. "Little One"
Prime Memory Bonus: *Lieutenant Ben Prieto*

MAXIMUM SCORE POTENTIAL: **21**
YOUR SCORE: _____

Look Who's Talking

1. B
2. C

3. B
4. A

5.	C		17.	A
6.	B		18.	C
7.	B		19.	B
8.	A		20.	B
9.	C		21.	C
10.	A		22.	A
11.	B		23.	B
12.	C		24.	A
13.	A		25.	C

14. B
15. C
16. B

17. A
18. C
19. B
20. B
21. C
22. A
23. B
24. A
25. C

Prime Memory Bonus: *Ian, Troi's alien child*

MAXIMUM SCORE POTENTIAL: **30**
YOUR SCORE: ____

Out of This World, Part I

1.	F		8.	H
2.	I		9.	D
3.	J		10.	A
4.	G		11.	E
5.	L		12.	B
6.	C			
7.	K			

Prime Memory Bonus: *Tau Ceti III*

MAXIMUM SCORE POTENTIAL: **17**
YOUR SCORE: ____

Out of This World, Part II

1.	B		8.	A
2.	F		9.	L
3.	H		10.	G
4.	J		11.	K
5.	I		12.	D
6.	C			
7.	E			

Prime Memory Bonus: *Paulson Nebula*

MAXIMUM SCORE POTENTIAL: **17**
YOUR SCORE: ____

To Everything There Is a Season, Part I

1.	4th	27.	5th
2.	1st	28.	2nd
3.	7th	29.	2nd
4.	2nd	30.	4th
5.	6th	31.	4th
6.	7th	32.	6th
7.	4th	33.	3rd
8.	4th	34.	2nd
9.	1st	35.	1st
10.	3rd	36.	2nd
11.	7th	37.	1st
12.	5th	38.	3rd
13.	6th	39.	5th
14.	4th	40.	4th
15.	5th	41.	3rd
16.	7th	42.	6th
17.	7th	43.	6th
18.	1st	44.	7th
19.	2nd	45.	7th
20.	2nd	46.	5th
21.	5th	47.	1st
22.	3rd	48.	1st
23.	4th	49.	6th
24.	6th	50.	6th
25.	6th	Prime Memory Bonus: *3rd*	
26.	3rd		

MAXIMUM SCORE POTENTIAL: **55**
YOUR SCORE: _____

To Everything There Is a Season, Part II

1.	1st	11.	6th
2.	6th	12.	3rd
3.	4th	13.	5th
4.	4th	14.	2nd
5.	2nd	15.	2nd
6.	1st	16.	5th
7.	6th	17.	1st
8.	2nd	18.	5th
9.	4th	19.	4th
10.	4th	20.	5th

21.	1st	44.	4th
22.	2nd	45.	6th
23.	2nd	46.	6th
24.	4th	47.	4th
25.	3rd	48.	5th
26.	2nd	49.	5th
27.	5th	50.	3rd
28.	2nd	51.	3rd
29.	2nd	52.	2nd
30.	6th	53.	2nd
31.	1st	54.	5th
32.	1st	55.	6th
33.	1st	56.	3rd
34.	5th	57.	3rd
35.	4th	58.	4th
36.	5th	59.	5th
37.	4th	60.	3rd
38.	2nd	61.	5th
39.	3rd	62.	6th
40.	4th	63.	1st
41.	3rd	64.	2nd
42.	5th		Prime Memory Bonus: *4th*
43.	4th		

MAXIMUM SCORE POTENTIAL: **69**

YOUR SCORE: _____

The Name Is the Game, Part I

1.	C	16.	C
2.	B	17.	A
3.	B	18.	B
4.	A	19.	C
5.	C	20.	B
6.	A	21.	A
7.	C	22.	C
8.	A	23.	B
9.	B	24.	B
10.	C	25.	C
11.	B	26.	A
12.	A	27.	C
13.	A	28.	A
14.	C	29.	B
15.	A	30.	C

31. C
32. A
33. B
34. A
35. B
36. C
37. B
38. A
39. C
40. B
41. A
42. B

43. C
44. A
45. C
46. B
47. A
48. B
49. A
50. C
51. A
52. B

Prime Memory Bonus: *Qui'Tu*

MAXIMUM SCORE POTENTIAL: **57**
YOUR SCORE: _____

Starfleet Intelligence Officer Dossier: Lieutenant Worf Rozhenko

1. Qo'noS
2. Worf
3. Sergey and Helena
4. B
5. True
6. Nikolai
7. False (Nikolai dropped out.)
8. C
9. A
10. Lieutenant, junior grade
11. Three
12. She was killed on Vagra II.
13. A
14. Their mothers
15. It had been severely damaged battling the Borg.
16. True
17. *Rokeg* blood pie
18. One
19. True
20. Alexander from the future

21. C
22. A
23. *Deep Space 9*
24. B
25. C
26. Duras
27. True
28. He would not otherwise have been permitted to take sides.
29. He had experienced a crisis of faith and wanted to visit a Klingon monastery
30. B
31. A
32. C
33. A
34. A dagger
35. Iceman

Prime Memory Bonus: *The Great Council Chamber*

MAXIMUM SCORE POTENTIAL: **40**
YOUR SCORE: _____

Starfleet Intelligence Federation Member Dossier: Klingons

1. Blade
2. B
3. 2, 8, 23
4. False
5. C
6. Courage
7. Klingonese
8. The eldest son or a trusted friend
9. *Sto-Vo-Kor*
10. B
11. C
12. C
13. *Kut'luch*
14. Phase
15. A warning for the dead to beware a Klingon warrior has arrived
16. A
17. Klingon Defense Force
18. True
19. Klingon *Bird-of-Prey*
20. Klingon battle cruisers
21. Klingon High Council

22. True
23. C
24. 2218
25. Poisoning
26. B
27. Boreth
28. The clerics of the Boreth monastery
29. Lursa and B'Etor
30. B
31. A
32. B
33. B
34. C
35. Vagh
36. They were sweaty and unpleasant. Such an irritation kept a warrior on edge at all times.
37. Kahless the Unforgettable

Prime Memory Bonus:

MAXIMUM SCORE POTENTIAL: 42
YOUR SCORE: _____

Klingon to Your Universal Translator

1. D
2. F
3. M
4. E
5. N
6. B
7. H
8. J

9. L
10. I
11. A
12. C
13. G
14. K
Prime Memory Bonus: *"I speak to you"*

MAXIMUM SCORE POTENTIAL: 19
YOUR SCORE: _____

Starfleet Intelligence Officer Dossier: Lieutenant Commander Geordi La Forge

1. Visual Instrument and Sensory Organ Replacement
2. Infrared
3. True
4. B
5. False (It was the Romulans.)
6. A
7. A
8. C
9. True
10. Five
11. His parents
12. B
13. True
14. A
15. C
16. B
17. Dr. Crusher
18. False (It was Picard.)
19. Flight controller (conn)
20. C
21. A
22. B
23. Iced coffee

Prime Memory Bonus: *Christi Henshaw*

Prime Memory Bonus: *"special insight"*

MAXIMUM SCORE POTENTIAL: **33**
YOUR SCORE: _____

Starfleet Intelligence Officer Dossier: Chief Medical Officer Beverly Crusher

1. B
2. A
3. Felicia Howard
4. Her grandmother
5. B
6. True
7. 2349
8. C
9. 2364
10. Starfleet Medical
11. A
12. She could not accept her love inhabiting a different body.
13. B
14. C
15. *Cyrano de Bergerac*
16. A
17. Riker

Prime Memory Bonus: *Reginald Barclay*

MAXIMUM SCORE POTENTIAL: **22**
YOUR SCORE: _____

House Calls

1. B
2. A
3. C
4. A
5. C
6. B
7. A
8. A
9. C
10. B
11. C
12. C
13. A
14. B

15.	B	20.	A
16.	C	21.	B
17.	B	22.	B
18.	A		
19.	C		

Prime Memory Bonus: *Nurse Alyssa Ogawa*

MAXIMUM SCORE POTENTIAL: 27
YOUR SCORE: _____

The Name Is the Game, Part II

1.	C	31.	B
2.	B	32.	A
3.	C	33.	C
4.	A	34.	B
5.	B	35.	A
6.	A	36.	B
7.	B	37.	A
8.	A	38.	C
9.	B	39.	C
10.	B	40.	A
11.	C	41.	B
12.	B	42.	C
13.	C	43.	A
14.	A	44.	B
15.	A	45.	B
16.	C	46.	C
17.	A	47.	A
18.	C	48.	B
19.	A	49.	C
20.	B	50.	B
21.	A	51.	C
22.	C	52.	A
23.	B	53.	C
24.	B	54.	B
25.	C	55.	A
26.	A	56.	A
27.	C	57.	B
28.	B	58.	C
29.	C	59.	B
30.	A	60.	C

61. A
62. B
63. A

64. C

Prime Memory Bonus: *He
    remained unnamed.*

MAXIMUM SCORE POTENTIAL: 69
YOUR SCORE: ____

Trek Tech Specs

1. A
2. Tritanium/duranium
3. Stardrive
4. Navigational
5. False (It was the primary
    hull.)
6. False
7. Bussard collectors
8. A
9. Sublight
10. Matter, antimatter
11. True
12. B
13. Matter/antimatter reaction
    chamber
14. Warp factor
15. C
16. Distortions
17. Tractor beam
18. Banks
19. C
20. Photon torpedo
21. B
22. Directly ahead of the
    Captain's chair
23. Conn
24. Turboelevators
25. B
26. Bearing
27. Jefferies tube
28. Transporter
29. Holographic Environment
    Simulator
30. A
31. C

32. True
33. C
34. B
35. True
36. A
37. B
38. Buffers
39. 3
40. False (It was invented over
    one century later, not two.)
41. C
42. True
43. Computer core
44. Conference lounge
45. Antigravs
46. A
47. B
48. False (It was a by-product of
    warp drive.)
49. Personal Access Display
    Device
50. Optical Data Network
51. C
52. True
53. A
54. Transporter ID trace
55. Tricorder
56. Autodestruct
57. Dermal
58. False (as high as 16)
59. Three
60. C
61. Emergency transporter
    armbands
62. Heisenberg compensators

63. Confinement
64. A
65. True
66. Battle section
67. C
68. B
69. B
70. Baryon sweep
71. True

72. A
73. Sonic shower
74. Kiloquad
75. B
76. A
77. 2
Prime Memory Bonus:
    Electroplasma system taps (or
    EPS taps)

MAXIMUM SCORE POTENTIAL: 82
YOUR SCORE: _____

Stacked Deck: Saucer Module

1. H
2. E
3. C
4. L
5. A
6. F
7. B

8. G
9. I
10. D
11. K
12. J
Prime Memory Bonus: *Deck 10*

MAXIMUM SCORE POTENTIAL: 17
YOUR SCORE: _____

Stacked Deck: Stardrive Section

1. N
2. A
3. E
4. L
5. K
6. D
7. F
8. H

9. I
10. C
11. O
12. B
13. G
14. J
15. M
Prime Memory Bonus: *Deck 25*

MAXIMUM SCORE POTENTIAL: 20
YOUR SCORE: _____

It's About Time, Part II

1. Worf
2. C
3. False (He went to the future.)

4. Blue
5. B
6. A

7. False (He had three.)
8. C
9. Leah heard the news at Starfleet Medical.
10. True
11. B
12. *Galileo*
13. False
14. A
15. C
16. B
17. True
18. C
19. False (It was 15 starships.)
20. A
21. For "distinction"
22. B
23. True
24. A blue miniskirt
25. C
26. C
27. Farpoint Station
28. True
29. A
30. B
31. False (They never went to the couch.)
32. B
33. True
34. Klingons
35. C
36. A
37. Governor
38. B
39. Child
40. Picard
41. C
42. A

43. A
44. B
45. Warp 13
46. Earl Grey tea
47. C
48. B
49. Beverly
50. True
51. A
52. A
53. Worf
54. U.S.S. *Enterprise*
55. False (Worf and Troi "never got together.")
56. It was never discussed.
57. Dr. Crusher's nurse, Alyssa
58. C
59. A
60. Microscope
61. True
62. B
63. True
64. C
65. Static
66. The past and present *Enterprises*
67. False (Q said, "The trial is never over.")
68. The Q Continuum's
69. A
70. C
71. Only Picard
72. Data
73. Stud

Prime Memory Bonus: *Isaac Newton*

Prime Memory Bonus: *Honor*

Prime Memory Bonus: *2395*

MAXIMUM SCORE POTENTIAL: **88**

YOUR SCORE: _____

Battlestations! Romulans

1. B
2. Valley, Sea
3. C
4. False (It was one light-year across.)
5. B
6. A
7. True
8. C
9. B
10. To test his loyalties
11. C
12. Romulan Star Empire
13. A
14. Proconsul
15. True
16. B
17. False (It was the Vulcan government.)
18. C
19. C
20. *Galaxy*
21. A
22. True
23. C
24. Blue
25. True
26. B

Prime Memory Bonus: *Three*
Prime Memory Bonus: *The two homeworlds, Romulus and Remus*

MAXIMUM SCORE POTENTIAL: **36**
YOUR SCORE: _____

Battlestations! Cardassians

1. C
2. True
3. B
4. B
5. False (2366)
6. Sarek, his father
7. A
8. A
9. True
10. False (millions)
11. C
12. Bajor
13. B
14. True
15. Gul
16. C
17. Gallitep
18. A
19. B

Prime Memory Bonus: *Thetaband*

MAXIMUM SCORE POTENTIAL: **24**
YOUR SCORE: _____

"Wanna Buy a Used Starship?" The Ferengi

1. A
2. Ferengi Rules of Acquisition
3. True
4. Betazoids
5. C
6. B
7. B
8. A
9. False (It's a two-person vessel.)

10. Ferengi Salvage Code
11. Ferengi pod
12. True
13. True
14. C
15. A
16. Clothing

17. B
18. C
19. B
20. DaiMon
21. Grand Nagus
22. A
Prime Memory Bonus: *285*

MAXIMUM SCORE POTENTIAL: **27**
YOUR SCORE: _____

Starfleet Intelligence Officer Dossier: Ensign Wesley Crusher

1. A
2. False (His primary interests were science and technology.)
3. Prodigy
4. True
5. A
6. C
7. Nanites
8. B
9. C
10. B
11. 15
12. A
13. Captain Picard's decision to let Jack Crusher die so that another man could live

14. True
15. Riker and Deanna and Lwaxana Troi
16. Picard granted him a field promotion to the rank of ensign.
17. False (2367)
18. C
19. A reprimand was entered into his academic record, and he was forced to repeat his freshman year.
20. B
21. True
Prime Memory Bonus: *Ancient Philosophies*

MAXIMUM SCORE POTENTIAL: **26**
YOUR SCORE: _____

Starfleet Intelligence Officer Dossier: Lieutenant Commander Tasha Yar

1. B
2. B
3. C
4. B
5. A
6. A

7. C
8. C
9. B
10. A
11. B
12. C

13. B
14. A

Prime Memory Bonus: *Telluridian
synthale*

MAXIMUM SCORE POTENTIAL: 19
YOUR SCORE: _____

Starfleet Intelligence Officer Dossier: Lieutenant Ro Laren

1. C
2. B
3. B
4. A
5. C
6. C
7. B
8. A
9. A

10. C
11. B
12. B
13. A
14. C
15. A
16. B
Prime Memory Bonus: *Deck 4*
Prime Memory Bonus: *Type 8*

MAXIMUM SCORE POTENTIAL: 26
YOUR SCORE: _____

Starfleet Intelligence Ambassador Dossier: Lwaxana Troi

1. Fifth, Chalice, Rings
2. Drowning
3. The Antidean ambassador
4. Picard and Riker
5. B
6. Campio could not accept the traditional Betazoid custom

of conducting the ceremony in the nude.
7. C
8. Guilt for blaming herself for Kestra's drowning accident
9. Mr. Homn
Prime Memory Bonus: *Rex*

MAXIMUM SCORE POTENTIAL: 14
YOUR SCORE: _____

Behind the Scenes, The Final Chapter

1. B
2. "Family"
3. A
4. Appeared as Picard on another series (*Deep Space 9*)
5. C
6. They all guest-starred on *TNG* in the first season.
7. B

8. One
9. B
10. The floor transporter pads
11. Inside on a Paramount set
12. A
13. True
14. C
15. *Heaven and Hell*
16. B

17. LeVar Burton
18. A
19. B
20. B
21. B
22. False (Data never played Zorro.)
23. James Worthy
24. Ray Walston
25. C
26. Ben Vereen
27. Shuttle astronaut, Dr. Mae Jemison
28. The "whoosh" of the opening and closing of doors
29. A
30. Richard James
31. B
32. A
33. Majel Barrett
34. "The Pegasus"
35. Supervising Producer David Livingston
36. B
37. Gates McFadden
38. True
39. True
40. Data
41. Eric Menyuk, a.k.a. the Traveler
42. C
43. B
44. Denise Crosby
45. A
46. False (It was Bob Justman's.)
47. True
48. C
49. Their 1979 novel of the same name
50. C
51. B
52. A
53. Dan Curry
54. "Birthright, Part I"
55. Cliff Bole
56. "The First Duty"
57. Cybernetic organism
58. B
59. C
60. A
61. True
62. "The Child"
63. *A Connecticut Yankee in King Arthur's Court*
64. Gene Roddenberry, whose middle name was Wesley
65. C
66. B
67. A
68. A
69. "Evolution"
70. C
71. B
72. True
73. Bob Justman
74. A
75. C
76. False
77. True
78. B
79. True
80. C
81. B
82. B
83. Draped over the back of his chair
84. A
85. C
86. The small craft/shuttle was re-dressed and utilized in all three episodes.
87. B
88. A
89. B
90. *Star Trek VI: The Undiscovered Country*

91. C
92. B
93. Berlingoff Rasmussen
94. Sydney Greenstreet
95. A
96. True
97. C
98. A
99. Only once (in the episode "Cause and Effect")
100. C
101. *Star Trek II: The Wrath of Kahn*
102. False (They were never given a name.)
103. It was assumed that Data was made in his creator's image.
104. Somali
105. A
106. B
107. C

108. Stephen Hawking
109. *Star Trek II: The Wrath of Kahn*
110. C
111. *Lost in Space*
112. *Star Trek: The Motion Picture*
113. Transporter
114. 52
115. A
116. True
117. B
118. True
119. False
120. B
121. C
122. An earthquake
Prime Memory Bonus: *May 14–20, 1994*
Prime Memory Bonus: *British psychotherapist Robin Skynner*
Prime Memory Bonus: *1,200*

MAXIMUM SCORE POTENTIAL: **137**
YOUR SCORE: _____

Star Search

1. B
2. A
3. B
4. C
5. C
6. A
7. B
8. C
9. A
10. C
11. B
12. C
13. A
14. A
15. C
16. B

Prime Memory Bonus: *Starbase G-6*
17. B
18. A
19. C
20. C
21. B
22. A
23. B
24. C
Prime Memory Bonus: *43657.0*
25. A
26. C
27. C
28. B
29. B

30. A
31. A
32. C
33. B
34. B

35. A
36. C
37. C

Prime Memory Bonus: *Order 104, Section C*

MAXIMUM SCORE POTENTIAL: 52
YOUR SCORE: ____

Transporter Scramble

1. Sarek
2. Riker
3. Perrin
4. Yar
5. Barclay
6. Locutus
7. Shelby
8. Timicin
9. Bok
10. Vash
11. Jellico
12. Wyatt
13. Elburn
14. Duras
15. Data
16. Aquiel
17. Toq
18. Gowron
19. McCoy
20. Deanna
21. Bynars
22. Alexander

23. Lore
24. Kurn
25. Geordi
26. Clemens
27. Picard
28. Brahms
29. Scotty
30. Crusher
31. Lwaxana
32. Worf
33. Pulaski
34. Hugh
35. Quaice
36. Quinn
37. Keiko
38. Ishara
39. Haftel
40. Mendon
41. Satie
42. Miles

Prime Memory Bonus: *Mark Lenard*

MAXIMUM SCORE POTENTIAL: 47
YOUR SCORE: ____

Trekkers' Top Ten
Number Ten: "Attached"

1. B
2. C
3. A
4. B

5. C
6. B
7. A
8. C

9. A
10. B
11. B
12. C
13. A
14. B
15. C
16. A
17. A
18. B

19. C
20. A
21. A
22. B
23. B
24. C

Prime Memory Bonus: *Shoved him through, leaving herself to be captured*

MAXIMUM SCORE POTENTIAL: 29
YOUR SCORE: _____

Number Nine: "Parallels"

1. B
2. C
3. A
4. B
5. C
6. B
7. A
8. C
9. A
10. B
11. C
12. B
13. A
14. C
15. B
16. A

17. B
18. C
19. B
20. A
21. C
22. B
23. C
24. A
25. B
26. B
27. C
28. A
29. C

Prime Memory Bonus: *Celebrate alone*

MAXIMUM SCORE POTENTIAL: 34
YOUR SCORE: _____

Number Eight: "Inheritance"

1. B
2. A
3. B
4. C
5. C
6. A

7. A
8. B
9. C
10. C
11. A
12. B

13. C
14. A
15. B
16. B
17. C
18. A
19. A

20. B
21. C
22. B
23. A
24. B

Prime Memory Bonus: *Synapic scanning*

MAXIMUM SCORE POTENTIAL: **29**
YOUR SCORE: _____

Number Seven: "Skin of Evil"

1. C
2. C
3. A
4. B
5. B
6. A
7. B
8. B
9. C
10. C
11. A

12. A
13. B
14. C
15. B
16. A
17. C
18. C
19. A

Prime Memory Bonus: *Mishiama wristlock*
Prime Memory Bonus: *La Forge's*

MAXIMUM SCORE POTENTIAL: **29**
YOUR SCORE: _____

Number Six: "I, Borg"

1. A
2. B
3. B
4. C
5. B
6. B
7. A
8. C
9. A

10. B
11. B
12. A
13. B
14. C
15. B
16. C

Prime Memory Bonus: *Foil*
Prime Memory Bonus: *23rd*

MAXIMUM SCORE POTENTIAL: **26**
YOUR SCORE: _____

Number Five: "Relics"

1.	B	15.	B
2.	A	16.	C
3.	B	17.	A
4.	C	18.	B
5.	B	19.	C
6.	A	20.	A
7.	C	21.	B
8.	B	22.	B
9.	B	23.	C
10.	C		
11.	A		
12.	A		
13.	B		
14.	C		

Prime Memory Bonus: *Marina Sirtis*

Prime Memory Bonus: *Isolinear optical chip*

MAXIMUM SCORE POTENTIAL: **33**
YOUR SCORE: _____

Number Four: "Yesterday's Enterprise"

1.	C	14.	C
2.	B	15.	B
3.	C	16.	B
4.	A	17.	A
5.	B	18.	B
6.	C	19.	C
7.	A	20.	B
8.	B	21.	A
9.	A	22.	B
10.	C	23.	C
11.	B		
12.	C		
13.	A		

Prime Memory Bonus: *Military Log*

Prime Memory Bonus: *Four*

MAXIMUM SCORE POTENTIAL: **33**
YOUR SCORE: _____

Number Three: "The Offspring"

1.	C	5.	C
2.	A	6.	A
3.	C	7.	C
4.	B	8.	A

9. B
10. A
11. C
12. B
13. A

14. C
15. C
Prime Memory Bonus: *Otar II*
Prime Memory Bonus: *Hallie Todd*

MAXIMUM SCORE POTENTIAL: 25
YOUR SCORE: _____

Number Two: "The Best of Both Worlds, Part I

1. B
2. B
3. A
4. C
5. B
6. C
7. A
8. B
9. C

10. A
11. B
12. C
13. B
14. A
15. C
Prime Memory Bonus: *Cliff Bole*
Prime Memory Bonus: *Transwarp conduit*

MAXIMUM SCORE POTENTIAL: 25
YOUR SCORE: _____

Number One: "The Best of Both Worlds, Part II"
(NOTE: Every correct answer counts as five (5) points)

1. Antimatter spread
2. Gleason
3. Emergency transporter armbands
4. Heavy graviton beam
5. Jupiter Outpost 92
6. NCC-65491
7. *New Orleans*
8. Mars Defense Perimeter
9. Microcircuit fibers
10. Multimodal reflection

sorting
11. Two to three
12. Shuttle escape transporter
13. 11,000
14. He would become "obsolete"
15. The Borg had "neither honor nor courage"
16. Regeneration
17. "Almost human, but with a headache"
18. "Everything"

MAXIMUM SCORE POTENTIAL: 90
YOUR SCORE: _____

Crews Through Time: *Star Trek Generations*

1. A
2. B
3. False (He replied "Staying busy.")
4. B

Prime Memory Bonus: *A woman reporter*

5. A
6. Pluto
7. B
8. True
9. Spacedock
10. False (They were headed for Earth.)
11. A

Prime Memory Bonus: *Scotty*

12. C
13. C
14. True
15. Crusher

Prime Memory Bonus: *3*

16. A
17. Three
18. Worf
19. B
20. False (Two were discovered.)
21. C
22. A watch
23. C
24. B

Prime Memory Bonus: *12*

25. His nephew, René
26. A
27. The Borg
28. B
29. La Forge
30. True

31. A

Prime Memory Bonus: *39.1*

32. C
33. False (Picard thus advised Data.)
34. Records showed that any ship that approached the energy ribbon was either destroyed or severely damaged.
35. A
36. C
37. C
38. The Borg

Prime Memory Bonus: *257.4*

39. C
40. True
41. A
42. The warp core
43. Data
44. B
45. Chopping firewood
46. McCoy

Prime Memory Bonus: *Seven*

47. Antonia
48. Kirk's uncle in Idaho
49. B
50. Kirk's Starfleet insignia
51. B

Prime Memory Bonus: *261*

52. Picard
53. C
54. A
55. A

Prime Memory Bonus: *Lakul*

Prime Memory Bonus: *Captain Harriman*

MAXIMUM SCORE POTENTIAL: **105**

YOUR SCORE: _____

678

111213

Behind-the-Scenes: *Star Trek Generations*

1. A
2. C
3. A
4. B
5. B
6. C
7. A
8. C
9. C
10. B

Prime Memory Bonus: *Nov. 18, 1994*

Prime Memory Bonus: *July 18, 1995*

11. A
12. A
13. B
14. C
15. A
16. B
17. C
18. A
19. B
20. C

Prime Memory Bonus: *Great Belles of Fire*

Prime Memory Bonus: *1701-B Science Officer*

21. B
22. A
23. A
24. C
25. B
26. C
27. A
28. B
29. C
30. A
31. A

Prime Memory Bonus: *We know, we know. It's a trick question. There is no rational explanation for this blatant continuity screw-up. Ronald D. Moore, who wrote* TNG *episode "Relics" and co-wrote the* Generations *screenplay, will be spending years trying to explain this sloppy mistake.*

MAXIMUM SCORE POTENTIAL: **56**
YOUR SCORE: _____

SCORING

After you have totaled the points from each section to calculate your overall score, determine your Starfleet rank as follows:

2134–1803	**Admiral**
1802–1438	**Captain**
1437–1100	**Commander**
1099–771	**Lieutenant**
770–457	**Ensign**
456–201	**Academy Cadet**

ADMIRAL

Congratulations! You've been promoted to Admiral and posted to Starfleet Command in San Francisco where you will oversee Starfleet Corps of Engineers, the special projects division responsible for the construction of Starbase 542, the massive planetside facility on Beto II.

CAPTAIN

Your Command Orders from Starfleet Command are as follows: Report immediately to Earth Station McKinley where the U.S.S. *Enterprise*-E is undergoing its final shakedown prior to launch. Henceforth and until further notice, you are the captain of the Federation's newest flagship. Heed the sage advice of one legendary *Enterprise* captain to another: "Don't let them promote you. Don't let them transfer you. Don't let anything take you off the bridge of that ship."

COMMANDER

Your new posting is Starbase 525 on the border of the Neutral Zone, where you will be the commanding officer of a joint Federation–Romulan defense perimeter guarding against intruding enemy spacecraft (such as the Borg and the Dominion). Diplomacy will have to be one of your virtues. The Federation and the Romulan Star Empire are presently engaged in peace treaty discussions, and there are subversive forces within Starfleet Intelligence and the Romulans' Tal Shiar espionage service who will stop at nothing to oppose the peace process. Watch your back!

LIEUTENANT

Starfleet has assigned you to the Inspector General's office to assist in the cover investigation of a Cardassian infiltration conspiracy deep in the heart of the Federation. Be careful who you choose to trust. As a matter of fact, trust no one!

ENSIGN

Your new posting is Relay Station 47, the remote Starfleet communications system near the Klingon border. Most of the operations of the station are automated, although a two-person crew provides non-routine operations and maintenance.

ACADEMY CADET

You need to spend more time studying. Obviously you're spending more time on the dom-jot tables in the recreation center. If you want to graduate and have a promising career in Starfleet, you'd better "ignite the midnight petroleum." (If you don't know which Commander said that, then you're worse off than we thought.)

200–0

If you scored less than two hundred you're either a stowaway on a Federation starship or a Cardassian spy for the Obsidian Order. Watch your step or you'll end up being exiled to a deep space starbase, where you'll make a simple living as a tailor with a history of alliances and betrayals that haunt you.

BIBLIOGRAPHY

Entertainment Weekly StarTrek: The Ultimate Trip Through the Galaxies Special Collector's Edition, November 1994.

Farrand, Phil. *The Nitpicker's Guide for Next Generation Trekkers.* Dell, New York: 1993.

Hackett, George. "Roddenberry Gets His Flight." *Newsweek,* 9 May 1994: 6.

Kim, Albert. " 'Star' Witnessed." *Entertainment Weekly,* 25 November 1994: 64–65.

Logan, Michael. "The Magnificent Seven." *T.V. Guide,* 14–20 May 1994: 10.

Marriott, Michael. "When Time Stands Still." *Newsweek,* 21 November 1994: 88–89.

Nemecek, Larry. *Star Trek: The Next Generation Companion* (Revised Edition). Pocket Books, New York: 1995.

Okuda, Michael, and Denise Okuda. *Star Trek Chronology.* Pocket Books, New York: 1993.

Okuda, Michael, Denise Okuda, Debbie Mirek, and Doug Drexler. *The Star Trek Encyclopedia.* Pocket Books, New York: 1994.

Oldenburg, Ann. "Kirk Out?" *USA Today,* 26 October 1994, Sec. 1–2: D.

Roush, Matt. "The Franchise is Forever Enterprising." *USA Today,* 23 May 1994, Sec. 1: D.

Sanz, Cynthia. "Beam Him Down." *People,* 28 November 1994: 179–180, 182.

Spelling, Ian. "Inside Trek." *Houston Chronicle,* 21 August 1993, Sec. 2: C; 4 September 1993, Sec. 2: C; 11 September 1993, Sec. 2: D; 18 September 1993, Sec. 2: C; 9 October 1993, Sec. 2: C; 16 October 1993, Sec.

2: C; 13 November 1993, Sec. 2: C; 11 December 1993, Sec. 2: C; 18 December 1993, Sec. 2: C; 8 January 1994, Sec. 2: C; 22 January 1994, Sec. 2: C; 29 January 1994, Sec. 2: C; 5 February 1994, Sec. 2: C; 26 February 1994, Sec. 2: C; 5 March 1994, Sec. 2: C; 12 March 1994, Sec. 2: C; 19 March 1994, Sec. 2: C; 9 April 1994, Sec. 2: C; 23 May 1994, Sec. 1: D; 2 July 1994, Sec. 2: C; 10 September 1994, Sec. 2: C; 8 October 1994, Sec. 2: C; 22 October 1994, Sec. 2: C; 3 December 1994, Sec. 2: C; 10 December 1994, Sec. 2: C.

Spotnitz, Frank, and Albert Kim. "Absolutely Nebulous." *Entertainment Weekly*, 7 October 1994: 8–9.

Star Trek Generations: The Official Movie Magazine, November 1994.

Star Trek: The Next Generation Official Magazine Series, June 1994.

Star Trek: The Official Fan Club Magazine, April/May 1994.

Sterback, Rick, and Michael Okuda. *Star Trek: The Next Generation Technical Manual*. Pocket Books, New York: 1991.

Svetkey, Benjamin. "Generation Ex." *Entertainment Weekly*, 6 May 1994: 16.

T.V. Guide Star Trek: Four Generations of Stars, Stories, and Strange New Worlds Collector's Edition, Spring 1995.

Westbrook, Bruce. " 'TNG' Cast Takes Over Film." *Houston Chronicle*, 13 November 1994, Sec. ZEST: 8.

Zoglin, Richard. "Trekking Onward." *Time*, 28 November 1994: 72–79.

APPENDIX

Quick Reference Episode Guide

SEASON 1 (FIRST AIRED 1987–1988)

1. and 2. *"Encounter at Farpoint, Parts I and II."* The new *Galaxy*-class *Enterprise*-D is dispatched to find out why the low-tech Bandi built a *very* sophisticated Federation base at Farpoint Station. The mission, however, is almost permanently sidetracked when the crew is put on trial for the crimes of humanity by a superbeing known simply as "Q." (These two episodes were originally aired as a two-hour T.V. movie, although for later airings it was divided into two hour-long segments.)

3. *"The Naked Now."* An intoxicating virus that causes the crew to lose their inhibitions contaminates the *Enterprise*-D crew after it makes contact with a dead science vessel that had been investigating a nearby star's collapse. It is discovered that the virus is similar to the Psi 2000 disease that affected James Kirk's *Enterprise* crew in 2266. An appropriate treatment is developed before the *Enterprise*-D becomes a ghost ship.

4. *"Code of Honor."* A plague on Styris IV sends the *Enterprise*-D crew to Ligon II, the only known source of a vaccine, where Tasha Yar is kidnapped by the planet's chief ruler after being impressed with her beauty and her strength. Yar must combat the ruler's current "First One" wife to satisfy the planet's tradition and obtain the vaccine.

5. *"Haven."* Deanna Troi's mother, Lwaxana, makes her first visit to the *Enterprise* when her late husband's best friends, the Millers, insist on seeing the childhood bonding vows be consummated between Deanna and Wyatt, their son. The wedding is set until a number of plague-ridden Tarellians arrive and Wyatt, a doctor, chooses instead to take up residence with them in hope of finding a cure for their plague. (This episode marked the first appearance of Majel Barrett, a.k.a. Mrs. Gene Roddenberry, and a.k.a. Nurse Chapel of *TREK-classic*.)

6. *"Where No One Has Gone Before."* A warp drive experiment by a supposedly brilliant Starfleet propulsion specialist propels the ship into another galaxy several million light years away. It is discovered that the gains in efficiency are not due to the specialist's modifications, but rather to the efforts of his assistant, known as "the Traveler," who befriends young Wesley Crusher and convinces Picard to grant Crusher the rank of "acting ensign."

7. *"The Last Outpost."* While pursuing first contact with a "new alien threat," the Ferengi, the *Enterprise*-D and the Ferengi vessel suddenly find themselves captured by the last outpost of the long-dead TKon Empire. The away teams must pass an important inquisition by a life form known as "the Portal" before being allowed to continue their journeys.

8. *"Lonely Among Us."* A mysterious energy cloud creature attempts to communicate with the *Enterprise*-D crew after inhabiting Picard's body and altering his personality. After apologizing for the damage it causes, the alien has Picard resign his command and divert the ship back to the cloud, where it beams out as pure energy. (Android Data displays his interest in Sherlock Holmes for the first time.)

9. *"Justice."* The *Enterprise*-D chooses the hedonistic planet of Rubicon III for shore leave, but R&R is cut short when Wesley inadvertently chases a ball into a forbidden zone, drawing the punishment of death. Attempts to negotiate a release for Wesley are unsuccessful and Picard violates the Prime Directive of noninterference by violating local laws to secure young Crusher's release.

10. *"The Battle."* DaiMon Bok of the Ferengi presents Picard with the derelict hulk of his old ship, the *Stargazer*, as part of an elaborate revenge scheme (Bok's son was killed after attacking the *Stargazer*). The supercapitalist Ferengi remove Bok from command for insanity, demonstrated by his giving away the *Stargazer* without remuneration.

11. *"Hide and Q."* The powerful but childlike Q makes a return appearance offering Riker the gift of godlike powers. Riker eventually yields to Q's persuasion and grants his friends their wishes: sight for La Forge, adulthood for Wesley, a Klingon mate for Worf, and humanity for Data. But, as Picard predicted, they all turn down their gifts. Humiliated, Q is called back to the Q Continuum for losing his bet, and Riker's power and the crew's wishes all disappear.

12. *"Too Short a Season."* Wheelchair-bound Admiral Mark Jameson attempts to make amends on Mordan IV, a planet where he traded weapons for hostages, thus sparking forty years of unrelenting civil war. Karnas, the ruling governor, is determined to exact retribution. (This episode marked the first appearance of a Starfleet admiral on *TNG*.)

13. *"The Big Goodbye."* Picard tries a little role-playing in his favorite holodeck program, featuring a 1940s gumshoe named Dixon Hill, but a glitch in the computer causes Picard and his friends to become trapped.

14. *"Datalore."* The *Enterprise*-D returns to Data's "home" planet to find the answer to why 411 of its colonists mysteriously disappeared 26 years earlier, but instead discover Data's twin brother, Lore, a psychotic and ruthless android. Lore turns Data off, assumes his identity, and summons the Crystalline Entity that destroyed the colony years before. Dr. Crusher reactivates Data and the two androids fight each other in a cargo bay until Lore is eventually transported into space. (Lore was originally scripted to be a female android, a non-lookalike love interest for Data.)

15. *"Angel One."* The crew of the *Enterprise*-D attempt to rescue survivors from the crash of a freighter and encounter a planet where males are second-class citizens. The survivors are found, but refuse to leave because they have taken wives from among the outcasts on the planet who don't like the status quo. The governing authorities allow the group to be exiled to a remote part of the planet.

16. *"11001001."* The *Enterprise*-D visits Starbase 74 for an upgrade to the ship's computer facilities by the Bynars, who attempt to hijack the ship in hopes of using its computer to restart their planetary computer system. (The four actors portraying the Bynars were all women dancers whose voice track was mechanically lowered in pitch.)

17. *"Home Soil."* When the *Enterprise*-D is asked to check up on a remote terraforming station on Velara III, the crew discovers that the project threatens the environment for a race of tiny crystalline life forms, a fact that the project administrator tries to hide. The life forms are discovered to be intelligent when they respond by seizing control of the *Enterprise*-D computer.

18. *"When the Bough Breaks."* The *Enterprise*-D discovers a planet completely cloaked from outsiders by a powerful force-shield, but the supposedly friendly inhabitants of the planet kidnap seven *Enterprise* youth, including Wesley, to perpetuate their race. They eventually agree to release the children, and the ship's personnel assist with the dismantling of the planet's shielding system and perform a reseeding of the ozone layer, a move expected to reverse the sterility of the planet's inhabitants.

19. *"Coming of Age."* As Wesley takes his long-awaited entrance exam to Starfleet Academy on Relva VII, Picard's old friend, Admiral Quinn, tests the captain's loyalty before offering to make him commandant of Starfleet Academy. Picard declines, citing his belief that he can best serve Starfleet as captain of the *Enterprise*-D. Although Wesley fails to gain admission to the Academy, his score is sufficient to allow him to resubmit his application the following year.

20. *"Heart of Glory."* The *Enterprise*-D rescues a group of rebellious Klingon warriors who try to persuade Worf to assist them in hijacking the ship. When one of the renegades threatens to destroy the warp intermix chamber in Engineering if he is not given the battle section of the *Enterprise*, Worf makes his choice, killing the Klingon. (Except for Worf, this episode marked the first appearance of Klingons on *TNG*.)

21. *"The Arsenal of Freedom."* When the *Enterprise*-D is sent to the uninhabited planet Minos to investigate the disappearance of the U.S.S. *Drake*, the ship encounters a technically sophisticated weapons system that threatens both an away team on the planet's surface, and the *Enterprise* itself. Further investigation reveals that this ancient automated weapons system was responsible for the destruction of the *Drake*, as well as for the entire Minosian culture.

22. *"Skin of Evil."* On Vagra II, a sadistic living tar pit being named Armus tortures Riker, taunts La Forge and Data, and senselessly murders Tasha Yar (the first regular *Trek* character ever to be permanently killed off, Spock notwithstanding). Worf and Wesley discover that Armus loses his power when provoked, and using that weakness Picard is able to get his crew off the planet. Back on board the *Enterprise*-D, crew members play a recorded hologram of Yar's will and her last thoughts on her friends.

23. *"Symbiosis."* The *Enterprise*-D discovers two planets, one of which is populated by the drug-addicted Ornarans, the other by Brekkians, who supply the narcotic felicium. Dr. Crusher discovers that the Brekkians have kept the unknowing Ornarans addicted for profit for two centuries. She demands to let the Ornarans know, but Picard rules that Prime Directive considerations prohibit Federation intervention. However, he does refuse to repair the Ornarans' disabled freighters, and trade with the Brekkians is now impossible. Realizing they will suffer withdrawal, Picard believes the Ornarans will conquer their addiction. (Though this episode was originally shown before *"Skin of Evil,"* it was filmed after, and Denise Crosby, who played the then-deceased Yar, can be seen breaking out of character and waving goodbye at the end, just before the cargo door closes.)

24. *"We'll Always Have Paris."* The *Enterprise*-D rescues a noted scientist and his wife, Jenice, who turns out to be an old love of Picard's, whom he stood up in Paris to ship out with Starfleet 23 years earlier. The scientist's experiments in nonlinear time are causing disturbances throughout the star system until Data is successful in repairing the temporal anomaly. Thanks to a Parisian holodeck program, Picard gives Jenice a proper goodbye after 23 years.

25. *"Conspiracy."* The threads of the plotline in *"Coming of Age"* are continued in the darkest, most notorious *TNG* episode ever filmed. When Picard orders the *Enterprise*-D back to Earth, Admiral Quinn is discovered to be controlled by a tiny intelligent parasite, whose presence is revealed only by a quill-like protrusion from the host's neck. Meanwhile, Picard and Riker, who have been invited to dinner with two other admirals and Quinn's former aide, Remmick, walk into a trap at Starfleet Command. The two *Enterprise*-D officers kill the admirals and Remmick (who hosted the mother alien) and are successful in thwarting the complete infiltration of Starfleet.

26. *"The Neutral Zone."* The *Enterprise*-D revives a group of cryogenically frozen humans who died in the 20th century while dealing with another challenge: a cloaked Romulan ship, the Federation's first contact with its old enemies in 53 years. A tense exchange reveals the destruction of both Federation and Romulan outposts along the Neutral Zone (which in later episodes would be found to be the work of the as yet unheard of Borg). The two sides agree to exchange information and the three passengers from the 20th century are returned to Earth.

SEASON 2 (FIRST AIRED 1988-1989)

27. *"The Child."* Troi is impregnated in her sleep by a glowing white light and bears a child, the offspring of a mysterious life form attempting to learn more about humans. The resulting child, which gestates and grows at a highly accelerated rate, is found to be a source of eichner radiation, compromising the safety of medical specimens the *Enterprise*-D is transporting. Seeking to avoid harm to the ship and her crew, the entity departs.

28. *"Where Silence Has Lease."* En route to the Morgana Quadrant, the *Enterprise*-D suddenly finds itself trapped in a "hole in space." Finally, the presence behind the void appears: a noncorporeal intelligence known as Nagilum, who is attempting to study human reaction to death. He announces he will use from one-third to one-half of the crew for his experiments and Picard regretfully initiates the autodestruct sequence with Riker. With just two seconds left before autodestruct, Nagilum suddenly frees the ship, saying he has learned enough about the crew's preparation for death.

29. *"Elementary, Dear Data."* Data's initial fascination with Sherlock Holmes (see *"Lonely Among Us"*) goes a step further in this episode when Dr. Pulaski challenges the android to solve a new, computer-generated mystery, but the holodeck simulation causes the character of Dr. Moriarty to take on a life of his own. Holmes' archenemy not only kidnaps Pulaski in an effort to become real, but also threatens to take over the *Enterprise*-D with a Victorian gadget that can control the ship from the holodeck. Picard convinces Moriarty that his efforts are in vain and orders the simulation program saved to avoid the destruction of what is apparently a self-aware sentient intelligence.

30. *"The Outrageous Okona."* Captain Picard mediates disputes between twin planets whose ruling families have filed claims against the roguish, but charming, young Captain Okona. Straleb's ruler accuses him of stealing their sacred jewel, while Atlec's raves that Okona got his daughter pregnant. Okona convinces the Straleb leader's son to admit that the two fearful young people used Okona as go-between for their romance and used the jewel as a nuptial vow. With the two planets now united with the upcoming marriage, Data attempts to understand the concept of humor and unintentionally cracks up the bridge crew. (Okona was played by William O. Campbell, who was originally almost cast as Riker.)

31. *"The Schizoid Man."* Data's "grandfather," a reclusive scientist named Dr. Ira Graves, transfers his consciousness into the android's brain just prior to his death, causing Data to act irrationally. Picard argues for the release of Data's body and the cyberneticist succeeds in recording the sum of his personal knowledge into the *Enterprise*-D computer system. (W. Morgan Sheppard, who portrayed Dr. Graves, later played a Klingon commander in *Star Trek VI: The Undiscovered Country*.)

32. *"Loud as a Whisper."* Riva, a hearing-impaired mediator, whose resume extended to negotiating early Federation–Klingon alliance treaties, is transported by the *Enterprise*-D to Solais V to resolve a bitter planetary conflict. Initial attempts to bring a cease-fire between the two warring parties are unsuccessful, but Troi inspires Riva to stay behind to continue efforts to bring peace to the planet.

33. *"Unnatural Selection."* Answering a distress call from the U.S.S. *Lantree,* the *Enterprise*-D discovers all the ship's personnel to be dead from hyperaccelerated aging. Investigation reveals that the aging disease was caused by genetically engineered children at the Darwin research station on Gagarin IV, where the *Lantree* had visited earlier. These children are found to possess an unusually powerful immune system that actually attacks potential causes for infection, including other human beings. Sadly, the "superchildren" must be isolated forever, and remains of the *Lantree* are destroyed to eliminate risk of further contamination.

34. *"A Matter of Honor."* In a new exchange program, Riker becomes the first Starfleet officer to serve aboard a Klingon ship. When the

Klingon Captain Klag orders an attack on the *Enterprise*-D, Riker uses an emergency transponder given to him by Worf to beam Klag off the bridge, making Riker captain long enough to demand the "surrender" of the *Enterprise*-D to preserve the Klingons' honor. (This episode scored *TNG*'s highest Nielsen ratings to date, and Colm Meaney's character, after seven appearances, finally got a last name—O'Brien.)

35. "The Measure of a Man." Data is put on trial and his rights as a sentient being are questioned when a cyberneticist wants to disassemble the android to make duplicates for Starfleet. Picard argues for Data's rights, and because of insufficient legal staff Riker is forced to act as prosecutor. Starfleet Judge Advocate General Phillipa Louvois subsequently rules that Data is indeed a life form with full civil rights, and that he, like all beings, are created but not owned by their creator. (We learn in this episode that Data's storage capacity is said to be 800 quadrillion bits with a rating of 16 trillion operations per second.)

36. "The Dauphin." A diplomatic mission provides the setting for Wesley's first romance when the *Enterprise*-D must transport young princess Salia to her homeworld, where it is hoped she can bring peace to warring peoples. When Salia is revealed to be a shape-changer, Wesley feels betrayed and deserts her. Finally he overcomes his pride and accepts her apologies. (The term "dauphin" comes from the title given in the 14th and 15th centuries to the heir apparent to the French throne.)

37. "Contagion." Crossing the Neutral Zone to answer a distress call from the U.S.S. *Yomato*, the *Enterprise*-D and a Romulan ship are threatened by an ancient computer software weapon. When the *Yomato* and its crew are destroyed by the weapon, the Romulan warbird *Haakona* is similarly infected by the software weapon, but assistance from the *Enterprise* averts destruction of the Romulan spacecraft as well as an interstellar war. (This episode featured the first-ever name of a Romulan ship in *Trek* history.)

38. "The Royale." After the *Enterprise*-D recovers a chunk of a 21st-century NASA spacecraft, an away team beams down on the nearest inhabitable planet, only to become trapped in a bizarre recreation of a setting from *The Hotel Royale,* a badly written pulp mystery. Their investigation determines the environment to have been created by an unknown alien intelligence in an effort to create a habitat for the survivor of the crashed NASA space vehicle. Unfortunately, the aliens used the trashy novel as their model.

39. *"Time-Squared."* In a time-travel story, Picard is confronted by his own duplicate from six hours in the future, out of phase, disoriented, and drifting in an escape pod in space, the aftermath of the *Enterprise-D*'s destruction in a vast temporal distortion. This distortion and the impending destruction of the *Enterprise-D* is disrupted when Picard orders the ship into the center of the phenomenon.

40. *"The Icarus Factor."* Riker's estranged father visits his son aboard the *Enterprise-D* and Worf becomes increasingly tense because he missed a ritual marking the decade since his Age of Ascension. The Klingon's shipboard friends surprise him by setting up a reenactment of the Klingon spiritual rite in the holodeck, and Riker and his father finally resolve their feelings for each other when they participate in an anbo-jytsu martial art match. Riker stuns the crew when he turns down an offer to command another ship in favor of remaining aboard the *Enterprise*. (John Tesh makes an appearance as a Klingon warrior.)

41. *"Pen Pals."* Data violates the Prime Directive by contacting a young girl on a planet experiencing dangerous volcanic stresses, then comes to her rescue when he learns the planet is about to be destroyed. Meanwhile, the *Enterprise-D* command staff give Wesley a real test of responsibility by allowing him to oversee a team checking into the dangerous geological events on the young girl's planet. Wesley's team reverses the volcanic activity, and Dr. Pulaski "wipes" the young girl's short-term memory, so she remembers nothing of Data or the ship that saved her planet.

42. *"Q Who?"* Q angrily hurls the ship thousands of light years away, where they first make contact with the half-humanoid, half-robotic Borg. The *Enterprise-D* is severely damaged and 18 crew members are killed during this first deadly encounter. Picard admits to a gloating Q that humans can't yet handle all that might exist in deep space and that he needs help before the Borg totally destroy them. Satisfied, Q returns the *Enterprise-D* to their own section in the cosmos and disappears. (The Borg were originally scripted as a race of insects, a concept dropped for budget reasons.)

43. *"Samarian Snare."* While Picard is off to a starbase for replacement of his mechanical heart, Pakleds kidnap La Forge when he beams over to give them a hand with repairs to their ship and demand that the *Enterprise*-D release all of its computer information to them. As the crew considers a show of force to rescue La Forge, Riker learns Picard is near death after surgery. Anxious to reach their captain, the crew members trick the Pakleds with a ruse of their own—"the crimson force field"—and rescue La Forge. Picard awakens in post-op to learn that an amused Pulaski is the doctor who pulled him through his near-death experience.

44. "Up the Long Ladder." The *Enterprise*-D serves as a rescue ship transporting the Bringloidi, a primitive rural farming community, and the Mariposans, an advanced race of clones, when stellar flares threaten their homeworld. The clones, fearful of degeneration due to replicative fading, rejoin the Bringloidi, their original fellow colonists, and breed on a resettlement world. (This episode's original title, *"Send in the Clones,"* actually survived until well after the scripts were printed.)

45. "Manhunt." While picking up the Antedian delegates on a diplomatic mission, Lwaxana Troi returns to the *Enterprise*-D with full ambassadorial status and the intention of finding a new husband. Lwaxana, who is in the midst of the Betazoid "Phase," a mid-life female cycle that enhances a woman's sex drive, unsuccessfully pursues Picard. Before transporting off the ship, Lwaxana shows off her telepathic powers by casually pointing out that the Antedian delegates are carrying undetectable explosives with which to disrupt the peace conference. (Mick Fleetwood shaved off his trademark beard to accommodate the makeup for his role as the Piscean Antedian terrorist.)

46. "The Emissary." Worf's well-disciplined life is interrupted by the first in a long series of complications when his former lover and special Federation emissary, K'Ehleyr, steps back into his life as she is dispatched to the *Enterprise*-D with orders to intercept a Klingon sleeper ship before the crew is automatically revived. (Returning from a 75-year mission of exploration, the Klingons on board would believe that a state of war still exists between the Federation and the Klingon Empire.) During the mission, K'Ehleyr and Worf renew their past romantic relationship, although she declines to take the Klingon oath of marriage.

47. *"Peak Performance."* To prepare for a Borg incursion into Federation space, Picard requests a battle simulation against Riker, who commands the revived derelict U.S.S. *Hathaway*. Riker scores an early hit using the holographic image of a Romulan warbird as a distraction, but the games turn deadly when Picard mistakes an incoming Ferengi ship for another illusion.

48. *"Shades of Gray."* Riker becomes comatose when an invading microbe reaches his brain. Dr. Pulaski discovers that the first officer's romantic dreams promote the microbe's growth and she enlists the aid of Troi to stimulate his negative memories to slow the organism. Pulaski risks the potentially fatal all-out induction of Riker's most primitive emotions, which rack his body with convulsions, but the microbe is finally defeated. (This "clip show" was designed to use scenes from earlier episodes for budget-saving reasons.)

SEASON 3 (FIRST AIRED 1989-1990)

49. *"The Ensigns of Command."* The isolationist Sheliak Corporate breaks its 111-year silence with the Federation to demand that the desert-like Tau Cygna V, ceded to it by treaty, be cleared of a "human infestation" within three days. Data is sent to negotiate with the colonists to evacuate their settlement in the time allowed by the Sheliak, but is unsuccessful until he shows the settlers the danger they face by launching a frightening, though restrained, show of force.

50. *"Evolution."* Wesley's science project goes awry when he allows two medical microbiotic robots to interact and evolve into an intelligent life form, almost dooming the *Enterprise*-D when they breed and escape into the ship's computer core. Data volunteers himself as a face-to-face communication conduit and satisfied with the goodwill shown them, the "nanites" ask for an uninhabited world to colonize. (Although filmed after *"The Ensigns of Command,"* this episode was aired first for the third season, marking the return of Dr. Crusher.)

51. *"Survivors."* Answering a distress call, the *Enterprise*-D arrives to discover a lonely couple, Rishon Uxbridge and her unfriendly husband, Kevin—the sole survivors of an attack by a massive ship that ravaged their planet leaving 11,000 colonists dead. The two say they don't know why they weren't killed and refuse to leave. Kevin finally confesses that he is actually an immortal superalien disguised as a human, and Rishon is nothing more than an image of his wife, a human who died in the original attack.

52. "Who Watches the Watchers?" A cultural observation team on Mintaka III is accidentally discovered by the planet's native humanoids when their holographic duckblind fails. The cultural contamination is worsened when one of the natives receives medical care from *Enterprise*-D personnel and interprets the experience as fulfillment of a prophecy, believing Picard to be their god, the "Overseer." When the captain is shot with an arrow and draws blood, the Mintakans become aware of the outworlders.

53. "The Bonding." A routine mission led by Worf to explore the ruins of a civilization ends in tragedy when a bomb left over from the planet's long war explodes, killing an *Enterprise*-D archaeologist, orphaning her 12-year-old son. A race of noncorporeal life forms from the planet offer to accept responsibility for the child's upbringing, but the offer is declined and Worf adopts the boy into his family through the Klingon *R'uustai* (bonding) ceremony.

54. "Booby Trap." The *Enterprise*-D sets out to explore an ancient alien battle cruiser discovered in an asteroid field and becomes trapped in an energy-draining device. As the ship's reserves are drained of power, La Forge comes across the original plans of the *Galaxy*-class designers. He then re-creates one of them, Dr. Leah Brahms, as an interactive holodeck character to help him find a way to escape the booby trap and feels strangely drawn to her. (Early scripts called for Picard, instead of La Forge, to become involved with the Brahms holodeck re-creation.)

55. "The Enemy." The *Enterprise*-D responds to the distress signal of a crashed Romulan vessel on a planet a half light-year within Federation space. One survivor later dies because of the unavailability of Romulan-compatible ribosomes. A warbird arrives to take custody of the other survivor and Commander Tomalak denies that the incursion into Federation space by the scout ship was a treaty violation, merely a navigational error. (Worf letting a Romulan die by refusing to donate blood met resistance from actor Michael Dorn, but the writing staff convinced him.)

56. "The Price." Troi falls for a soft-spoken, but charismatic, Betazoid negotiator who comes aboard the *Enterprise*-D to bid on an apparently stable wormhole on behalf of a strategic alliance between the

Chrysalians and the Ferengi. During the negotiations, an expedition of shuttle vehicles from the *Enterprise*-D and the Ferengi vessel finds that the wormhole does change endpoints, and they escape just before it collapses, stranding the Ferengi far from home. (Troi's "bed scenes" were the first in the *Trek* series.)

57. *"The Vengeance Factor."* The *Enterprise*-D crew investigate the attack on a Federation science outpost by the Gatherers, a thieving band of renegades who split off from Acamarian society a hundred years earlier. Captain Picard tries to negotiate an end to the raids by healing the split between the two groups. As both sides discuss a mutual alliance, Riker falls for an attractive young woman who is actually a centuries-old weapon of death whose mission is to win revenge on a rival clan. Riker hinders one of her long-planned assassination attempts with three phaser shots and the peace talks continue, but peace is the last thing Riker feels.

58. *"The Defector."* Jarok, a Romulan defector, asks for asylum and brings news of a planned Romulan attack on Federation space. The crew later discover that Jarok is the victim of a ploy by the Romulan government to test his loyalty as well as an attempt to capture the *Enterprise*-D. Jarok, knowing his fate, commits suicide by poison. (At one point during rewrites of the script, Dr. Crusher and Jarok were to become romantically involved.)

59. *"The Hunted."* In this analogy to Vietnam veterans, the *Enterprise*-D captures an escaped convict whose only crime was not fitting in to normal society after having been transformed into the "perfect soldier." His escape is part of an uprising by prisoners to demand rehabilitation for the veterans. Picard cites the Prime Directive in declining Starfleet intervention, but agrees to consider the planet's petition for Federation membership, pending outcome of the prisoners' uprising.

60. *"The High Ground."* While helping victims of a terrorist bomb blast on Rutia IV, Dr. Crusher is taken hostage by a terrorist who hopes to draw the Federation into his struggle for his planet's independence. (Data reveals that the reunification of Ireland on Earth occurs in 2025.)

61. *"Deja Q."* Picard has his hands full trying to keep Bre'el IV's moon from crashing into the planet when Q shows up powerless, expelled from the Q Continuum and on the run from the Calamarain, who have a score to settle with the now defenseless former superbeing. When Q displays a selfless act, another member of the Q Continuum restores Q's powers and he circularizes the Bre'el moon's orbit at a safe altitude. Q rewards Data for trying to protect him from the Calamarain with a one-time belly laugh as a lesson in humanity.

62. "A Matter of Perspective." The holodeck is used to re-create the scene of a crime at a science station when Riker is accused of murder. Riker is finally vindicated after it is discovered that the murdered scientist was secretly trying to develop a new weapon he could sell on his own to the highest bidder.

63. "Yesterday's Enterprise." The *Enterprise*-C, lost with all hands 22 years earlier, emerges from a temporal rift, creating an alternate time line. In this alternate universe, Tasha Yar is still alive, the *Enterprise*-C was not destroyed, and the Klingon–Federation alliance never occurred. Instead, the two governments are engaged in a decades-old conflict that has claimed billions of lives. Only Guinan can detect the changes in history and she persuades Picard to return the *Enterprise*-C through the temporal rift to meet its destiny. Yar, who learns of her senseless death in the "real" time line, volunteers to go back with the doomed ship and Picard grants her permission to do so. (Because of time constraints, a longer, bloodier battle scene, in which Wesley's head was blown off and Data electrocuted, was cut. "To this day I do not understand 'Yesterday's *Enterprise*.' I do not know what the f— happened in that episode," says Jonathan Frakes.)

64. "The Offspring." Data ignites another legal firestorm when he constructs a female "child" and she surpasses even Data's programming. Starfleet requests the transfer of his daughter to the Daystrom Institute for study, but Data declines on grounds that he does not wish to relinquish custody of his child, and Picard defends him citing issues of civil rights. The argument becomes moot, however, when the new android develops emotions that cause a systemwide failure, resulting in death.

65. "Sins of the Father." Worf and Kurn, the younger brother he never knew he had, return to the Klingon homeworld to defend their family name when their late father is branded a traitor behind the Romulan attack at Khitomer that killed thousands. Council leader K'mpec refuses to admit evidence Worf uncovers implicating the father of council member Duras, citing the political fallout of exposing this powerful family. A compromise is reached in which Worf is branded an outcast for his father's alleged acts of cowardice, but is allowed to go free to live for another day when he can clear his family's name.

66. "Allegiance." To study the concept of authority, alien scientists kidnap Picard and replace him with a near-perfect replica aboard the *Enterprise*-D while the real captain is trapped with three humanoids in a bizarre cell like lab rats. The false Picard arouses suspicion, however, when he joins in the officers' weekly poker game, leads the crew in a drinking song, and acts seductively toward Dr. Crusher. The scientific experiment is discontinued when the real Picard and his fellow captives refuse to participate and the captain returns to the *Enterprise*-D just as Riker is leading a "mutiny" against the imposter Picard.

67. "Captain's Holiday." Picard, on vacation at a *Fantasy Island*-type resort planet, becomes involved in archaeological intrigue with a beautiful woman named Vash, a typically unethical Ferengi entrepreneur, and two time-traveling alien criminals in search of the Tox Uthat, a 27th-century artifact hidden in the past and believed to have enormous potential as a superweapon. Although the search for the Uthat is successful, the artifact is destroyed in the *Enterprise*-D transporter to prevent it from falling into the hands of the criminals. (All this because Patrick Stewart wanted his Picard character to experience more "sex and shooting.")

68. "Tin Man." The *Enterprise*-D takes on board a Betazoid first-contact specialist to establish relations with a living spacecraft that is dying of loneliness. A lonely man himself, the Betazoid elects to remain with Tin Man.

69. "Hollow Pursuits." Socially awkward engineer, Reginald Barclay, retreats to the holodeck and in violation of protocol surreptitiously creates simulations of his crewmates, ranging from his seduction of Troi to the casting of La Forge, Data, and Picard as the Three Musketeers. Meanwhile, the *Enterprise*-D's matter–antimatter injectors freeze open, catapulting the ship forward with a sudden burst of warp speed, threatening to self-destruct the starship in minutes. Nervous and shy, Barclay realizes the problem and helps La Forge get the ship back under control just in time. Now filled with self-confidence, Barclay bids farewell to his holodeck fantasies, with the exception of his seduction of Troi.

70. *"The Most Toys."* Data is presumed destroyed when his crew-mates watch his shuttlepod explode while returning from another ship, but in reality the android has been captured by Kivas Fajo, an eccentric and cruel collector who decides he must add Data to his collection. The *Enterprise*-D officers research Fajo's record and guess the truth regarding Data's "death." The starship intercepts Fajo's vessel and rescue Data. The collector himself is placed under arrest for kidnapping and theft, and his prize stolen collection is confiscated. (The role of Kivas Fajo had to be recast when veteran actor and well-known little person David Rappaport committed suicide.)

71. *"Sarek."* Spock's father, renowned Vulcan ambassador Sarek, travels aboard the *Enterprise*-D for a crucial diplomatic mission, but he suffers from an Alzheimer's-like disease that erodes the aged Vulcan's emotional control and causes outbreaks of violence aboard the starship. Picard agrees to a mind-meld in hope of reinforcing the ambassador's emotional control for a brief time. Dr. Crusher braces the captain for the onslaught of Sarek's full life of repressed emotions. The mind-meld is successful and the diplomatic agreement negotiated by Sarek is hailed as the final triumph of his long and distinguished career.

72. *"Ménage à Troi."* During a trade agreements conference on Betazed, Riker, Troi, and her mother, Lwaxana, are abducted by the Ferengi DaiMon Tog, who wants to take advantage of Lwaxana's Betazoid empathic abilities in trade negotiations. She convinces Tog that Picard is her old flame and will use all the firepower of the *Enterprise*-D to gain her freedom. The captain pretends to be her jilted lover and his Shakespearean performance on the bridge is good enough to scare Tog into giving Lwaxana up without an interstellar incident. Acting Ensign Wesley Crusher, who has been accepted to Starfleet Academy, is granted a field promotion to full ensign. (Gene Roddenberry presented Wil Wheaton with his own ensign's bars, which he had earned in the U.S. Navy some 30 years earlier. General Colin Powell, a dedicated *Trek* fan and chairman of the Joint Chiefs of Staff at the time, attended the ceremony on the set.)

73. *"Transfigurations."* Dr. Crusher saves a severely injured humanoid found in the wreckage of an escape pod, but the serene "John Doe" recovers much faster than expected. En route to the departure origin of his vessel, Doe begins evolving into a noncorporeal energy being, and he departs the *Enterprise*-D, returning to his people to tell them of their own coming rebirth.

74. *"The Best of Both Worlds, Part I."* Admiral Hanson assigns Lieutenant Commander Shelby to the starship to assist with tactical preparations for an incursion by the Borg in Federation space. When a Borg ship is sighted to be headed to Sector 001 at high warp speeds, the admiral orders every available Starfleet ship to rendezvous at Wolf 359 to mount a defense. Unfortunately, the Borg beam aboard the *Enterprise*-D, kidnap Picard, and assimilate him into one of their own. The episode and the season end with Riker ordering the *Enterprise*-D to fire on Picard and the Borg immediately or lose their only chance to destroy the invaders before they reach Earth.

SEASON 4 (FIRST AIRED 1990–1991)

75. *"The Best of Both Worlds, Part II."* And now for the exciting conclusion. The *Enterprise* is unsuccessful in stopping the Borg, who continue at high speed toward Earth. An armada of 40 Federation and Klingon starships is nearly annihilated and 11,000 personnel (including Admiral Hanson) are killed at Wolf 359. It is believed that the Borg tapped into Picard's knowledge of Starfleet defenses and human nature. Captain Riker, inspired by Guinan's advice to turn the tables on the Borg by using their own hostage, designs a daring plan with the help of Commander Shelby, now serving as his first officer. Worf and Data successfully rescue Picard and, by studying his Borg modifications, are able to trigger a self-destruct command on the Borg vessel. A shaken and devastated Picard begins rehabilitation.

76. *"Suddenly Human."* The *Enterprise*-D discovers a failed Talarian craft adrift. Among the survivors is a young human, Jeremiah Rossa, the grandson of Starfleet Admiral Connaught Rossa. The boy was kidnapped a decade earlier when his parents were killed and his colony attacked by Talarians. The Talarian captain who adopted and raised him after his own son was killed threatens war when Admiral Rossa requests that the boy be brought back home. Picard rules the child's interests would be better served by returning him to his adoptive family, since he now considers the Talarian captain to be his father.

77. *"Brothers."* Data isolates himself on the *Enterprise*-D bridge and changes course when he and his brother, Lore, are unknowingly "called home" to a secret location by their reclusive creator, Dr. Noonien Soong. The scientist has at last perfected an "emotions" circuit chip for Data, but Lore disables him and tricks Soong into installing the chip in him, then goes on a rampage, fatally injuring his creator. Lore escapes and Dr. Soong dies after an *Enterprise*-D away team retrieves Data, leaving him to wonder how his life would have changed with the emotion chip.

78. *"Family."* In the only episode in *Trek* history with no scenes on the bridge, Picard returns to his hometown of Labarre, France, to heal his emotional wounds from the Borg encounter and visit his brother, sister-in-law, and nephew. There, Picard declines an offer to serve as director of the Atlantis Project, choosing to remain with Starfleet. Meanwhile, Worf's adoptive parents visit their son aboard the *Enterprise*-D, and Wesley Crusher views a holographic message from his late father, recorded when Wesley was only ten weeks old. (This show, the second aired for the season, was actually the fourth produced for that year, but was a direct continuation of *The Best of Both Worlds, Parts I and II*.)

79. *"Remember Me."* When Wesley's warp physics experiment goes awry, it seems that his mother is trapped in her own private universe wherein everybody is slowly beginning to disappear, but actually it is Beverly who has disappeared for several hours inside a static warp bubble. She is rescued by Wesley, with the assistance of the Traveler, just as her alternate universe collapses.

80. *"Legacy."* The *Enterprise*-D attempts to rescue two Federation engineers lost on the late Tasha Yar's homeworld, where the crew is surprised to discover her sister involved with one of the two warring factions. The two engineers are discovered to have been captured by the other rival gang in control of the colony and with Ishara Yar's assistance the rescue mission is successful. When Data learns she is actually trying to disable her enemy's power plants and cripple their defense, he dares her to shoot him. She is about to do so when Riker stuns her, giving the android first-hand experience with betrayal.

81. *"Reunion."* In a continuation of Worf's story in *"Sins of the Father,"* K'mpec, the Klingon leader, has been poisoned by one of his enemies and appoints Picard to mediate the rite of succession. Klingon emissary K'Ehleyr, Worf's former lover, comes aboard the *Enterprise*-D with a child, Alexander, his son from their encounter during her previous visit to the starship. After K'mpec dies, Picard hears claims to the leadership by council member Duras and political newcomer Gowron, but when K'Ehleyr uncovers suppressed evidence that Duras' father had betrayed the Klingons at the Khitomer Massacre, Duras murders her. Claiming the right of vengeance, Worf kills Duras and is officially reprimanded by Picard. Gowron is subsequently installed as Leader of the Klingon High Council.

82. "Future Imperfect." After having passed out during an away team mission, Riker awakens with no memory of the past sixteen years, including the facts that he is captain of the *Enterprise*-D and a widower with a teenage son. Finally, the boy reveals that he is an alien who captured Riker and devised the elaborate memory-loss scenario to offset his loneliness while he was in exile. He eventually agrees to release Riker, and the *Enterprise*-D officer invites him to return with him to the starship.

83. "Final Mission." On a last mission with Picard before he heads off to Starfleet Academy, Wesley and the captain crash-land a mining shuttle on a desert moon. Wesley figures out a way to keep Picard alive until the *Enterprise*-D finally rescues them.

84. "The Loss." Troi's empathic powers disappear and despite the protests of her friends that she still has her professional training, she resigns as ship's counselor. Meanwhile, Data and Riker realize that a warp drive malfunction is being caused by a school of two-dimensional life forms returning to a nearby cosmic string fragment. Troi's empathic powers come rushing back and she realizes that the strength of the two-dimensional creatures' feelings completely overwhelmed her powers. She returns to her post as ship's counselor with renewed spirit. (Kim Braden, who guest-stars as Ensign Janet Brooks, later played Picard's Nexus "wife" in the *Generations* movie.)

85. "Data's Day." Keiko and O'Brien get cold feet and then get married; Dr. Crusher tries to teach Data how to dance; a Vulcan ambassador is revealed to be a Romulan spy in Federation territory. A typical day of life aboard the *Enterprise*-D is seen through the eyes of Data. (This is the show's first glimpse of the ship's barber shop and of people shopping at the replication center.)

86. "The Wounded." In an episode introducing new adversaries, a renegade Federation starship commanded by Captain Maxwell is destroying Cardassian ships, threatening the fragile peace between the Federation and the Cardassian Union, because he believes that the Cardassians are about to launch an unprovoked military strike against the Federation. After Maxwell is relieved of command and taken into custody, Picard informs the Cardassians that Starfleet is aware that Maxwell's charges of military preparations are grounded in truth.

87. "Devil's Due." An emergency transmission from a science station sends the *Enterprise*-D to Ventax II, where the crew discover the planet's inhabitants are about to hand over their peaceful world to Ardra, a devilish supernatural being whom they made a pact with a thousand years earlier. After La Forge locates her cloaked orbiting ship and Picard taps into its power systems, the captain is able to convince the local authorities that Ardra is not the legendary, shape-changing devil, just another con artist.

88. "Clues." As the *Enterprise*-D is on its way to investigate a mysterious planet, the ship falls through a suddenly appearing wormhole, knocking the crew unconscious for apparently thirty seconds. Clues such as a botany experiment recording 24 hours' growth and the ship's chronometer having been tampered with provide evidence that the crew was out much longer—an entire day, in fact. Data reveals that the ultra-reclusive Paxans routinely stun intruders to their planet and send their ships on their way, but Data's immunity as an android foiled their plan. The Paxans demanded that the *Enterprise*-D be destroyed. However, Captain Picard successfully won an agreement to erase all human and computer memories of the incident, with Data ordered to never reveal the encounter. During the second visit, Picard assures the Paxans that the minor problems would be corrected so that their existence will remain confidential.

89. "First Contact." On a first-contact reconnaissance mission on Malcoria III in native disguise, Riker is captured by the paranoid inhabitants of the planet and placed in a hospital where they soon discover his true identity. Local authorities are alerted of the Federation presence, and plead with Picard that contact with the outworlders will cause serious cultural shock at this stage in the planet's social development. Picard agrees and the planet's ruler quietly puts his world's fledging space program on hold, while granting his science minister's wish to leave with the *Enterprise*-D. (We learn in this episode that a botched first-contact mission was the reason behind decades of Klin-gon–Federation hostilities.)

90. "Galaxy's Child." La Forge finally meets the *real* Leah Brahms (whose holodeck image he once fell in love with) when she comes aboard the *Enterprise*-D for an inspection tour. Meanwhile, an object is discovered orbiting Alpha Omicron VII, and is determined to be a spaceborne life form. When the creature is accidentally killed, Worf and Dr. Crusher must perform a phaser-fired "caesarean section" to deliver the dead life form's unborn offspring. The child believes the *Enterprise*-D is its mother and insists on using the ship as a source of nurturing, drawing power from the ship's engines, until La Forge and Dr. Brahms devise a sour harmonic frequency, which weans the baby away just in time.

91. "Night Terrors." When the *Enterprise*-D finds the missing U.S.S. *Brattain* adrift in space and 34 of its crew having died under violent but unexplained circumstances, the ship becomes trapped in a Tyken's Rift, a spatial rupture causing failure of the ship's power systems. Cooperation with an unknown alien ship trapped on the other side of the rift permits the two ships to escape. Proximity to the alien intelligence is found to be responsible for severe dream deprivation of all *Enterprise*-D personnel, a side effect of the aliens' attempt to communicate with them. The dream deprivation is believed to have been the cause of the insanity that drove the crew of the *Brattain* to die so violently.

92. "Identity Crisis." La Forge and his former shipmate from the U.S.S. *Victory,* Susanna Leitjen, are compelled to return to Tarchannen III, a planet they visited five years earlier, where they start to mutate into another species. Dr. Crusher finds a way to remove the parasite causing the mutation from Leitjen and La Forge before their transformation is completed.

93. "Nth Degree." When the *Enterprise*-D is sent to repair the malfunctioning Argus Subspace Telescope Array, an energy surge from an alien probe turns milquetoast Reginald Barclay into the most advanced human ever seen. His expanded intellectual capacities are of significant value in saving the Argus Array from a series of critical malfunctions, and later allows Barclay to modify the *Enterprise*-D warp drive system so that he can pilot the starship some 30,000 light-years toward the galactic core. A previously unknown race called the Cytherians use the technique to bring visitors to their home system for cultural exchange. Barclay is restored to normal as Picard agrees to be scanned in exchange for information about the Cytherians, who then return the *Enterprise*-D to Federation space.

94. "Qpid." Q transports Picard, his archaeologist lover Vash, and the *Enterprise*-D senior officers to Sherwood Forest, where Q challenges the captain to risk his crew's lives for the woman he loves. The Merry Men come to their captain's aid and Picard, a skilled fencer, skewers Sir Guy, Vash's captor, and rescues her (claiming he'd do the same for anyone). Back on the *Enterprise*-D, Vash announces she plans to travel with Q through the galaxy.

95. "The Drumhead." An explosion in the *Enterprise*-D's dilithium chamber initiates a search by Admiral Norah Satie for evidence of a subversive conspiracy. Picard openly challenges her, which leads her to question him as a possible traitor. When she begins a groundless tirade, her rage shocks everyone in attendance and Admiral Henry rules her investigation unconstitutional, and, in the absence of further evidence, orders it discontinued.

96. "Half a Life." Lwaxana Troi falls in love with a scientist who must decide between saving his world's dying star or conforming to his society's expectation of "Resolution," ritual suicide at age 60. Enraged, Lwaxana asks him why doom his entire world by committing suicide when his research is so close to success. Eventually he agrees with her and seeks asylum aboard the *Enterprise*-D. Threatening a diplomatic incident, the scientist reverses his decision and Lwaxana accompanies him home to join in the celebration of the Resolution.

97. "The Host." In the first episode featuring the "joined species" Trill, Dr. Crusher falls in love with Ambassador Odan. When Odan is fatally injured, Dr. Crusher learns that the actual intelligence known as Odan is a parasitic being occupying a humanoid host's body. Riker volunteers to serve as a temporary host until a new permanent host body can arrive. Ambassador Odan, now using Riker as a host, successfully mediates the diplomatic talks. When the new Trill's host body arrives and turns out to be a woman, Dr. Crusher admits to Odan that she can't take the constant changes even though she loves him. (Writer/producer Brannon Braga calls this "the best love story we ever did.")

98. *"The Mind's Eye."* La Forge is kidnapped and undergoes mental reprogramming by the Romulans who intend to use the engineer in a plot to split the Federation–Klingon alliance. Klingon emissary Kell meets with Kriosian governor Vagh to discuss allegations of Starfleet aid to rebels fighting for independence on his colony. When La Forge tries to assassinate Governor Vagh, it is revealed that Kell is a Romulan sympathizer manipulating La Forge's implanted programming.

99. *"In Theory."* Data continues his quest to understand humanity by developing a romantic relationship with security officer Jenna D'-Sora. After creating a special program to provide a guide to love, he and Jenna have their ups and downs, but she finally realizes that though he can approximate emotion he will never really feel it. Data agrees and erases his special love program. (This is the first episode directed by Patrick Stewart.)

100. *"Redemption, Part I."* In a direct continuation of *"Sins of the Father"* and *"Reunion,"* Worf resigns his Starfleet commission to become involved in a Klingon civil war between the powerful Duras family and forces loyal to Klingon leader Gowron, who has restored Worf's honor. The Duras sisters, B'Etor and Lursa, meet with Romulan allies, including a woman who looks just like the dead Tasha Yar, to assure Duras' son ascends to the leadership of the Klingon High Council.

SEASON 5 (AIRED 1991–1992)

101. *"Redemption, Part II."* Worf fights at Gowron's side in the Klingon civil war but begins to suspect Romulan involvement in the conflict. Starfleet authorizes Picard to lead a nonaggressive armada of 23 starships along the Neutral Zone in an attempt to blockade a Romulan convoy. The Romulan commander identifies herself as Sela, the daughter of Tasha Yar, claiming that the former *Enterprise*-D security officer had been sent into the past and had been captured after the destruction of the *Enterprise*-C some 24 years earlier and Sela was the product of a relationship between Yar and a Romulan general. Exposed, the Romulans withdraw, leaving the Duras family challenge to leadership of the High Council a failure. Captain Picard accepts Worf's request for reinstatement as a Starfleet officer.

102. *"Darmok."* Eight attempts by the *Enterprise*-D to establish communication with the Tamarians have been unsuccessful, even with the use of the universal translator. The Tamarians beam Picard and their own captain Dathon to a rugged planet nearby. The abduction, at first believed to be a hostile act, is later learned to be an attempt at communication by Captain Dathon; Tamarian language consists of metaphors derived from abstract narrative images based on mythology.

103. "Ensign Ro." After Bajoran extremists attack a Federation colony, convicted criminal and Starfleet officer Ensign Ro Laren, is released from prison and joins the crew of the *Enterprise*-D in exchange for her participation in a covert mission against her fellow Bajorans. After Ro assists in locating him, the Bajoran leader Orta meets with Picard and presents evidence that the attack on the Federation colony was not the work of his terrorist cell, but rather the Cardassians. Picard offers Ro an opportunity to remain in Starfleet as flight controller (conn) of the *Enterprise*-D, and she accepts. (Although it was not planned at the time it was scripted, this episode would lay much of the foundation for the forthcoming *Deep Space 9* series.)

104. "Silicon Avatar." Xenologist Dr. Kila Marr, a scientist whose son was killed by the Crystalline Entity on Omicron Theta, comes aboard the *Enterprise*-D to assist with a Starfleet directive to locate the alien life form and establish communication. Dr. Marr is cold to Data, whom she blames for her son's death because his brother, Lore, lured the entity to Omicron Theta, until she learns he has the stored thoughts of the colonists, including her son. The *Enterprise*-D baits the Entity with graviton pulse emissions, and the ship and the creature appear to be communicating until Dr. Marr covertly modifies the frequency of the pulse and shatters the entity.

105. "Disaster." As Picard is playing host to three young winners of an *Enterprise*-D science contest, damage from collision with a quantum filament causes an almost complete shutdown of the ship's systems, trapping the captain in the turbolift and placing Troi in command on the bridge. O'Brien and Ro are successful in assisting engineering crew members in averting an explosion despite a major power failure in the engineering section. Meanwhile, Keiko gives birth to a baby girl in Ten-Forward with the assistance of Worf.

106. "The Game." During his first visit to the *Enterprise*-D since leaving for Starfleet Academy, Wesley falls for Robin Lefler, a young engineering ensign, while the rest of the crew falls for a highly addictive video game which rewards its players with a pleasurable sensation.

The devices employ sophisticated neural-optical conditioning techniques to control the behavior of the ship's crew and later are discovered to be part of a Ktarian attempt to conquer Starfleet one starship at a time. Data, who is not affected by the device, and Wesley and Robin, who fake addiction, are successful in developing a neuro-optic burst device whose flash reverses the game's effects. (Robin was played by Ashley Judd, the youngest sister of country and western singer Wynnona Judd.)

107 and 108. "Unification, Parts I and II." Starfleet is shocked to learn that legendary Vulcan scientist and ambassador Spock appears to have defected to the Romulan Empire. Picard and Data secure a cloaked Klingon ship from Gowron and, disguised as Romulans, journey to Romulus to seek out Spock's contact, Senator Pardek. En route, Picard receives word that Sarek has died from a degenerative brain disorder. The captain attempts to fulfill his friend Sarek's request by telling Spock of his late father's love. Spock reveals that he is undertaking an unauthorized mission to pursue the reunification of the Vulcan and Romulan peoples. Later, Spock and Picard learn that the support of some members of the Romulan government, including Senator Pardek, has been part of a Romulan attempt by Commander Sela to conquer Vulcan. Spock elects to remain on Romulus to work in the underground, and the Vulcan bids his father a poignant "good-bye" by sharing Sarek's previous mind-meld with Picard.

109. "A Matter of Time." While trying to reverse the nuclear winter–type effects caused by a crashed asteroid on Penthara IV, the *Enterprise*-D is visited by a time-traveling professor from 26th-century Earth. While investigating reports of numerous small items discovered missing on the ship, Data searches the professor's time-travel pod and discovers that he is nothing more than a petty thief from the past. He confesses that his goal was to return to the 22nd century with 24th-century technology. The "professor" is trapped in the 24th century, however, when his pod's timed return mechanism sends it back in time without him.

110. "New Ground." Worf receives an unexpected visit from his foster mother, Helena, and his son, Alexander, who has had difficulty adjusting to life on Earth. When Alexander continues to act disruptive aboard the ship, Worf threatens to send him to a rigorous Klingon school, but when a fire breaks out aboard the ship and Worf and Riker must save Alexander, the Klingon officer realizes how much he would miss his son if he were sent away. Alexander remains aboard the *Enterprise*-D with his father.

111. *"Hero Worship."* A young boy whose parents were killed in a terrible disaster on the U.S.S. *Vico* copes with the grief by deciding he is an android, just like his rescuer, Data. When the *Enterprise*-D is buffeted by gravitational distortions within a black cluster, it is determined that a similar phenomenon caused the destruction of the *Vico* and the boy's recollection of the ship's final moments aid Data in devising a means to avoid a similar disaster for the *Enterprise*-D.

112. *"Violations."* The *Enterprise*-D transports three Ullians, members of a race of telepathic historians, while a series of unexplained neurological disorders is reported by several members of the ship's crew, including Troi, who lapses into a coma. One of the Ullians is found to be responsible for both the disorders and a number of hideous mind-probing rapes on other planets. He is returned to Ullian authorities for prosecution and rehabilitation.

113. *"The Masterpiece Society."* While monitoring the progress of a threatening neutron star's core fragment, the *Enterprise*-D discovers a previously unknown colony composed of perfectly planned and genetically engineered humans who refuse to relocate. The starship successfully utilizes its tractor beam to partially deflect the core fragment, and thus reduce its seismic effect on the planet. Colony authorities, however, strongly disapprove of the decision of 23 colonists to leave their home and accept passage aboard the *Enterprise*-D, causing irreparable damage to the fragile colony.

114. *"Conundrum."* After being scanned by an alien ship, the *Enterprise*-D crew realize both their own and the computer's memories have been selectively erased, so they have no way of knowing if Starfleet's orders to attack a Lysian space station are genuine. They eventually uncover the Sartaaran plot against the Lysians and Dr. Crusher finds a way to restore the crew's short-term memories.

115. *"Power Play."* When Troi, Data, and O'Brien investigate an old-style distress call on an uninhabited planet, their minds become possessed by alien criminals condemned to a penal colony some 500 years earlier who plan to use the *Enterprise*-D in an escape attempt. Taken hostage by the three, Picard accompanies them to a cargo bay where the rest of the criminal entities are beamed up. The captain then threatens to open the outer cargo bay doors and kill all of them, including himself, rather than allow the entities to possess his crew. The criminals back off and return to their prison on the planet below. (This episode has "no socially redeeming value," said screenwriter Brannon Braga, "but it sure is action-packed!")

116. "Ethics." When Worf is left paralyzed from the waist down after an accident, the Klingon asks Riker to help him commit ritual suicide while Dr. Crusher and a neurospecialist clash over a proposal to use an experimental genetonic replication to replace Worf's spine. The Klingon agrees to the life-threatening spine replication procedure proposed by the neurospecialist. Worf dies in surgery, but the redundant Klingon physiology jump-starts the body like a back-up system and mourning turns to joy. (We discover in this episode that Worf has 23 ribs, 2 livers, and an 8-chambered heart.)

117. "The Outcast." The J'naii are an androgynous race who consider gender orientation a crime. Riker falls in love with Soren, a J'naii who reveals she has female tendencies. The government accuses Soren of aberrant behavior, alleging a socially unacceptable sexual relationship with Riker. Picard cites the Prime Directive and refuses to intervene with the J'naii judiciary. Despite the captain's warnings that a rash act could ruin his career, Riker tries to free her with Worf's help, but it is too late; Soren has been found guilty of forbidden behavior and is rehabilitated with "therapy."

118. "Cause and Effect." The *Enterprise*-D is trapped for 17 days in a temporal causality loop in which it is destroyed over and over again by colliding with the U.S.S. *Bozeman*, a 90-year resident of that same disruption in the space–time continuum. The disaster between the two ships is averted on the final cycle as the result of a message transmitted via a dekyon field to Data by the crew on its next-to-last cycle.

119. "The First Duty." Just prior to arrival at Starfleet Academy, where Picard is scheduled to deliver the commencement address, he is notified of an accident involving Wesley Crusher's flight squadron. Initial testimony by members of the Nova Squadron suggests the fatal accident was due to pilot error, but a statement by Cadet Crusher reveals the cause of the crash to be an unauthorized Kolvoord Starburst, a spectacular exhibition of stunt flying banned for over a century. Squadron leader Nick Locarno is expelled, while Wesley and the other two Nova Squadron members are reprimanded and ordered to repeat the past academic year.

120. *"Cost of Living."* After the *Enterprise*-D helps destroy a rogue asteroid, Lwaxana Troi beams aboard the ship and announces that she is getting married to a planetary dignitary she has never met. Meanwhile, the crew discovers that parasitic life forms that had lived in the asteroid have settled on the *Enterprise* hull, resulting in significant damage to the ship's structure and systems. Data barely gets the ship back to the creatures' home and beams them away. With disaster averted, Lwaxana proceeds with a traditional Betazed wedding—in the nude! Counselor Troi is delighted when her mother's stuffy and old fiancé runs away.

121. *"The Perfect Mate."* A sexually empathic "metamorph," is chosen by a Kriosian ambassador to be a peace offering to the ruler of Valt Minor to end years of war between the two worlds. She has been prepared from birth to bond with Valt's leader, but falls in love with Picard. However, they decide duty and honor must come before their desires, and the bonding between the woman and the Valt leader occurs with a visibly shaken Captain Picard participating in the ceremony.

122. *"Imaginary Friend."* Troi tries to assure an officer that the imaginary friend created by his young daughter is a normal reaction to constant changes in her childhood, but her playmate is actually a previously undiscovered life form materialized in human form. It is eventually discovered that the entity is indigenous to a nebula the *Enterprise*-D passed through and is attempting to evaluate the potential of the ship as an energy source. The spaceborne entity, which has become friends with the little girl, departs the starship when made aware of its negative impact on the child.

123. *"I, Borg."* The *Enterprise*-D rescues an injured young Borg from a crashed scout ship. When the crew begins studying his biochip implants to yield information on the Borg's collective intelligence, the Borg, known as "Third of Five," begins to exhibit individual behavior characteristics. Although an invasive programming sequence believed capable of destroying the entire Borg race is developed, Picard deems it unethical to use a sentient being as a weapon of destruction and orders the Borg, renamed Hugh, to be returned to the crash site. La Forge, observing Hugh's rescue by a second Borg scout craft, later reports his belief that the young Borg retained his individuality.

124. *"The Next Phase."* Ro and La Forge apparently die in a transporter accident, but in reality have merely been made invisible by a new Romulan cloaking device. Finally they manage to reappear during the ship's memorial service for its two supposedly "fallen comrades."

125. *"The Inner Light."* An unassuming probe transmits a nucleonic beam that manages to penetrate the *Enterprise*-D's shields and leaves Picard comatose on the bridge. He awakens on the drought-stricken planet Kataan, where days become years, and the aging Picard watches his children grow, his wife and friend die, and his planet dry up. Finally, Picard regains consciousness on the bridge and reports having experienced a lifetime of memories from a native of Kaatan. The purpose of the probe was to transmit these memories from that long-dead civilization and thus reveal their story to some future historian.

126. *"Time's Arrow, Part I."* In the cliff-hanger finale to the fifth season, the *Enterprise*-D crew is amazed to find Data's head among ancient artifacts in excavations under San Francisco. Clues point to Devidia II as the source of the relics. Data is accidentally entrapped in an opening time vortex and transported back to Earth in the 19th century. An away team follows Data into the past in an effort to prevent the Devidia II life forms from invading Earth and Data's destruction.

SEASON 6 (FIRST AIRED 1992–1993)

127. *"Time's Arrow, Part II."* Picard and his senior officers find Data, but attract the attention of the curious Mark Twain, who is convinced that Guinan and Data are themselves an alien threat and follows them to the cavern where the android's head will be found in the future. There, the blast of the "time door" opening decapitates Data. Seemingly trapped in the 19th century, Picard keys a crude escape message in Data's head that he hopes will be found in the 24th century. Back aboard the *Enterprise,* La Forge reconnects Data's "old" head and reads Picard's message. The "time door" is opened, and a reassured

Mark Twain volunteers to go back to the 19th century so that Picard can come forward into the future. The aliens' doorway to the past is destroyed.

128. *"Realm of Fear."* The ever-nervous Reginald Barclay, who is scared to death of the transporter, is attacked by creatures living in the transporter beam, but keeps the story to himself. During another beaming, Barclay grabs one of the creatures, which turns out to be one of the crewmen of the lost U.S.S. *Yosemite.* Barclay is hailed as a hero when others are rematerialized too. (Screenwriter Brannon Braga penned this script out of his own fear of flying.)

129. *"Man of the People."* After the *Enterprise*-D assumes the transport of a famous Federation mediator to the site of an interplanetary war's peace talks, Troi begins hyper-aging following the death of the ambassador's aged mother. It is discovered that he has been "dumping" his negative thoughts in her in order to keep his mind clear for negotiating. The dead woman was not his "mother," just his previous victim. Picard waits until near the end of the peace talks before faking Troi's death. The broken "link" with Troi leaves the ambassador to die the same kind of agonizing death as did all of his victims.

130. *"Relics."* The *Enterprise*-D discovers an immense artificially constructed habitat around a star and the legendary Starfleet engineer Montgomery "Scotty" Scott kept alive for 75 years in a transporter beam after his transport ship crashed. But depression sets in for the old "miracle worker" when La Forge makes him feel he is "in the way." When the *Enterprise* is drawn inside the artificial sphere's tractor beam, it is Scotty who figures out a way to open the sphere's doors long enough for the starship to escape. Picard "loans" Scotty a shuttle as gratitude for saving the ship and its crew, and the legendary engineer departs for worlds unknown. (Scotty was the Kirk-era character chosen for this episode because the producers felt he had the most "fun" quotient.)

131. *"Schisms."* Riker reports extreme exhaustion, Worf and La Forge experience sharp pains and anxiety, and even Data apparently dozes off for 90 minutes he can't account for when aliens from another time continuum kidnap the officers during their sleep. Armed with a stimulant and a homing signal, Riker volunteers to track where the crew is being taken. He awakens in a lab to find insect-like aliens battling to close a "rupture" between universes that the *Enterprise* crew has tracked and now opened on their own. Riker grabs the last missing crewmate and escapes before the rupture closes.

132. "True Q." A young student intern is stunned when she realizes during her tenure aboard the *Enterprise*-D that the powers she has been trying to ignore mean she is actually a member of the Q Continuum. Q himself turns up to take the girl back with him, and admits that her parents were executed as renegades from the Continuum and the same fate might befall their daughter. She decides to remain with humans and pledges not to use her powers, but her intervention in a planetary disaster helps her realize that her place is in the Q Continuum.

133. "Rascals." After they are beamed off an endangered shuttle through a mysterious energy field, Picard, Guinan, Keiko, and Ro are transformed into the physical equivalents of 12-year-old children. When renegade Ferengi in Klingon warships disable the *Enterprise*-D and declare ownership, the "young" *Enterprise* officers gain control of the ship through the school's computer. O'Brien and Dr. Crusher discover how to use the transporter to reverse the masked effect on the genetic code of the "youngsters."

134. "A Fistful of Datas." Worf and Alexander become trapped in a malfunctioning holodeck program of the "ancient West," wherein the fantasy won't stop, the weapons failsafe won't work, and the "bad guys" all look like Data and have his android abilities. La Forge discovers that Data's memory has been crossed with the ship's holodeck database. Even though the program turned out to be too real, Worf promises Alexander that they will return once again to the Western days of yesteryear. (Originally this Patrick Stewart-directed episode was to be titled "The Good, the Bad and the Klingon.")

135. "The Quality of Life." Data threatens his Starfleet career when he refuses to send exocomps to do hazardous tasks because he believes the problem-solving computer tools to be sentient life forms. When Picard and La Forge are trapped aboard an orbiting mining station, Data locks out the transporters and refuses orders to use the exocomps as slaves to rescue them until Riker requests their help.

136 and 137. "Chain of Command, Parts I and II." Picard, Crusher, and Worf are reassigned for a secret search-and-destroy mission on Celtris III, where Starfleet fears the Cardassians are developing a metagenic weapon. Captain Edward Jellico takes command of the

Enterprise-D and must negotiate with the Cardassians during a time of cold war tensions. On Celtris III, the covert mission team realizes the virus story is nothing more than a hoax. Worf and Crusher escape, but Picard is captured in the ambush. Although Picard is able to resist his interrogator, he tells Troi he was so brutalized by the experience that he would have done anything had he not been freed. (This episode introduced the news of the Cardassians' Bajoran withdrawal to set up the events of *Deep Space 9*'s pilot episode.)

138. *"Ship in a Bottle."* Continuing the story of Professor Moriarty begun in *"Elementary, Dear Data"* from the second season, Barclay comes across the stored holodeck file of Holmes' fictional nemesis, who traps the crew in a Holodeck simulation and takes control of the ship's computer. The officers outwit Moriarty by creating their own false reality and have the professor and his paramour, Countess Barthalomew, "beamed" into it. Believing they have been given a shuttlecraft, Moriarty returns the ship's controls to Picard. In reality, the two lovers are allowed to live and interact in countless programs within a protected file.

139. *"Aquiel."* La Forge falls in love with Lieutenant Aquiel Uhnari, a technician on a subspace two-man relay station, even though the woman is strongly suspected in the disappearance of her crewmate. Aquiel is cleared when a coalescent creature, which had taken the form of her dog, tries to kill La Forge and take his form. (This episode was jokingly referred to by producers and writers as *"Murder, My Pet."*)

140. *"Face of the Enemy."* Troi is kidnapped from a conference and awakens to find herself aboard a Romulan warbird, disguised as a Tal Shiar special intelligence officer in a plot to smuggle out three high-level defectors to the Federation. Meanwhile, the *Enterprise*-D picks up a Romulan defector, whose message from Spock and the underground leads them to Troi's cloaked warbird. She beams over the three high-level defectors and herself just as the Romulan commander discovers the plan.

141. *"Tapestry."* After Picard is severely wounded by terrorists, he awakens in a stark white environment to find Q announcing that the captain is in the Afterlife and that Q will allow him to relive his regretful younger years. Determined to change history, Picard is returned to the fight where, as a cocky but green ensign, he was stabbed through the heart in a brawl. But avoiding the fight changes his life for the worse. Eventually, Picard regains consciousness in sickbay, actually grateful to his old nemesis Q for "opening his eyes."

142 and 143. "Birthright, Parts I and II." While the *Enterprise*-D is docked at *Deep Space 9*, Worf is shocked to hear news that his father may have survived the attack at Khitomer and may still be held in a secret Romulan prison camp. Worf locates the camp, but the Klingons there have raised a new generation and don't consider themselves prisoners. When Worf begins telling the young Klingons about their heritage, the Romulan commandant over the camp decides to kill him rather than lose the historic peace of the village. But the youths and the elders stand with the proud Klingon. (Part I was the first crossover episode using elements from both *TNG* and *Deep Space 9*.)

144. "Starship Mine." When the *Enterprise*-D is shut down and its crew evacuated for a routine but deadly baryon purging sweep, Picard plays a cat-and-a-mouse game with six thieves who plan to drain off the warp engine's toxic waste for use as a weapon. (Tim Russ, who played one of the thieves, later portrayed a 1701-B crewman in the *Generations* film and, of course, the Vulcan Tuvok on the *Voyager* series.)

145. "Lessons." Picard becomes romantically involved with the chief of stellar sciences, but their relationship is threatened when he finds himself ordering her to her possible death on a firestorm-ravaged Federation outpost. When she and her crew are presumed dead, Picard finds it difficult to control his emotions. After she is discovered to be alive, the two realize they cannot remain lovers while working as commander and subordinate, and she reluctantly transfers off the *Enterprise*-D.

146. "The Chase." Picard's old archaeology professor, Dr. Galen, sends the captain on a quest to solve a four-billion-year-old mystery, based on clues from prehistoric DNA. When the last DNA clue is decoded with the assistance of Cardassians and Klingons, they trek to the specified location (only to be "welcomed" by Romulans) and discover a message from a long-dead race that had seeded the DNA across the various races' home planets, creating a common genetic heritage among the numerous humanoid species in the galaxy. (This show marked the first time that *Trek*'s humanoids, Klingons, Romulans and Cardassians appeared together in the same scene, much less the same episode.)

147. *"Frame of Mind."* Riker is captured and tortured in an insane asylum, where he is finally convinced that his Starfleet career is an illusion and that he will soon stand trial for murder. Worf and Data retrieve him, but aboard the ship he still refuses to believe he's a Starfleet officer. Sensing he can't trust any of these "realities," Riker mentally breaks through each one in turn to elude his captors and return to sanity.

148. *"Suspicions."* Dr. Crusher becomes a crime-solving doctor when a Takaran scientist is killed during an experiment. Violating the Prime Directive in her search for clues, she is relieved of duty until her investigation reveals the culprit. (The *Enterprise*-D morgue is seen for the first time.)

149. *"Rightful Heir."* Worf finds Kahless the Unforgettable, his people's mythic spiritual leader, returned from the dead on the planet where clerics await his promised return. When Kahless is defeated by Klingon leader Gowron, the clerics confess that Kahless is just a clone of the original. But with word of Kahless' spiritual presence spreading throughout the Klingon Empire, Gowron agrees to let this "heir" to Kahless rule as emperor and spiritual leader.

150. *"Second Chances."* Returning to the site of an eight-year-old mission, Riker is amazed to find an exact duplicate of himself created by a rare transporter mishap. "Lieutenant Riker" resumes the passion with Troi they shared at the time, and the two Rikers clash. As Lieutenant Riker prepares for his new posting aboard the U.S.S. *Gandhi* (using his middle name, Thomas, to distinguish himself from his "twin") Troi promises to consider marrying him. (Originally, *TNG* writers wanted to kill off Commander Riker and install his career-climbing duplicate at the helm, greatly enhancing the Riker–Troi romance.)

151. *"Timescape."* Returning from a conference aboard a runabout, Picard, Data, Troi, and La Forge are shocked when they find the *Enterprise*-D frozen in time while engaged in battle with a Romulan warbird. Upon inspection of a strange vortex in the warbird's engine core, an entity from another time dimension reveals that his young are attracted to the core's artificial gravity well, which is causing time to "freeze." The alien entities are sent back to their dimension and the *Enterprise*'s "time" is successfully reset. (The runabout, which was created for *Deep Space 9,* was built on *TNG*'s budget to help out the new spin-off series.)

152. *"Descent, Part I."* Answering an outpost's distress call, the *Enterprise*-D encounters a new mass of self-aware fanatical Borg, who seek vengeance rather than assimilation. The *Enterprise* pursues the shuttlecraft of two escaping Borg to a sensor-shielded planet, and Dr. Crusher is left in command when most of the crew leave the starship to conduct a massive ground search. Picard's team is captured and is shocked to find Data and his evil twin brother, Lore, who proclaim they will destroy the Federation with their new army of followers.

SEASON 7 (FIRST AIRED 1993–1994)

153. *"Descent, Part II."* Picard and his senior officers devise a way to defeat Lore when they realize that the evil android is controlling his brother with the negative aspect of Dr. Soong's emotion chip. Riker and Worf are discovered by Hugh's underground Borg forces, who abandoned Lore when his experiments left many born mutilated. Hugh aids the crew in infiltrating Lore's complex, and engineers a Borg revolt where Data deactivates his brother and keeps the emotion chip only at the insistence of La Forge. (It is clarified that Hugh's local unit of the Borg are the only ones affected by the "individuality" concept and could conceivably create another *Enterprise*-D encounter with a "Borg collective" group in future *TNG* movies.)

154. *"Liaisons."* Two Iyaaran ambassadors covertly study the concepts of pleasure and antagonism aboard the *Enterprise*-D, while Picard and his Iyaaran pilot depart in a shuttle to meet with their planetary leader. The shuttlecraft crashes on a hostile world where Picard is cared for by a human woman. Picard tries to escape when he realizes he is not badly injured, but his "lovesick" host plans to keep him captive. As it turns out, the Iyaaran shuttle pilot took the form of the human woman to study the concept of love.

155. *"Interface."* La Forge grieves when his father calls to tell him that his mother, Captain Silva La Forge of the U.S.S. *Hera,* is missing and presumed dead. But while trying to retrieve the wreckage of another ship by use of a new virtual reality probe, La Forge is shocked to discover his mother alive. Despite suffering neural shock from the probe—and against a direct order from Picard and the belief of his friends, who believe he is hallucinating—La Forge risks one more contact with his mother. (LeVar Burton bought out a day of Ben Vereen's Broadway show so he could make a cameo appearance as La Forge's father on this episode.)

156 and 157. *"Gambit, Parts I and II."* Picard poses as a renegade archaeologist and Riker as a black sheep Starfleet officer aboard an intergalactic pirate ship seeking to steal a psionic resonator, an ancient superweapon. No one aboard the pirate ship is who they pretend to be and a Romulan, who turns out to be a Vulcan agent who then double-crosses Picard, kills the other mercenaries with the resonator just as Picard realizes its power source is negative thought. The captain alerts the *Enterprise*-D and, left useless, the weapon is destroyed by the Vulcan government.

158. *"Phantasms."* Data is troubled by a disturbing nightmare, which causes him to stab Troi. In sickbay, Dr. Crusher finds interphasic, leechlike creatures on Troi's wound and discovers that the creatures, largely invisible, are all over the crew, fatally extracting cellular peptides. Interpreting his dreams for clues to their removal, Data successfully drives out the creatures.

159. *"Dark Page."* Lwaxana Troi experiences the Betazoid equivalent of a nervous breakdown. Deanna uncovers her mother's feelings of guilt over the drowning of a previously unknown older daughter many years earlier and helps her to heal.

160. *"Attached."* Sparks between Picard and Crusher are finally explored when the two are taken hostage by an isolated and xenophobic cult group and physically shackled together with devices that open up uncontrollable telepathy between them. They discover they are strongly attracted to each other, but once back aboard the *Enterprise*-D, Crusher informs the captain that she wishes to remain no more than friends—for the time being. (Nick Sagan, son of the well-known physicist Carl Sagan, wrote this episode.)

161. *"Force of Nature."* A brother and sister Hekaran science team board the *Enterprise*-D forcibly to demand that the use of warp drive be halted before it destroys the fabric of space near their planet. Data finds their theories to be accurate, but the sister half of the scientific team grows impatient and sacrifices herself dramatically to prove her point, almost destroying the ship in the process. The Federation initiates a new warp five speed limit.

162. "Inheritance." Dr. Juliana Soong Tainer tells Data she was once married to Dr. Soong, his creator, and thinks of herself as the android's mother. But Data discovers that she is actually an android. A microchip found in her brain plays a holographic image of Dr. Soong explaining that his real wife died after they fled Omicron Theta, but he constructed his most perfect android to house her mind without her knowing the difference. Accepting his creator's wishes, Data decides not to tell his "mother" of her true nature.

163. "Parallels." Worf is nearly driven insane when he returns from a victorious *bat'telh* contest and realizes he is shifting from one alternate universe to another. In these different universes, Picard is dead, Riker is commanding the *Enterprise*-D, Lieutenant Wesley Crusher is at ship's tactical, and Worf is first officer and married to Troi. Data and Wesley discover a quantum fissure that trapped the original Worf and is aggravated by La Forge's VISOR's subspace pulse. After Worf is returned to his correct universe, the quantum fissure (where many universes intersect) is repaired, and the Klingon sees his relationship with Troi in a different light.

164. "The Pegasus." In an episode that finally nails down the eternal question, "Why not a Federation cloaking device?", Admiral Pressman, Riker's former commander aboard the *Pegasus,* leads the *Enterprise*-D on a mission to retrieve their old ship before the Romulans discover they were experimenting with a phased cloaking device that allows a ship to pass through solid material. The Romulans seal the *Enterprise* inside the fissure of a huge asteroid, but Riker reveals Pressman's secret and the *Enterprise* uses the banned technology to escape. Pressman is arrested for violating the original Treaty of Algeron with the Romulans and an inquiry to expose his Starfleet allies is promised.

165. "Homeward." The *Enterprise*-D officers are shocked to discover that Worf's foster brother, Nikolai, has sheltered the primitive natives of Boraal II in duplicate caves in the *Enterprise*'s holodeck to protect them from the planet's suddenly dissipating atmosphere until a new home planet can be found. Picard and Worf are furious over this blatant violation of the Prime Directive, but now feel forced to go along, especially since Nikolai reveals he has fathered a Boraalan child and plans to stay with his people on their new planet.

166. "Sub Rosa." Following her grandmother's funeral on Caldos IV, Dr. Crusher resigns Starfleet and becomes passionately involved with a handsome young "ghost" who has romanced her family's women for centuries. Picard, Data, and La Forge finally shock Beverly with the truth: he is really an anaphasic plasma being who has used her family to stay alive. Beverly destroys the "ghost" and returns to the *Enterprise*-D. (The title of this romance novel in space is Latin for "undercover" or "not out in light.")

167. "Lower Decks." Two young *Enterprise*-D ensigns find their friendship strained during personnel evaluations, as Sam Lavelle and Sito Jaxa learn they are both up for the same job. Worf respects and has faith in Sito, even though she receives a verbal lashing from Picard, who reminds her of the role she had in the Nova Squadron cover-up by Wesley Crusher's Academy flight team in *"First Duty."* After a lesson from Worf, Sito stands her ground with the captain and volunteers to pose as a Bajoran captive taken by the Cardassians on a covert Starfleet mission. Sadly, Sito is lost on the assignment, leaving behind only scattered escape-pod debris.

168. "Thine Own Self." Sent to retrieve radioactive debris from a downed probe on a preindustrial planet, Data loses his memory and unknowingly spreads the fragments throughout the village, thus infecting the inhabitants with radiation sickness. Even though Data discovers a cause and a possible cure, an angry mob blames the android for the outbreak. When they reveal his inner circuitry, the mob finally "kills the monster" and buries him, but Riker and Crusher arrive to beam up the long overdue android. Upon reactivation, Data cures the villagers of the radiation sickness, and Troi passes the bridge officer's test, outranking the android.

169. "Masks." In one of *TNG*'s most confusing and least popular episodes, a comet discovered by the *Enterprise*-D is found to be an archive of an ancient society. As a replication program converts areas of the starship into a Mayan-like culture of jungles and foliage, Data becomes "possessed" with multitudes of characters from the ancient civilization. With time running out after Main Engineering is transformed and override impossible, La Forge finally locates the archive's transformational program and both the ship and Data return to normal.

170. *"Eye of the Beholder."* Troi detects an overwhelming empathic echo in one of the nacelles, where a promising young *Enterprise*-D officer committed suicide and "relives" in her mind a love triangle between the dead Enterprise officer, his girlfriend, and a mysteriously menacing man.

171. *"Genesis."* After recovering a stray demonstration torpedo, Picard and Data find the starship slowly looping through space powerless and the crew transformed into various life forms. Data discovers that a synthetic T-cell injected by Crusher into Barclay to help fight a flu bug has activated the crews' dormant introns and de-evolved them to various lower life forms. The android's cure allows a rapid return to normal for the entire crew just as the Worf-beast corners Picard inside a Jefferies tube.

172. *"Journey's End."* Picard is forced to relocate a Federation colony of Native Americans outside the newly redrawn border between Federation and Cardassian territories. Meanwhile, a disenchanted Wesley Crusher arrives on leave from the Academy and, after encountering a vision of his father telling him to seek his own way, resigns from Starfleet. The Indian colonist who helps Wesley fulfill his destiny transforms into the Traveler and the young man chooses to live among the colonists in favor of self-exploration with the guidance of his transdimensional friend. Meanwhile, Picard, the Indians, and the Cardassians reach a compromise: the colonists stay on the planet, trading Federation for Cardassian supervision. (The original script had Wesley abandon his Starfleet career to become a Maquis resistance fighter against the Cardassians.)

173. *"Firstborn."* When young Alexander shows little interest in warrior training, K'mtar, a trusted family friend, attempts to pique his interest, but Worf discovers that K'mtar is actually Alexander from 40 years in the future. Worf's son reveals he has time-traveled back to change the upbringing that allowed him to become a pacifist diplomat duped into allowing Worf's eventual assassination on the Klingon High Council floor. "K'mtar" returns to his proper place in the future when Worf helps him to realize that he can only die honorably if he allows Alexander to become his own person.

174. *"Bloodlines."* Resolving the unsatisfied vengeance of DaiMon Bok from the first season episode *"The Battle,"* the Ferengi bribes his way out of prison to taunt Picard again that he plans to kill the son the *Enterprise*-D captain never knew he had. Even after Picard determines the boy is not his son, he races against time to free the boy, and reveals Bok's profitless insanity to his mercenary crew, who depose him in typical Ferengi fashion. Picard and his "son" acknowledge their bond forged from the experience and agree to visit each other in the future.

175. *"Emergence."* After the *Enterprise*-D suddenly goes into warp for no reason, Data and La Forge discover a network of self-erected nodes cross-connecting the ship's functions, similar to a life form's neural web. In the holodeck, the crew finds a symbolic train program running with a conductor, engineer, and characters from various other programs, which the crew realizes represent different ship's functions. When the characters all prevent Data from shutting down the power grid within the program, he realizes that the ship is fostering its own embryonic intelligence. When the ship begins a trip that will exhaust the life-support system, the crew convinces the train "passengers" to try a nearby nebula as their source for vertion particles instead, but they disappear when a life form found in a cargo bay departs into space fully matured.

176. *"Preemptive Strike."* Newly promoted Lieutenant Ro Laren returns to the *Enterprise*-D when Starfleet asks her to infiltrate the rebel Maquis as a Cardassian-killing Bajoran fugitive. She gains the local cell's full confidence by staging a daring raid against the *Enterprise* for medical supplies, but finds herself more and more sympathetic to the Maquis' rebellion. When her elderly Maquis mentor is killed by a surprise Cardassian raid at their base, Ro abandons Starfleet to join the Maquis. (The elderly Maquis leader, Macias, was inspired by a Cuban freedom fighter in that nation's War of Independence from Spain.)

177 and 178. *"All Good Things . . . Parts I and II."* Twenty-five years in the future, a frail and bearded Picard begins to travel through time, with Q secretly controlling his trips, but the past he visits is not as he remembers. History seems to be changing itself and the Captain believes the problem with time might be caused by trouble in deep space. He enlists his former crewmen, La Forge (now an author) and Data (a Cambridge professor) to help him find out what's wrong. The men hitch a ride on the *Pasteur*, a medical ship captained by his ex-wife, Beverly Crusher, and with the help of Worf (now governor of a

Klingon outpost) and Admiral Riker, Data uncovers a rupture in space that seems to be causing the time-shifting phenomenon. Q reveals that the rupture is wiping out all of history and if Picard can't fix the problem, humanity will be obliterated. In a climatic sequence, he orders *Enterprise*-D crews of the past, present, and future into the void at warp speed in a maneuver that means almost certain death. The past and present starships explode, and as Picard waits in the future for his ship to explode, too, Q appears and Picard finds himself back in the superbeing's courtroom. The *Enterprise*-D survives and Q confirms that the captain has saved humanity. Picard says he hopes it's the last time he will find himself in the courtroom. But Q tells him, "The trial never ends." (These two episodes were originally produced as a two-hour series finale, although in later airings it was divided into two hour-long segments.)

ABOUT THE AUTHORS

James Hatfield is the former film critic for *The Texas Women's News* and a frequent contributor to other Lone Star State regional publications. Having returned to his native Arkansas from Dallas in 1994, where he was for many years the vice-president of a large real estate management company, he now lives in a small town at the foothills of the Ozarks. He divides his time between writing books, computer trouble shooting, reviewing movies, hunting for antiques, and fishing on Beaver Lake for "that trophy Bass."

George Burt, Ph.D. (affectionately known as "Doc") is a computer consultant to major businesses and industries in Texas, specializing in software application development. Doc met his co-author while working on a major computer project for one of America's largest retail companies and, after discovering they both were diehard Trekkers, have been writing partners ever since. Doc makes his home in Dallas, Texas, where he spends his leisure time reading law books (he's also a paralegal) or indulging in his real passion—cheering for the Super Bowl champion Dallas Cowboys!